ONCE A COPPER

THE LIFE AND TIMES OF BRIAN 'THE SKULL' MURPHY

VIKKI PETRAITIS

Published by Wild Dingo Press
Melbourne, Australia
books@wilddingopress.com.au
www.wilddingopress.com.au

First published by Wild Dingo Press 2018
Text copyright © Vikki Petraitis
The moral right of the author has been asserted.

Except as permitted under the Australian Copyright Act 1968, no part of this book may be reproduced, stored in a retrieval system, or transmitted in any form or by any means, electronic, mechanical, photocopying, recording, or otherwise without prior permission of the copyright owners and the publisher of this book.

Cover design: Debra Billson
Editor: Catherine Lewis
Printed in Australia by Griffin Press

Petraitis, Vikki, 1965- author.
Once a copper / Vikki Petraitis.

A catalogue record for this book is available from the National Library of Australia

ISBN: 9780648066330 (paperback)
ISBN: 9780648066392 (ebook: pdf)
ISBN: 9780648215905 (ebook)

I dedicate this book to my mum, Helen Burke, for her endless support, encouragement, and proofreading; to my friend Sandra Nicholson who first introduced me to The Skull, and to the two most special boys in my life, Archer and Jenson.

— VP

My story is dedicated to my beautiful wife, Margaret, who has always stood by me, and to the memory of one of my dearest friends, Paul Higgins. May he rest in peace.

— BFM

Praise for *Once a Copper*

What was policing really like before technology changed it forever? Vikki Petraitis takes us there with her vivid portrayal of 'old school' cop Brian Murphy, who grew up on the mean streets of South Melbourne during World War II and walked the beat as the inner suburbs slowly gentrified. Murphy was often unconventional and occasionally found himself in hot water, but he always got the job done. A fascinating read.

— Cheryl Critchley, journalist, true crime writer

A very compelling insight into the Police Force of yesterday. In the early part of The Skull's story, I kept thinking of what Winston Churchill said in the British Parliament pointing to the benches opposite, 'The opposition occupies the benches in front of you, but the enemy sits behind you'. That's how dysfunctional things were because of the corruption. Skull is the Australian version of Eliot Ness and has contributed to today's policing being far more proactive restoring faith in our police force.

— Les Twentyman, AOM, National youth advocate

FOREWORD

Brian Francis Murphy is one of the last of a breed of coppers we'll never see again in Australia. Some may consider this a big plus, but the old-style methods got results, with very little interference from the 'bosses' and not much help from modern science. During his time in the job, Murphy shot 40 crooks and suspected crims, without killing any of them, saving his own life on many occasions. He never went anywhere without a gun.

Brian's close mate, Paul Higgins, summed up those 'bad old days' for me during a chat we had after he got out of prison, after 'serving time for other guilty people'. He said that when he and Murph were in the job they could 'batter down front doors, give crooks a knee in the knackers, or a biff in the breadbasket and if all else failed, take them to the infamous fifth floor at Russell Street Police Headquarters, where if a few clouts with a phone book didn't produce the right answers, they could hang them upside down out the window, to give them a chance to revise their story'. Higgins said that these days cops have to knock politely, be viewed through the front-door peephole and by the time, or IF, the door is opened, 'the suspect is standing in the hall on his mobile phone, already getting lawyered up'.

Brian's recollections, as told to my friend and colleague Vikki Petraitis, using the old-time police vernacular, are not only about tough policing, but about his disdain for bent coppers, the unorthodox methods used to achieve results and the sometimes unbelievable incidents that seemed to only happen to Brian. His stories remind us that in those days police had to find a phone box or a wall phone in a pub to call for backup or to relay information. They also recall a time when the Breakers, the Consorters, the Robbers and the Doggies consisted of blokes just as tough as the crooks they were chasing.

But like all tough guys, Brian has a soft spot—his unfailing respect for the women he encountered in the job, and in particular, his enduring love for his large family, from his parents to his own children and his Catholic faith, which has sustained him on many occasions. I'm pleased Margaret, Brian's loyal and long-suffering wife, gets more than a mention. She has been his rock and he has protected her and his family throughout his dangerous career.

Now in his eighties, he's been retired for around thirty years, nearly as long as he spent in the job. But he has not been idle. He has many clients who engage his 'negotiating' services and a mobile phone that rings incessantly, bringing him all the 'good mail' from his huge network. In his dapper suit and trademark fedora hat, he is recognised by many as he keeps himself busy around town. But what he actually gets up to? Well, that would fill another book.

I hope you enjoy reading this engrossing tale about Brian 'The Skull' Murphy as much as I did. He is not only one of the last old time coppers still standing, but a gentleman as well.

Robin Bowles, award-winning true crime writer, Melbourne

INTRODUCTION

It was Christmas 2014 and I'd just finished writing my latest book, *The Dog Squad*, about Victoria Police dog handlers and their dogs. Over lunch with retired Assistant Commissioner, Sandra Nicholson, I talked about finding a new writing project.

'You should write a book about Brian,' Sandra said.

'Brian who?' I asked.

'Brian Murphy—The Skull. He was my old boss back in the 80s.' Sandra got up from her chair, went to her bookshelf, and returned with a book called *The Skull* by journalist Adam Shand. The cover was red with a picture of a bald man in dark glasses on it. The subtitle read: *Informers, hitmen and Australia's toughest cop*.

I have to admit, informers and hitmen are not my favourite topic, but I had recently dabbled in the dark side of organised crime in my writing.

'This was written by a journalist,' said Sandra, 'but Brian always wanted to tell his own story.'

I told Sandra that I would read *The Skull* to get a feel for Brian's story, and if I was interested, she could put me in touch with him.

I found *The Skull* intriguing more for what it didn't say than what it did. Adam Shand had done a fine job creating the rogue that Brian Murphy was as a copper—a dashing man, fast with his fists, breaking the rules and getting the bad guys in the end. By the time I reached the final page, I wanted to meet the man himself. There was a lot of *what* he had done, but not so much *why* he had done it.

My interest always lies in the method behind the madness.

Brian Murphy lives at an address that, just by sitting quietly immovable in Middle Park for the last hundred or so years, had morphed in location from undesirable to highly desirable. It's a family home with stained-glass windows and high ceilings. It is here that Brian met me at the door. For a writer, I'm not particularly good at describing people and have wondered in idle moments if I could describe members of my own family to a police artist with any accuracy.

My first impression was that Brian reminded me of my dad; around the same vintage, give or take half a dozen years. But there is something recognisable in men of that age. Politeness, a ruddy glow to their cheeks, a lack of hair, a gait swayed by a dodgy hip. And because I adore my dad, and because I trusted the judgement of my friend Sandra Nicholson, I felt an immediate fondness for Brian 'The Skull' Murphy.

We started writing over summer. Brian was 82 and sharp as a tack. His memory for times and dates was phenomenal. But writing someone's story takes patience and a fair bit of wrangling. With a project like ours, there always needs to be a rapport. What did I have in common with The Skull? We were both Catholic, knew people in common, and were interested in some of the same criminal cases, but there was something else. He was a natural-born storyteller and so was I. We both understood that words spoken in just the right way, at just the right time, can change lives.

I always like to start at the beginning.

I knew The Skull ended up with the reputation for being Australia's toughest cop in his heyday, but what were the early hints? What were the suggestions in the child of the adult he became?

'So, where did it all begin?' I asked.

1

GENESIS

A week after Brian Francis Murphy entered the world on 12 March 1933, his parents took him home to a double-fronted weatherboard in South Melbourne. Their house was built by his great-grandfather and once had an uninterrupted view to the lagoon where longboats brought passengers from the ships to Port Melbourne. But by the time Brian arrived, the area was built up and the outlook more industrial than bay views.

Brian grew and thrived in a no-nonsense world of lots of kids and strict but kind parents. In those days, South Melbourne was a mixture of working-class families, factories and tiny run-down workers' cottages. The local Dunlop Factory sounded a whistle each morning at 7.25 to mark the start of the working day. For the Catholic kids like Brian, it was also the signal that 7.30 Mass was about to start. He would race off towards St Peter and Paul's Catholic Church in South Melbourne, trying not to breathe too deeply if there was a north wind; the stink of the nearby Lever and Kitchens factory that made soap from the fat of the boiled-down horse carcasses was the perfume of his suburb.

Some days, the stench hung over South Melbourne like an ill wind.

Brian was born into a world where you knew where you stood. There was good. There was bad. And sometimes there was a grey area in the middle where you had to stretch the rules a little for the greater good.

His mother, Maggie Murphy, was an astute woman; she was

South Melbourne born-and-bred, and a staunch follower of Dr Mannix and the Catholic Church. She hadn't had a good education, but she could read people better than anyone, a psychologist from the school of hard knocks. A strong woman of Irish descent with a couple of generations of Australian thrown in, Maggie had a tough life growing up. The worst thing that ever happened to her began one Saturday night after Maggie and her sister had been to Saturday night Confession, and skipped home without a care in the world. On approaching their house, a horse and cart from the fire department stood outside. A woman from the neighbourhood stepped out in front of them to stop them from getting closer.

Maggie's mother had fallen asleep in bed and the newspaper she was reading caught fire when it slipped onto the hurricane lamp. Her hair had caught alight; so by the time she woke up, she was engulfed in flames. She was said to have run out into the street screaming horribly.

She was taken to hospital where she died a couple of days later, her grieving husband by her side. From that moment on, the girls took on their mother's role and became unpaid servants to their demanding male siblings.

One night, Maggie's brother, Bill, lost his temper when his dinner wasn't ready on time and he had a union meeting to go to. He waited impatiently at the table wearing an open-necked shirt. Stirring a pot of rice, Maggie suddenly flung a ladleful at his face. Rice stuck to the hairs on his chest as he wildly tried to brush the gluggy white scorchers from his flesh. Maggie took off out the door and hid for hours until her dad came to find her and take her home. It was the first time she really flared up. Her brother had blisters on his chest for a week. Once she got over the fright of what she had done, Maggie felt empowered by her anger.

Brian, too, would come to know this intoxicating feeling.

When she had her own children, Maggie swore she would treat them equally. Accordingly, Brian grew to be an expert at doing dishes, and polishing linoleum floors with Wonder Wax every

Genesis

Saturday till they shone like glass. Maggie always said, 'Water is free and soap doesn't cost much more. Just because you live in a slum, doesn't mean you have to be part of it.' Her six children were always spick and span. So was the house.

The Murphys had a slight financial advantage over others in the neighbourhood in that they owned their own house, handed down from two generations. Even so, the family was as poor as everybody else's. Socks were darned and trousers were patched.

Brian was number four in the order of kids in the family, which made him the king of hand-me-downs. He would never forget the first new item of clothing he ever received; he was six years old when he was given a brand new chocolate-coloured coat with brown velvet pockets and lapels. It was the most beautiful thing he had ever seen and he wore it at every opportunity, feeling like a little gentleman. He had the coat for about a year when one Sunday morning, before Mass, he searched but couldn't find it anywhere.

'Where's my coat?' he yelled.

'Just put your school coat on,' said Maggie. 'Hurry or we'll be late for Mass!'

They set off up the street, heading for St Peter and Paul's, but Brian's thoughts were panicked: *where was it?* Just as he was working himself up, thinking maybe he'd lost it, Brian saw a kid he knew called Jimmy, sitting in the gutter wearing a brown coat with velvet lapels.

'Hey! That's my coat!' he shouted.

Maggie swiped the back of his head. 'Shut your mouth and keep going!' she growled.

'But—'

'He needs it more than you do,' she hissed.

Brian fell silent. Backchat was rare in the Murphy house. As he drew closer, he got a better look at Jimmy, feet bare in the chill of the morning. The only thing keeping him warm was the brown coat. He knew Jimmy. He'd played with him. Both Jimmy's parents were boozers, and there was little joy in the boy's life.

In his mind, Brian said goodbye to that coat. Even though the Murphys had very little, there was always someone with much less. His mum and dad did their best to bring a little comfort wherever they could, Maggie often feeding stray kids from their street. She always said, 'When you're feeding eight, everyone can have a little less so that someone else gets to eat.'

Brian's dad, Reg Murphy, was a volunteer at St Vincent de Paul, and he was also a probation officer for the Catholic kids in the area who got into strife. He'd organise to meet them right after Mass—his way of ensuring they all *went to* Mass—and he tried to keep them on the straight and narrow. He'd even ride his pushbike around the street at night and, if his probation kids were out playing cricket, he'd stop and ask them if they'd done their homework.

By day, Reg was a despatch clerk at Carlton and United Breweries. While the brewery allowed workers to have a couple of beers each day—perhaps to cut down on theft—Reg always came home ramrod straight. Sometimes, Maggie would say, 'You've been drinking!' And Reg would always say, 'Yes. I've had two.' It was a bit of a family joke. They never knew if it was two glasses, or two bottles, or two dozen. However much he drank, he held it well because Brian never once saw his father drunk.

One day, in his first year of school—known as 'the babies'—Brian was walking to school and, as little boys do, stomping in the wet gutters. He couldn't believe his luck when he noticed that a ten-bob note had stuck to his shoe. He told everyone at school of his good fortune. When he showed it to his teacher, she took it from him and posted it into the tin for African babies that sat on her desk. When Brian got home and told Maggie, she said, 'Bugger the African babies! We need it more.'

The money was more than Reg made in a week, but Maggie never would have gone to the school to ask for it back. She wouldn't want the teachers to think they were poor. Even though everyone was poor, it was important to hide the fact. Maggie went to church in gloves and a hat, looking the best she could. In those days, poverty often only existed behind closed doors.

Poverty wasn't the only scourge. Polio was a blight in the days before a tiny spoonful of medicine wiped it out. One of the kids in the neighbourhood, Paddy Brown, was stricken, then pushed around by his mum in a big wooden pram for years before he began waddling around on his own calipered legs. He never played football or cricket but the local kids tried to include him in games whenever they could. The first words from the lips of any Catholic mother when confronted with the crippled or the lame were: *There, but for the grace of God, go I.* An important reminder that calamity could strike anyone at any time, and since medicine offered few solutions, strict adherence to the Church and the power of prayer were some of the few options available to worried mothers.

Melbourne is about as physically far away from the war as a place could be, but war's dark tendrils reach out across oceans and touch the lives of all. Brian's was no exception. He was six years old when war was declared in 1939. It was announced on the wireless. Soon afterwards, food was rationed and mothers everywhere pasted dark paper over their windows. Street lighting was reduced at night to dim the streets should enemy planes ever make their way to South Melbourne. While London was in the grip of nightly blackouts, the shadowy dimming of Melbourne's streets was known as the 'brownout'.

Every day at school, children prayed for the soldiers and that the Germans didn't take over the Vatican and kill Pope Pius XII. One of Brian's classmates, Allan Carey, lost his dad when the *HMAS Perth* was sunk by the Japanese in March 1942. Allan disappeared from school for a couple of days. While he was absent, they all said prayers and had a Mass for his dad; every kid in the class cried. When Allan came back to school, his classmates made an extra effort to make his life a bit better. He was picked first for teams and people were nice to him. Another boy, Porky Martin, lost his dad too. He looked so bereft and miserable.

The loss of dads made the war overseas feel very close to home.

Before the war, vanilla slices were the staple of any good bakery in Australia, but as sugar and butter became scarce with rationing, they too became a casualty of war. Every now and again, though, this favourite delicacy would inexplicably appear in shop windows. Some kids had money to buy them, and others were cunning enough to follow their cashed-up friends to the cake shop. There was always a kid who would share, and they all munched on chunks of custard and pastry and talked dreamily about a time in the future when peace reigned, dads were safe and there was a steady and constant supply of vanilla slices.

Every newspaper was filled with the war during these years. The wireless gave local and BBC bulletin updates; and at the pictures, Cinesound showed newsreels of the battles being fought on the other side of the world. Brian's understanding boiled down to this: Hitler was bad and the Allies were good. He bought war savings stamps and stuck them onto a collector's board scrawled with the motto: 'Every stamp stuck on is another nail in the Axis coffin!'. Even nuns collected pennies to 'put a nail in Hitler's coffin'. The way young Brian saw it, dads, brothers and uncles went off to war to fight against Hitler's way of life. For a while, it seemed Hitler and his German youth could march all over Europe with impunity. Conversely, there was never any doubt that the Allies would win, because they were on the side of right.

The big question was: *when was it going to finish?*

During this time, the availability of apples and pears was limited, too, because Australian produce was sent overseas, principally to Britain, to help the war effort. Inevitably though, a black market sprung up; if people could afford it, they could buy anything, from ration books to highly-sought-after car tyres.

Maggie always said: *anything that's got rotten, goes rotten.* And while she would never dob anyone in for buying extra ration books, she didn't like the fact that it went on. At a time when everyone should be contributing to the war effort, she would often grumble about those making money from the desperation of others. Around the corner from the Murphys was a man who became a black marketeer at this time. Maggie never spoke to him again, nor did anyone else in the family.

One day when Brian was about nine years old, he went into Taylor's Produce Store in Albert Park to buy some things for his mum. The lady behind the counter beamed at him. 'Are you from the Catholic school?' she asked.

'Yes,' he answered, politely standing in front of her in his patched uniform.

'My son went to the Catholic school,' she said with a sad smile. 'But he's overseas now.' That meant he was a soldier.

Brian stood awkwardly, not knowing what to say to her.

The shopkeeper took Maggie's list and prepared the order. When she came around the counter and gave it to Brian, without warning, she enveloped him in a big hug. Even though he was only young, he knew that when she wrapped her arms around him, she was really hugging her own far-away son.

He hugged her back.

American soldiers appeared, generous and clean-cut in their smart uniforms, and were quick to hand out chocolate. The kids had great fun running alongside them as they marched from Port Melbourne to their tent city at the South Melbourne football ground—one of the many that sprang up in ovals and parks across Melbourne.

However, Brian's Aunty Mary had a brush with an American soldier that the family would never forget. She lived near the Fitzroy Gardens and used to walk through there every Sunday and often during the week on her way to 7 a.m. Mass in the city. One day, in late May, 1942, she made her way through the leafy avenues and was approached by a dishevelled Yank. He was disorientated, unshaven, and looked as if he'd slept in his clothes. Something about him made the hairs on the back of her neck stand up.

When he came closer, he slurred a question. 'Where are you going?'

Thinking quickly, Aunty Mary said: 'I'm on my way to the Cathedral to pray for all of you brave American soldiers.' Every fibre of her being told her to get away from this man, and yet, in her heart was the compassion of a church-going woman. She looked into his eyes. 'And I will pray for you especially, young man.'

The man began weeping. He fell to his knees, then grabbed her hand and kissed it.

Aunty Mary wriggled her hand free and went on her way.

A couple of days later, there was an announcement on the radio; the so-called Brownout Strangler had been caught. Three women had been murdered in Melbourne within a couple of weeks. Mrs Ivy McLeod was found strangled in Albert Park, Mrs Pauline Thompson was murdered outside a boarding house in the city, and finally, Mrs Gladys Hosking was found murdered in Royal Park near an American army tent city.

When a photograph of American soldier, Edward Leonski, was published in the newspaper, Aunty Mary gasped. It was the man she had seen in the Fitzroy Gardens. In the telling and re-telling of the story, Aunty Mary was sure that it was her use of the word 'brave' that saved her when she said she would pray for the brave American soldiers.

Because of Aunty Mary's connection to the Brownout Murders, the Murphys followed the case in the media. It was only a couple of months since Brian's classmate, Allan Carey, lost his dad on the *HMAS Perth*. Allan's dad died a hero. Leonski would die a murderer. Brian was nine years old and the deaths all swirled into one. At home, the Murphys prayed as hard for Leonski as they did for the lost and missing dads in their nightly Rosary.

When Leonski was hanged, they prayed for his soul.

2

THE CHURCH

Every first Friday of the month, Brian went to a special Mass with the nuns. The little kids would sit at the front. One day, as Monsignor Collins raised his arms, making the sign of the cross, then joined his hands in prayer, Brian copied his hand gestures, mesmerised. The Monsignor noticed and, after Mass, scuffed Brian's hair fondly. In response, the excited youngster stood up and spun around, losing himself in the folds of the priest's voluminous robes.

As soon as the priest was out of earshot, an old nun, Mother Joseph, scolded him. 'What did you think you were doing?' she hissed.

Brian looked up at her several layers of whiskery chins and said, 'You need to shave.'

Mother Joseph stared at him, aghast. Brian's two sisters were horrified; they broke land-speed records to get home to tell on him. By the time Brian walked in the door Maggie stood, hands on hips.

'I've heard all about you today and I don't want any of your lies!' she said.

After Brian spluttered that he was just telling the truth—Mother Joseph did have whiskers—Maggie grabbed his arm and wrenched him outside. 'That's it! I'm taking you to the orphanage!'

While she had threatened to take her brood to the orphanage before—not an uncommon threat in those days—her frustrations had never taken her to the point of acting on the threat until now. Brian was terrified, and struggled in vain as she dragged him off in the direction of the St Vincent de Paul orphanage in Cecil Street, South Melbourne, ranting all the while about how she was going to leave him there, forever. Mrs Glen from up the road, saw her and asked what she was doing.

'I'm taking him to the orphanage,' said Maggie, her voice shaking with fury. 'He's been very naughty.'

'Oh don't do that,' Mrs Glen said in a kind voice.

Brian grabbed the lifeline. 'Listen to Mrs Glen!' he pleaded.

'Shut your bloody mouth! You're in enough trouble!'

Maggie kept it up until they stood at the huge gates of the orphanage, her neighbour following.

Mrs Glen took her gently by the arm and led her away from the gates. 'You'll regret it if you leave him,' she said, leading them both back home.

Maggie might have calmed down by the time they reached the house, but not enough *not* to repeat the story to the whole family. Brian learnt a very important lesson: he had to be very respectful when he spoke to ladies. And nuns were ladies, too.

As soon as Brian was old enough, he became an altar boy. At school, the Christian Brothers taught children that God was all-seeing and all-knowing. He was ever-present, but nowhere more so than at St Peter and Paul's church, built from the donations of the working class a hundred years before Brian darkened its doorway.

Being an altar boy posed challenges for the hyperactive youngster. He tried his best to behave, given that God was watching, but sometimes the temper that he'd inherited from his mother got the better of him. Once, he knocked another altar boy out.

During Mass.

Here's how it happened. Brian was innocently kneeling alongside an altar boy called Dennis, trying to follow the service in his Mass book. At school, he found learning difficult and had developed lots of tricks to help. During the church service, his Mass book was a godsend because it helped him know which bits were coming up next and when he had to swing into action.

The Church

Mass was going swimmingly until Dennis pinched his book.

'Give it back to me!' Brian said in a low voice, trying to hide his panic.

'No,' sniggered Dennis.

'Be quiet, you devils!' snapped the old Irish priest, interrupting Mass. For a moment, there was an echoing disapproving silence.

From her front-row seat, Maggie glared at Brian with her laser-beam eyes.

Brian looked from his mother to the priest—who had resumed saying Mass—to Dennis who looked smug. 'Give me back my book!' he whispered again, trying to wrestle it from his grip.

Dennis grinned and clutched the Mass book to his chest.

That was when Brian hit him.

His fist connected with Dennis's chin and the boy hit the deck, sprawled like a snow angel. Brian looked at the prone figure in horror, too scared to do anything.

I'm in trouble, he thought. *And I'm going to cop it.*

Along with the rest of the congregation, he watched as Dennis wobbled slowly to his feet. He moved back to his kneeling cushion in a daze. Brian did his best to ignore him, and squeezed his eyes shut against the consequences of what was sure to come.

During Communion, Maggie came up to the altar and knelt down, face like thunder. As the only still-functioning altar boy, it was Brian's job to hold the small gold plate under the chins of the faithful as they came up to kneel for Communion. When she got close enough, she whispered, 'I'm going to kill you!'

When it was her turn for Communion, Brian pushed the gold plate roughly into her neck. He was going to cop a hiding when he got home, so he figured he had nothing to lose.

It was a bittersweet irony that the hiding Maggie gave him at home after Mass, was cut short by the parish priest knocking on the door. He had come to tell Maggie that her son's altar-boy services were no longer required.

He might have visited sooner if he had known about the coffin incident.

Brian hadn't meant to knock the coffin off its stand. But when you're a young boy and there are kneeling pillows, anything can happen. On this particular night, all the altar boys were at the church practising Latin. There was a coffin set up in front of the altar in preparation for a funeral the following day. Brian's brother was the head altar boy and he was conducting the practice. He criticised one of the other boys for mispronouncing a Latin word, then the boy whacked him over the head with a kneeling cushion. Naturally, Brian's brother grabbed his own cushion and retaliated.

All hell broke loose and it was on for young and old.

Pillow fighting altar boys scrambled through the church looking for weapons. It was great fun until the coffin got knocked off its stand. Panicked boys scrambled to pick it up again and undo the damage. Working together, they all took an edge of the dark wooden box and hoisted it back to its rightful place. Luckily, the lid didn't open and they all tried not to think about the person inside, whoever they might be.

Afterwards, the boys were all too spooked to stay around. As Brian hurried out the door, a trainee priest on his way in, scuffed his head by way of greeting and stopped in his tracks.

'You feel hot, young man,' he said, concern in his voice.

'I think I'm coming down with a fever,' Brian replied. The small lie was better than the awful truth.

Later, he debated the incident with a friend. The big question under discussion was whether or not to tell the priest what happened next time he went to Confession.

'Nah,' Brian reasoned. He had long figured that what Father didn't know couldn't hurt him.

'But it could be a mortal sin,' the friend suggested.

'A venial sin at most,' Brian said, shrugging. He had developed a theory about Confession. He reckoned that if you did something and got caught and copped a hiding, it was over and you didn't need to worry God about it at Confession. And if you didn't get

The Church

caught, maybe that was the way God meant it to be.

Even though his altar-boy services at St Peter and Paul's were no longer required, Brian still went to Mass with his family every Sunday. There was something about the place that made him feel safe. The dark wooden seats, big marble altar and the stained-glass windows were mesmerising to a small boy from the humblest of homes.

3

THE BLOKE WHO HUNG AROUND THE CHURCH

The expulsion from his local parish brought 11-year-old Brian and his nine-year-old brother, Kevin, to Melbourne's St Francis' Church which stood grandly on the corner of Lonsdale and Elizabeth streets. St Francis' Church was regarded as the pinnacle of altar serving, and when Brian was accepted for service, he prayed this time would be more successful. On the altar, Brian was in his element. He loved the theatre of it; the Sunday High Mass included three priests, a choir, and six acolytes to hold the candles. The Blessed Host was exposed in a gold monstrance on the altar and the congregation would kneel before it reverently. His duties weren't just in the church services. Every Saturday morning, Brian and Kevin would go to St Francis and polish and clean, set out hymn books, and generally make themselves useful. Brian was particularly good at making the brass candlesticks gleam. After chores at the church, the two brothers would go home and do chores for their mother.

On Sunday mornings, Brian and Kevin would pocket their tram money, choosing instead to make the 45-minute walk into the city. In between the early Mass and the later one, altar boys were treated to breakfast in the adjoining monastery. The kitchen was a bustling affair, serving the twenty priests who lived there. Every type of food was freely and abundantly available. Brian and Kevin loved the bacon and eggs. They never had bacon at home, but the wartime rationing and budget constraints suffered by every housewife in Melbourne didn't seem to reach the priests' kitchen.

The bloke who hung around the church

Luckily they were generous with their bounty and used it to feed the altar boys, as well as the line of beggars who arrived daily at their big wooden doors.

After the second church service, all the other altar boys headed across the road to a shop in Elizabeth Street called Ryan's Milk Bar where they would spend the money they didn't spend on trams. The big attraction was the amazing pineapple milkshakes. They were so thick with ice-cream and fresh pineapple, you couldn't drink them through a straw. The boys would pool their money and order one to share.

One Sunday, Brian and Kevin and a couple of other altar boys were sitting along the milk bar counter when a man approached. Brian recognised him from church but didn't know his name.

'G'day boys,' he said in a friendly voice, putting a hand on Brian's shoulder. 'You're altar boys at St Francis, aren't you?'

Brian nodded. The man looked like his dad—probably around the same age—but his voice was clipped and proper like a school teacher.

'I've seen you over at the church. You've probably seen me there too.' He walked around Brian and sat on the other side of Kevin who ignored him on account of being shy.

'My name is Robert Taylor,' the man said in a friendly voice.

'My name is Brian Murphy,' Brian said.

'Is he your brother?' Taylor nodded at Kevin.

'Yep. He's Kevin.'

The other altar boys introduced themselves to the man from the church, and Taylor asked a stream of questions in a friendly way that quickly elicited where they all lived, and how many children were in their families. The boys happily answered him, even though Maggie always warned her offspring against 'carting yarns'—or repeating family secrets.

When the proprietor approached to serve the boys, they asked for a milkshake to share.

'There's no need to do that,' Robert Taylor said. He smiled at the man and ordered a milkshake for each of the boys, then paid.

What a great bloke! Brian thought. The only people who ever bought him anything were his parents. He'd never met a generous adult before, or indeed one who was interested in him and asked him questions about himself.

Taylor sat with the boys from midday till around quarter to one, and then Brian and Kevin had to fly out the door because Maggie's Sunday roast was served promptly at 1 p.m.. Because they hadn't paid for the milkshakes, they still had their fare money and raced to the tram, making it home a couple of minutes after 1 p.m.

Hands on hips, Maggie demanded to know why they were late.

Brian did the talking. 'A man from the church spoke to us all after Mass and he said he wanted to buy us a milkshake.'

Maggie wasn't happy. During the meal she fired sharp questions at Brian about the man from the church. She didn't like the fact that he had bought them milkshakes and she didn't want him doing it again.

'B-but I think he's all right,' Brian stammered.

'You're too young to judge,' said Maggie. 'Your father and I want to meet this man.'

'Okay,' Brian said. He thought it would help. Maggie liked church people.

The following Sunday, Maggie and Reg came to Mass at St Francis. Maggie sought out the altar boy trainer and quizzed him about Robert Taylor.

'He's in here all the time,' he told her. 'He seems like a nice chap.'

'He bought all of the altar boys milkshakes.' The tone of Maggie's voice was clear; she wasn't happy.

'Maybe it wasn't a good thing,' he agreed, 'but he's a daily communicant, and he often returns for Benediction in the afternoon.'

Maggie's shoulders relaxed a little. In her book, any man who went to Mass every day must be a good man.

The bloke who hung around the church

As soon as the service ended, Robert Taylor materialised beside Maggie and Reg. He introduced himself, all smiles and handshakes. Within minutes of meeting them, he had complimented them on their boys. 'They must have a fine family life!' he declared.

Maggie asked Robert—'call me Bob'—Taylor where he had come from.

He told her he was from interstate. 'Coming to Melbourne and finding St Francis …'—he paused for effect—'has given me a great sense of coming home.'

Maggie beamed. On the way home, she declared Bob Taylor a fine chap. 'He's probably lonely,' she concluded, turning to Brian. 'Give Bob our phone number and invite him around for a family meal.'

The following day, Brian saw Bob at afternoon Benediction. After the service, he passed on Maggie's message. Bob phoned later and they settled on the Wednesday two weeks from now; he would come for dinner.

A couple of days later, Bob Taylor turned up again at Benediction. He invited Brian out for a pot of soup. 'Would you like me to ring your mother?' he asked in a friendly way.

'Well … I suppose,' Brian replied, hardly daring to hope that Maggie might say yes. She said no to so many things, but since he had never been asked out to have a pot of soup, he had no idea what her stance on soup might be.

They rang her from a public phone box. Hearing Bob's side of the conversation, Brian gathered that Maggie agreed. When he hung up, Bob told him it was fine as long as he was home by 6 p.m. He led Brian to a basement beneath a shop on the corner of Little Collins and Elizabeth streets. A sign outside said: Hoddle's Restaurant. Stepping down from the street was like entering a different world. Brian had never been into a restaurant before and didn't know what they usually looked like, but this one could have been out of the movies. There were linen napkins on the tables, and the lighting was soft and honey-coloured. As soon as they entered, a man with a white shirt and black trousers covered by a long black apron greeted Bob Taylor as if he were a regular patron and led them to a table.

As Brian tucked in his linen napkin, he felt like the luckiest boy in the world. Bob sat down beside him and put his hand on Brian's thigh and rubbed it.

'You're cold,' he laughed, rubbing a little harder. 'Lucky we're here to get some hot soup.'

What a nice bloke, Brian thought.

Bob ordered minestrone soup which Brian had never heard of before. It sounded like something from outer space to him but when it arrived, he realised it was similar to a soup his mum made. The soup came with Italian bread, crispy and served in fist-sized pieces. He went to cut it but Bob said it was supposed be torn apart in your hands. He demonstrated, showering crumbs everywhere. Brian could never do this at home—Maggie would have had a fit at the mess. Nonetheless, he copied Bob, then spread soft butter from a butter dish across the fluffy bread. As they ate, Bob told him about his travels. He'd been to Ireland and had visited all the Catholic churches there. He had even been to Rome. Having rarely left South Melbourne, Brian was impressed.

He was home safely by 6 p.m. that night.

Soon after, Bob again approached him after Benediction. 'I want to take you and show you a boat!' he said excitedly.

Brian didn't even bother to ring Maggie this time. He went with Bob on the tram to a house in North Melbourne. He was a little puzzled because he had expected Bob to lead him towards the bay, not to a house.

'Your eyes will pop out of your head when you see this!' said Bob enthusiastically once they'd settled on the tram.

Grabbing his hand, Bob didn't let go for the entire trip. Brian tried to wriggle it away without seeming rude or ungrateful. He was 11—too old for anyone to hold his hand. Maggie's friends used to hold his hand if they all went on a trip to the Shrine, but that was

The bloke who hung around the church

a while ago. Maybe Bob Taylor didn't understand when boys got too old to have their hands held.

When they got to the house in North Melbourne, Bob knocked on the door and introduced Brian to the man who answered it. They shook hands. The man seemed like a regular sort of fellow, but he smelt musty; so did the house. There was a strong kerosene odour that must have come from a heater somewhere in another room. The man led them into the musty-smelling front room that had a single bed, and was full of dirty cups and clothing on the floor. Brian had never seen such untidiness. He realised then that it was a boarding house and that the man lived in this room. His eyes were drawn to the boat in the window. At that moment, Bob moved in behind Brian and put his hands on his shoulders. He pulled the boy back closer to him, and away from the boat, perhaps worried Brian would get too close to the fragile model which was about a metre long and made totally from matchsticks. It had masts and flags and tiny sailors, and reminded Brian of the pictures of the Titanic or one of the huge cruise ships that he often saw from the beach at Port Melbourne.

While Brian was captivated by the boat, the two men murmured things that he didn't hear and wasn't interested in. They stood in the room a while and then Bob decided it was time to go, so they hopped a tram into the city and from there, Bob put Brian onto a bus and paid for his ticket home. Thoughts of the incredible model boat filled Brian's head and he couldn't wait to get home to tell all his brothers and sisters about it.

Reg listened as he described the boat, but didn't say a word. He just listened.

The following Sunday, Bob offered to take Brian and Kevin to the Botanic Gardens. Maggie said it was all right, but she wanted them home by 5 p.m.

When Bob arrived, Maggie invited him in for a cup of tea. Brian was impatient because Bob's socialising with his parents was eating into their outing time. Finally, they began walking up Park Street.

Usually, they caught the tram, but this time, Bob kept walking. He stopped outside a house on the corner of Palmer Street. Brian and Kevin didn't ask any questions; they just followed him around to a bungalow out the back. To their shock, the door to the bungalow was opened by a one-legged man.

Bob was effusive. 'I've just brought Kevin and Brian here to meet you.'

The one-legged man looked nervous but invited them in. There wasn't a chair for Brian and the man told him to sit on top of a little table. The boy obliged, hopped up, and swung his legs back and forward. The one-legged man shook his head, as if he was gesturing *no*. Brian didn't understand what was going on but all of a sudden, Bob came over to him and kissed him – not on his cheek like his mother might, but in a way that a man might kiss a lady in the movies. Bob moved his hands down and spread Brian's legs. The boy's heart beat so fast; he was terrified.

Bob's hand moved downward.

Kevin stood up abruptly, in shock.

Brian wriggled away and jumped off the little table, too. 'C'mon, Kevin, we need to get going if we want to get to the Shrine.'

Bob stepped back and pulled his coat around his front.

Brian could sense the danger. Something bad was going to happen if they didn't get out of the dark bungalow. Bob followed them out to the street. While every fibre of Brian's being wanted to run home to Maggie, he turned and headed towards the Shrine as if nothing had happened.

'I just love you so much,' Bob told him, taking his hand.

At the Shrine, Bob asked Brian if he needed to go to the toilet. Brian did but shook his head vehemently. A survival instinct had kicked in; he now knew with certainty that Bob was dangerous—if he went into the toilets and Bob followed, he imagined the man would probably kill him. When Bob left them to walk home alone, Brian told Kevin not to tell Maggie what had happened in the bungalow.

The bloke who hung around the church

'Why?' Kevin was not a curious boy.

'Because we'll get into trouble for going to someone's house,' Brian told him.

At home, Maggie asked about the afternoon.

'E-everything was good,' Brian stammered. 'Mr Taylor had to go into the city. He apologised for not bringing us home, but he had to catch a tram.'

Maggie went on with cooking the dinner and didn't say another word about it.

For the next three nights, Brian hardly slept. He was terrified. His mind swirled as he tried to apply his knowledge of the world to what had happened, but he came up short. He knew that there was something wrong with what Bob had done, kissing him and pressing against him, and worse; Brian was sure it was a mortal sin. The Catechism he recited every day at school taught about sin.

He wondered if he should tell the priest at Confession but the thought horrified him. As soon as it entered his head, he realised that he could not tell the priest about it because he wouldn't even know *how* to tell him; he didn't have the words. As Brian tossed and turned in the small hours of the morning, he wondered if he was still in a State of Grace—because if he wasn't, he wouldn't be able to go to Communion. But if he didn't go to Communion, Maggie and Reg would know that there was something wrong.

His thoughts were like a rat on a wheel, spinning round and round and getting nowhere.

Brian's state of panic that began when Bob Taylor kissed him, nearly exploded when Bob knocked on the door on Wednesday night for dinner. Bob cheerfully greeted Brian and Kevin and asked how they were.

'Fine,' Brian lied. His heart was pumping like a steam train and his guts were twisted into knots.

Maggie had cooked a roast as a special treat for the visitor and, as soon as Bob arrived, she called everyone to the table. To Brian's horror, Maggie gestured for Bob to sit next to him. She brought the impressive roast to the table and began to carve.

As soon as he sat down, Bob slid his hand under the table and groped Brian's private parts. Brian was so panicked, his world went silent—the only sound was the pounding of the pulse inside his head. Like looking down a tunnel, he stared at Maggie, willing her to know what was happening.

And then sound returned. Loud sound. Maggie. Screaming something. 'Get your hand on the top of the table or I'll stick this knife through your heart!' Maggie held the huge carving knife in front of her. Brian had never seen her so enraged.

Bob's hand whipped away from Brian's leg. He jumped up from his seat and ran from the room.

Clutching the carving knife, Maggie moved like lightning around the table. At the same time, Reg jumped up so fast, his chair tipped over. With a voice of steel, Maggie said to him, 'I'll look after this!' She raced to the front door, still carrying the knife. Seconds later, the front door slammed.

Maggie reappeared. 'He's gone!'

There was a stunned silence among the Murphy children.

Moments later, it was broken by Kevin. 'When are we going to eat?' he said.

Maggie put down the knife, looked at Brian, and nodded towards the front room. He climbed off his chair and followed her. Reg came too. Brian was trembling. He didn't know if he was in trouble, but he suspected that he might not be since it was Bob who Maggie had chased with the knife.

'I'm going to tell you something,' Maggie said, 'That man had his hand on you where he shouldn't have it. Don't you ever let anyone put their hand on you like that.'

'Yes, Mum,' he said. And then he told her what had happened on Sunday. After he finished the story, he whispered the question that had been plaguing him: 'Will I go to hell?'

'You won't go to hell,' said Maggie in a firm voice, 'because you've done nothing wrong—apart from being a bloody fool for not coming to me in the first place. If anything like that happens again, you come and tell me and your father.'

Then it was Reg's turn: 'There are plenty of people around like that, and if anyone does anything like that to you again, come and tell us immediately. With blokes like Taylor you can run faster than him. Just run away.'

Brian nodded.

'Now, forget what happened,' said Maggie. 'We'll sort it out with the rest of the family later on. I'll go and see the priest at St Francis and tell him. Don't blame yourself. That man set out to use you; but you can learn a good lesson from this.'

It was funny that such a leaden weight could be lifted by a short parental conversation and a knife-wielding mother.

When Maggie told the family what Bob had done, Brian's sisters hugged him, and his older brother wanted to find Bob and beat him up. Brian felt better knowing that they knew. His relief was absolute; he hadn't sinned. It wasn't his fault. His family loved him. Life could return to normal.

4

WAR AND PEACE...AND A SMALL CLASSROOM BATTLE

Ironically, Brian's battles began once the actual war was over. Victory in the Pacific was declared on 15 August 1945—Catholics took it as a sign of God's intervention that the war ended on the Feast of the Assumption. Their prayers had been answered. On that day, a teacher hurried into the classroom and announced to everyone that the war was over. The Germans had surrendered back in May, and now it was the turn of the Japanese. Two atomic bomb attacks on their soil had clinched the deal.

Cheering echoed throughout Brian's school. The streets of Melbourne were alive with pandemonium. Like hundreds of other kids, Brian headed into town where there was dancing and singing, and every serviceman was surrounded by women, leaving their cheeks covered in red lipstick kisses. Musicians brought instruments and struck up popular songs of the time. Speakers here and there blasted the happy music into the night. Brian watched it all in awe.

Slowly, the ration books were no longer needed. Mothers everywhere peeled brown paper from their windows and polished the smudged glass with methylated spirits and newspaper until it shone. Hour-long queues at the butchers for a couple of sheep shanks became a thing of the past, and vanilla slices once again graced the shelves of bakeries everywhere.

School teachers could be quite brutal in the 1940s, and kids like Brian were often on the receiving end of their wrath. Like hating the Protestants, it was just the way things were; you either accepted

War and peace...and a small classroom battle

it, or you developed a loathing for it that boiled and rose in your throat every time it happened. In those days, most kids remained silent, but Brian noticed that bullying of any kind just got worse when the victim said nothing. After all, it was a David and Goliath battle; children against Christian brothers who, at a moment's notice, armed themselves with straps or canes, ready to belt the living daylights out of you.

Not long after the end of the war, a smaller battle played out in a little classroom set up as a boxing ring. Brian was in Form 2 (Year 8) when Brother Doyle made the exciting announcement that he was setting up a boxing troupe. Brian jumped at the chance. Along with his classmates, he helped Brother Doyle set up a makeshift boxing ring in one of the classrooms. Once it was done, they all stood around waiting for instructions. There was no love lost between Brian and his teacher, so he was surprised when Brother Doyle chose him to stand in the ring first.

Brother Doyle sent in four boys, one after the other, to take him on. While he might have considered Brian a smart alec, or a kid who should be taken down a peg or two, what Brother Doyle clearly hadn't realised about Brian was that he never shied away from anything. Never showed fear. This attitude always won out against kids who tentatively approached a fight. Sure enough, one boy after the other gave up, and Brian beat all four of them.

Brian felt smug. Brother Doyle's face was thunderous. He walked over to Brian, swinging a pair of boxing gloves, then whacked them hard into Brian's head.

Without giving it a thought, Brian took a flying jump and punched Brother Doyle in the face, hard. As blood flowed from his teacher's nose, Brian tore off his boxing gloves, grabbed his bag, and ran out of the classroom. It took him some moments to realise the full horror of what he'd done. He sat on the front steps of the school, shaking like a dog. A kid called Johnny Attard had just taken his bike out of the bike rack and Brian jumped up and grabbed him. 'Mate, I need your bike!'

Johnny Attard handed it over. Before he knew it, Brian was pedalling furiously towards home.

Although he didn't expect any sympathy from his mother, Brian knew it would be better if she heard the story from him, not from the school. He talked madly to himself all the way home. *He hit me first for no reason. No, she won't believe me. She'll go and talk to Brother Doyle.* By the time he rode Johnny Attard's bike up the lane to the back gate, he knew that whatever he said, he was in trouble.

Maggie heard him out, then gave him a whack across the ears and told him to ride the bike back to school. She would meet him there. Maggie headed straight to school and soon stood face to face with Brother Doyle. Brian caught up breathlessly.

'Did he hit you?' she asked, pointing to Brian.

A look that might have been shame crossed Brother Doyle's face. 'No, he didn't,' he said in a quiet voice. Brother Doyle didn't know that Brian had already told Maggie what he'd done. That meant another biffing for lying. Then another one from Reg when he got home. Brian couldn't believe his bad luck. It all seemed so unfair. He had no idea why Brother Doyle had lied for him.

Oddly, the reaction at school was not what Brian had imagined. He was the school hero. Every Catholic school kid lived under the shadow of the anger and canes of the Brothers who taught them. Brian had bucked the considerable weight of authority. It was every kid's dream. Brother Doyle treated him differently after that. Every time he'd walk past, he'd scuff Brian's head in a friendly manner and say, 'How's it going Murphy?' Something had changed; there was a bond that stemmed from their encounter in the boxing ring. Perhaps things changed when the underling fought back and the balance of power was made even.

Brian went on to great schoolboy successes in the boxing troupe and represented the school against the kids from St Augustine's Orphanage in Geelong and St Vincent de Paul's Orphanage in South Melbourne. Boxing against these boys taught Brian another lesson. Those kids were tough. They had been

War and peace...and a small classroom battle

beaten from arsehole to breakfast and they had nothing to lose. They were fighting for their school and for accolades and kudos in a life devoid of them. Those boys were the toughest competition he ever faced.

There was a ruthlessness in kids with nothing to lose.

Another small battle had a long-lasting effect. The day began with a fight and ended with Brian nursing a black eye, leaning on the wall of a pub, waiting for his tram home. A week earlier, a bigger boy had issued a challenge which Brian had to accept. He was small but always fought back like a fiend. When the bigger kid stood opposite him in the schoolyard, fists raised, Brian thought: *he's gonna beat me*!

But then he had an idea. Brian looked over the boy's shoulder, made his eyes go a little wider, and shouted, 'Hi Brother!'

Thinking a teacher was approaching, the boy looked behind him. That's when Brian hit him. Big and hard. The kid went down like a sack of spuds. While Brian might have won that battle, the boy's mates declared war. Hence the black eye. And hence Brian leaning painfully against the pub wall waiting for his tram. With his good eye, he spied Brother Hackett coming around the corner, scowling.

'Have a look at you!' he snarled. 'This is what you'll be doing every Saturday afternoon for the rest of your life, Murphy—propping up a pub wall.'

Brian saw red. If he wasn't nursing a black eye, he might have given Brother Hackett one. At the heart of his fury was that Hackett judged him incorrectly. Alcohol was the scourge of his neighbourhood. Blokes drank too much at the pub and went home, taking their grog-fuelled rage out on their families. Kids went hungry while dads spent their wages on beer instead of food. As far as Brian could see, drinking made people angry and violent.

'That will never ever fucken happen,' he muttered under his breath, fuming.

He swore that day never to touch a drop.

5

JOINING THE COPPERS

For Brian, the road to the police force had a few detours. As soon as he left school, his parents took him to the Catholic Vocational Guidance Office in the city. His vocational test result suggested he should be a stonemason or a watchmaker. In due course, Brian began an apprenticeship with a watchmaker. It was 1948. He was fifteen years old. The war was over and the future looked bright. But for a kid who found the confines of the classroom hard, he ended up sitting at a watchmaker's bench for six hours a day. The other two hours, he walked the city streets making deliveries and collecting parts for repairs.

Add a self-righteous boss to the mix, and things were bound to end in tears. Over his two years as an apprentice, the boss needled away at Brian, who needled right back. The whole thing ended when Brian smashed a clock in a fit of anger.

A stint of National Service and a short-lived career as an auctioneer, made Brian think about what he really wanted to be when he grew up. As a kid, he had always idolised coppers, but was terrified of them in equal measure. When he was young, his greatest crime was a game of street cricket, with neighbours complaining about the threat to their windows. A huge cop would ride up on his wonky bicycle, puffing, and give the local kids a serve. Some days, when he was feeling particularly nasty, he'd get the kids to pump up his tyres—while he sat on his bike.

In his childhood, Brian had seen plenty of street fights. South Melbourne was rife with them, especially outside hamburger shops

Joining the coppers

or pubs. These fights always started when the blokes involved had drunk a bellyful of alcohol. All the neighbourhood kids would come out to watch with the kind of detachment that allowed them to judge the strength of each opponent. 'Have a look at this bastard,' one kid would say. 'He's going to clobber that other bloke!'

Some of Brian's greatest heroes were the coppers who would ride their bicycles into the fray every Friday and Saturday nights and take on packs of fighting bastards. Police officers were tougher and stronger than everybody else. They looked as if they had no fear; to the youngsters of Brian's suburb, they were even braver than Gene Autry or Hopalong Cassidy.

The fly-in-the-ointment of Brian's decision to join the Victoria Police was that his dad hated coppers. Reg was as law-abiding as the next man, but he had been a part of the wharfies' strike of 1928, and had been standing next to a unionist who was shot dead in one of the protests. When the cops and the wharfies clashed, Reg got clobbered with a baton and thrown into the sea near Station Pier. Some fellows dived in and grabbed him and pulled him onto the top of a large outlet pipe while they continued the battle. The men who knew he was there had scarpered when the fight wound down, and Reg lay there unconscious for 18 hours.

By the time some of his mates returned and carried him home, Reg was on death's door. Maggie took him up to the hospital. The doctors shook their heads. Said there wasn't much hope; he had a fractured skull.

Maggie sat devotedly by Reg's bedside for days until she had an altercation with a nurse. It happened after she brought a scapular––a small religious picture sewn onto a leather backing—into the hospital for Reg. The English nurse had said sarcastically, 'You're going to need more than that to save his life.'

After Maggie gave the nurse—who was clearly a Protestant––a piece of her mind, she decided to take Reg home. She walked her pneumonia-ridden husband to the tram stop, then helped him up the steps onto the tram. At the end of the journey, she helped him walk the three blocks home, where she lay him out in their bedroom and nursed him herself. Sympathetic neighbours were quick to offer advice. One suggested feeding Reg the blood from a half-cooked steak. Maggie stretched the budget to a daily piece of steak and did just that. Reg slowly returned to health.

The day in 1954 when Brian brought his brand new handcuffs home and put them proudly on the table, Reg lowered his newspaper and said, 'If you're going to be a copper, be a good one.'

Brian spent three months at the Police Depot[1], cleaning out the stables, washing floors and keeping fireplaces stacked with wood. Considering his humble origins and leaving school at 14, he did well against people who had matriculated and others who had been in the regular army. Some of the new police recruits had good educations from private schools, but they didn't have the street smarts that Brian did. That levelled out the playing field, especially on the mean streets of Melbourne.

In the first couple of weeks at the Depot, Brian was doing guard duty at Parliament House with another trainee who stood guard on the front steps while Brian walked a circuit. On one of his rounds, Brian saw a bloke walking past carrying a wooden fruit box on his shoulder, but his shoulder was down too low for it to be fruit. He'd seen this kind of thing a million times before where he came from.

'He's got stolen goods in that box,' Brian said.

'Don't bloody make trouble,' said the other trainee.

Brian ignored him and approached the fruit-box fellow and told him to put the box down. Sure enough it was full of stolen car radios. After a bit of a scuffle Brian arrested him, then looked around for his partner who'd vanished.

Shortly afterwards, CIB detectives roared up and took the bloke into custody. They'd been looking for him and clapped Brian on the back.

When Brian got back to Russell Street, it turned out that

---

1 The Police Depot, located on St Kilda Road, pre-dated the current Police Academy.

Joining the coppers

his partner had reported him for fighting. Luckily, the boss took Brian's side.

'Be careful of him,' said the boss. 'Don't trust that bastard.'

Brian learnt a good lesson that day. Even though police recruits were drilled to stay together and support one another, he realised he couldn't always rely on a partner to stick around when things got rough. But since Brian got the pats on the back, he also realised that he had done the right thing by following his gut feeling when it came to the man with the fruit box.

At the Police Depot, recruits had to study police briefs of past cases to familiarise themselves with the language of statements. The briefs ranged from traffic incidents to murder. The file that made the biggest impression on Brian was that of the murder of 21-year-old Constable George Howell by William James O'Meally in February 1952, just two years before Brian joined the police force. Constable Howell had been on night-shift patrol near the Crystal Palace Theatre on Dandenong Road, trying to catch the thief who had been breaking into cars near the cinema. Howell approached O'Meally who was loitering near some parked cars. O'Meally dropped a hat, a torch, and some keys he had been holding and ran off. Constable Howell gave chase and caught up with the suspect soon afterwards. O'Meally raised a sawn-off .22 calibre rifle and shot Howell at point blank range. The mortally wounded young constable tried to continue the chase but, as O'Meally disappeared into the night, Howell collapsed in the middle of Normanby Road. The dying police officer gave a description of the shooter to people who stopped to help him; Howell then repeated it to police who arrived on the scene. Despite emergency surgery to his abdomen, George Howell died in the small hours of the morning. What made this tragedy such incredible reading was that the information Howell provided on his death bed helped police capture O'Meally and gain a conviction against him. Brian read the case from cover to cover and vowed never to go on patrol without a gun.

Not surprisingly, Brian found himself bucking against authority at the Depot, usually when it was arrogant and unfair. His squad leader, Brian Kelly, was both. Twice a week, the recruits caught the tram to go to swimming training at the City Baths. One day, on the way to swimming, Kelly told everyone he had a cold then proceeded to whinge about it. One of Brian's fellow recruits leaned over and said, 'Murph, he's giving us the shits. Why don't you do something about it?'

'Do something about it, yourself,' Brian said, a little tersely. He had quickly gained a reputation for doing stuff others wouldn't do. Everyone knew he didn't suffer fools gladly. While he didn't ever start anything, by jingo, he'd give anything a go once it had started.

Brian was practising freestyle when Kelly appeared by the side of the pool and told him he should be doing the breaststroke instead. Trouble was, he said it in a poncy voice.

'I've got a cramp,' Brian told him, stopping and putting on a pained expression. 'Can you help me?'

'Sure,' said Kelly, leaning over and offering his hand.

Of course, Brian pulled him in. Fully dressed in his starched uniform. And, of course, Kelly reported it.

Back at the Depot, when Brian stood in front of the squad lecturer, he decided to go with the 'I-didn't-mean-it-Sir;-I-really-did-have-a-cramp' defence.

'You pulled him into the fucking pool!' yelled the man. He told Brian that if he didn't admit it, the matter would go further up the chain and he would probably get kicked out of the Depot.

Brian threw his hands in the air, as if to admit that he really did pull Kelly into the pool, but kept his mouth shut. It was enough for the squad lecturer.

'All right,' he said. You're going to lose 45 marks.'

Physical training was worth 100 marks, and losing 45 was a blow. Luckily, Brian slipped through with just enough marks to pass.

6

BEHIND CLOSED DOORS

Putting on the uniform for the first time as a graduate from the Police Depot, Brian felt as if he ruled the world. The first shift, he pulled over a motorist for not coming to a complete stop at a stop sign. He gave the man a good talking to about the dangers of disobeying road signage, and vigilantly took down the particulars of his car. He even carefully noted the reason he had gone through the stop sign. Walking up the street later, full of his own self-importance, Brian suddenly stopped in horror. He flicked open his notebook and realised he had forgotten to ask the man his name and address.

Back at the station, he confessed his error to his boss.

'Don't worry about it,' said the boss, laughing. 'We all do that sometimes. Let the bloke sweat while he waits for the summons that will never come.'

Brian was relieved. Forever after, name and address were the first things he asked.

Brian's first domestic violence job came on a night he was partnered with a cop called Billy Banks. Neighbours had reported the sounds of fighting and the two police officers hurried to the address. When the husband flung open the door at their insistent knocking, it took the enraged man a moment to realise it was the coppers. It took him another moment to process what that meant. For the smallest time, Brian was frozen to the spot. They all were. It seemed as if the slightest movement in the tableau would start it all up again.

It didn't last. The man was ready to take them on. He had entered another world—a world of red rage where he was the king of all his surrounds. Yelling and bellowing, spitting and swearing, eyes sticking out like organ stops, he was way past common sense.

Billy Banks got the first punch in.

And then it was on. The first couple of punches brought him back to reality. Bullies like him weren't used to being hit back; they can give but they can't take.

'What are you fucken doing this to me for?' he yelled. 'I'm a good bloke. All I did was belt my fucken moll of a wife.'

By the time they got him in handcuffs, the man was begging for mercy.

Inside the house, the wife was bleeding from blows to her face. Kids huddled beneath the kitchen table, whimpering; the little ones were so frightened, they'd wet their pants.

As they walked the man back to the police station, Banks provided him with a vivid description of what would happen to him if he attacked his wife again. After the violent husband was locked up, Brian and Billy returned to the house to make sure the wife was all right, then stayed for a cup of tea.

She was safe now, and her anger began to boil. The coppers took advantage of this.

'Who does he hang around with?' Banks asked.

Through swollen lips, she carefully sipped her tea and told them all the no-good characters her husband hung around with.

Billy Banks wrote the station phone number on a slip of paper. 'If he lays a hand on you, ring me and he'll get better than what he got today.'

The wife shook his hand gratefully.

'Never get called back a second time,' Banks said on the way back to the station, 'because it's always worse the second time.'

7

BELTING BOB

About six months after Brian became a copper, he was walking down Elizabeth Street on patrol when he noticed a man coming towards him. The man was holding the hand of a boy about ten or eleven years of age. As he got closer, Brian felt a stab of recognition.

It was Bob Taylor. Last seen fleeing Brian's knife-wielding mother.

Brian looked at the boy and couldn't believe Bob was still up to his old tricks. As they got closer, Bob turned and said something to a couple walking behind, close enough to suggest they were the boy's parents.

The distance shortened.

'Robert Taylor!' Brian boomed, quickly closing the gap.

Bob Taylor stopped in his tracks and dropped the boy's hand. 'I-I don't know you,' he stammered.

'But I know *you*,' Brian said, pointing his finger at Bob's chest. He turned to the couple: 'Take your boy away and don't ever let him near this man. He's no good.'

Brian swung hard and slapped Bob Taylor, open handed, across the face. The sound clapped like thunder. Bob's head jerked sideways. Then Brian whacked him with the other hand and sent his head jerking the other way. The couple grabbed their boy and took off. Bob didn't fight back. Instead, he ran off much like he had all those years ago.

'I hope you run into a bus!' Brian called after him. Probably best he ran. With the rage Brian felt, he could have killed him. Walking back to Russell Street, his hands stinging in a very satisfactory manner, Brian realised that if someone reported him, he could be sacked. Weighing it up, whacking Bob Taylor had been worth it. It was no small consideration that he had also saved the boy as well.

Not long after, another piece of the Bob Taylor story fell into place. Brian walked out the back entrance of the North Melbourne police station and realised it was right near the house with the matchstick boat. He found the house and knocked on the door. A woman answered and just from the smell, Brian could tell the place was no longer a boarding house. He asked her about the man in the front room.

'We've heard about him,' she said, frowning. 'He used to bring kids in there.'

Brian wasn't the first adult to come looking for him. Men who target boys never seem to think about the day those boys become men. And sometimes, policemen.

Brian's time as a police officer had made him realise that the matchstick boat he saw that day was probably made in prison. He had seen similar models but few as large—which meant the man he'd visited had probably done serious prison time. The matchstick boat was a good 18 months of work.

8

BLOODY LOU RICHARDS

Being a non-drinker among some hard-drinking coppers always put Brian a little on the outer. Ironically, on one afternoon shift, it was a pub that got him into trouble.

Brian escaped the confines of the North Melbourne police station and started foot patrol on his own. He headed to the Town Hall Hotel to check that all was well. When he got there, he found a car parked across the footpath outside the hotel on busy Errol Street. The publican was famous Collingwood ex-footballer, Lou Richards.

At the car, Brian found the man himself unloading boxes to take into the pub. 'Excuse me, sir,' he said, 'you'll need to move your car. It's blocking pedestrian access.'

A look of scorn crossed Lou Richards' face. He looked Brian up and down as if he was nothing. 'I can do whatever I want!' he snarled. 'I'll shift it when I'm ready!'

'Give it to 'im, Lou!' yelled one of the drinkers.

Moments later, there was a handful of drunk pub patrons egging Lou Richards on. Lou didn't disappoint. He ranted and raved and finally told Brian to stay where he was. Brian was gobsmacked.

Lou disappeared inside, then emerged a couple of minutes later. 'I've rung your boss and he wants to see you,' he said smugly. 'Go back to the police station and get your bum smacked.'

The crowd congratulated Lou Richards because he'd stuck it up a copper. Meanwhile, Brian found it hard to believe that his boss would want him back at the station in the middle of a shift. Just to be sure, he left the pub to the jeers and catcalls of the drunks, and found a public phone to ring the station. His boss, Senior Constable McSweeney, did indeed want to see him back at the station.

'Was it all necessary?' McSweeney asked when Brian appeared in front of his desk. 'Mate, you don't go upsetting the local traders. I talked to Lou and he's thinking about reporting you.'

Brian couldn't believe his ears. At the Police Depot, recruits were told that coppers always stuck together. But looking at his boss's drinker's nose, Brian had concerns about McSweeney's loyalties.

'We'll go there after closing time and sort this out,' said McSweeney,

Brian couldn't believe such a small thing could escalate when he was just doing his job. He stewed on it until 6.30 p.m. when he and McSweeney made their way to the Town Hall Hotel. Brian had no idea how this would play out. Would he be made the villain? If he hadn't been so angry, he might have been nervous, but anger trumps nerves every time.

By the time they got to the pub, the place was closed and McSweeney rang the bell near the doorway. Lou Richards answered the door.

'Come in, Joe,' he said in his deep voice, referring to McSweeney by his first name.

That's when Brian knew he didn't stand a chance. The two coppers followed Lou into the empty bar. A couple of employees were cleaning up and the smell of stale beer and cigarette smoke was pungent.

'Beer, Joe?' asked Lou.

McSweeney nodded.

'What about you, sonny?' Richards turned to Brian.

'I don't drink,' Brian said, in no mood for small talk.

Lou moved around to the business side of the bar and pulled a cold ale for McSweeney who accepted it without paying. He took a generous sip, then wiped the foam from his mouth.

McSweeney turned to Brian and said, 'For what happened today, I think you need to apologise to Mr Richards.'

'For what?' Brian exploded. He stared at Lou Richards, a smug man in charge of his world. Brian made a decision. 'I'm not fucken apologising to him! I've done nothing wrong!'

McSweeney choked on his beer. 'Get back to the police station!' he spluttered.

Brian gladly marched out, furious that a man wearing the same uniform as him would take the word of a smart-arse publican over a fellow police officer. McSweeney hadn't even asked for his side of the story and Brian had no idea what Lou Richards had told him. All he had done was ask Lou to move his car off the footpath.

When Brian got back to the station, he bumped into the watch-house keeper, Fleshy Beak Coombs, so-called because he looked like a turkey with a red beak nose and a wobbly bit under his chin. He asked why Brian was back by himself. Brian told him the whole story.

'Don't worry about it,' Coombs said, assured. 'Nothing will happen.'

Brian found that hard to believe. He had ignored an order from a superior in front of a civilian.

It turned out that Fleshy Beak Coombs was right.

McSweeney staggered in a couple of hours later, three sheets to the wind, arms wrapped around half a dozen long-neck bottles of beer in brown paper bags and a bottle of whisky. 'I got a bottle of whisky for you, boy,' he said.

Brian took in his dishevelled boss, and took things one step further: 'I don't drink! You can stick it up your arse.' He stormed off, trying to figure out why he'd been offered whisky after disobeying his boss. He suspected that McSweeney had compromised himself on prior occasions, taking free booze from Lou Richards; and this was the dance with the devil. Lou would expect a return on his 'investment'.

The return in this case was for McSweeney to turn on a fellow officer.

The Lou Richards incident taught Brian an important lesson. While backing down is the path of least resistance, standing up for what you believe—while hard at the time—gives you a feeling of strength. Ever since hitting Brother Doyle all those years ago, Brian had tasted the power of resistance. It was a game of strategy. This time, he stood up to the bullies and they offered him whisky. That night he vowed he would never let anyone stand over him. They might try, but he would never cop it like that again.

He was 22 and beginning to establish his own ground rules.

The incident spread like wildfire around the police station. It became a standing joke; young coppers would come in and say, 'Hey, I saw Lou Richards today and he sends his regards.' Then they would all have a laugh.

In a case of revenge being a dish best served cold, twelve months later, Lou Richards got his car stolen outside the new Channel 7 television station in Wells Street, South Melbourne. The stolen car was soon located in Dow Street, South Melbourne and Brian got the call from the police telecommunications centre, D24. When he searched the car, he found £5,000 in cash in a calico bag under the seat. It was a huge amount of money—enough to buy two houses in Middle Park. Brian and his police colleagues counted it twice and logged it through the property book.

When Lou Richards and his daughter arrived at the station to collect the car, Brian gave him a moment alone to check it out. When he finished, Lou's mood was as black as thunder. 'There's something missing,' he roared as his daughter tried to calm him down.

'What's missing?' asked Brian innocently. He wanted Lou to admit his idiocy in leaving such a huge amount of money in his car. Lou clearly didn't recognise him, and Brian was not going to make things easy.

'None of your business!' snapped Lou.

'Maybe the thief stole it,' Brian said, dryly.

'Nobody would know it was there!' Lou screamed. 'I want an inspector here! Someone has stolen something from my car!'

Brian made Lou and his daughter wait in the muster room while an inspector was summoned from town. Meanwhile, he went out the back and had a good laugh with his police mates.

'He's a trouble-making little prick,' said one of the constables. 'Hope he doesn't cause you any trouble.'

Brian laughed.

The inspector arrived, not happy at being summoned.

'He wants you here,' Brian told him. 'He reckons someone has pinched something out of his car. Won't tell us what it is. I don't trust this bastard and I don't know what kind of allegations he's going to make.' He led the inspector to the muster room.

'Inspector,' said Lou jumping up and shaking his hand.

'G'day Lou,' said the inspector. 'What's the problem?'

'I've had something stolen out of my car.' Lou's change of attitude when talking with someone higher in rank was remarkable.

'What is it? Why did you need me to come here?' There was a hint of impatience in the inspector's voice.

'I don't know who stole it, but it's missing,' said Lou.

The inspector looked puzzled.

'What's missing?' Brian said, trying to bait him, enjoying the show.

'There's £5,000 missing!' Lou said.

The boss looked at Brian, eyebrows raised.

Brian slapped his forehead. 'Why didn't you tell me it was £5,000? We've got it in the safe.'

'Has the money been put through the property book?' the inspector asked suspiciously.

'Of course,' Brian said.

'Well then, what am I doing here?' The inspector sounded more impatient.

Brian nodded towards Lou Richards. 'He wouldn't tell us what was missing and he wanted an inspector. So here you are.'

Lou Richards looked as if he realised he'd made a goose of himself.

The inspector started laughing. 'Looks like we've got your money, Lou. Maybe you shouldn't have left it in the car.'

'Well I haven't seen it yet,' grumbled the ex-footballer.

The inspector and Lou followed Brian to the safe where he ceremoniously removed the money.

The inspector inspected the property book. 'Looks like it's all there, Lou,' he said.

Just as Lou Richards reached for his bag of cash, Brian stopped him. Clearing his throat, he said: 'I'd like Mr Richards to count it. We don't want him coming back later and telling us some of it's missing.'

The boss gave Brian a *you're-a-shit-stirrer* look.

'It's all right,' said Lou.

'No, it's not,' Brian insisted. 'We don't want any false allegations, do we?'

The boss agreed and made Lou Richards count the whole thing. It took over half an hour. Every now and again, the boss would give Brian a wink. They both knew that this kind of shit-stirring put people in their place, even when they were a famous local identity. If people wanted to throw their weight around, sometimes, a couple of suburban coppers could politely throw it back at them.

Finally, Lou Richards stuffed the notes back into the calico bag and said, 'Yeah, it's all there.'

Brian made him sign the property book to acknowledge that he'd collected the money. Even though the police had recovered both his car and his cash, Lou took both without a word of thanks. He collected his daughter from the muster room.

As Lou left the building, Brian thought to himself: *up yours, Lou*!

What goes around, comes around.

9

A BRUSH WITH CORRUPTION

Brian had been in the police force for about 12 months, when he was on bike patrol with his mate, Constable Ronnie Taylor, in South Melbourne. The heavy black bikes had 'VP' painted on the crossbar marking them as the property of Victoria Police. Shops were closed but streetlights illuminated colourful signs on milk bars advertising Four'n Twenty pies, Cottee's Passiona, Coke, and Fanta. Young coppers loved swapping the stuffy police station and two-finger typing for the fresh air and exercise of bike patrol. They could head out on their own and poke about at the backs of factories and up laneways to see what was going on in the world. If they were lucky, they could catch some crooks.

On this crystal-clear night, Ronnie Taylor and Brian rode around the streets of South Melbourne and Middle Park. Despite their best efforts to seek out ne'er-do-wells, things were quiet. They had diligently stopped off at phone boxes to make their hourly phone calls to the South Melbourne police station with nothing to report.

It was 1.00 a.m. when they rode slowly past the Post Office in Montague Street and noticed a flickering light in the window—the kind of flickering made by an oxyacetylene torch.

'I reckon there's someone in there cutting a safe,' Brian said, trying to keep the excitement out of his voice. Post Offices were a common target for thieves; they carried a lot of cash so pensioners could both collect and cash their pension cheques on the premises.

'We'd better take a look,' said Ronnie grinning and keen for a job. He offered to take the front. Brian went around the back. The back door was ajar by a couple of inches. Without hesitating, he walked straight in. Once inside, the air was pungent with the smell of melting metal. The hissing and crackle of the blow torch masked his arrival, and the bloke on his knees in front of the safe didn't hear him coming; his first inkling of Brian's presence was a gun behind his ear.

'Don't make a move, or I'll shoot you!' Brian growled, trying to sound older than his 22 years.

The safebreaker turned off the gas and dropped the torch, knowing he was caught.

Brian called out for Ronnie who had seen what was happening through the front window and had run around to the back to gain entry.

'Are you all right?' asked Ronnie.

'Yep,' Brian said, pulling out his handcuffs and snapping them around the wrists of the thief. Ronnie checked the rest of the building in case there was an accomplice.

The man looked a bit older than the two police officers, athletic build, with blonde hair. He had a sharp look about him, pointy nose and chin. Brian had never seen him before and considering he'd grown up three blocks away, he knew most of the crims in the area, so the man definitely wasn't local.

Brian was just about to ask him his name when he heard a voice yelling through the back door. 'Hang on! Hang on!' The voice was quickly followed by a huge bloke who looked swarthy, as if he was from the Middle East. Brian immediately took him for a copper. He was followed by two other cops in suits.

'We're from the Breakers Squad,' said the boss. 'We've been after this bastard for six months.' The Breakers were a legendary squad of tough detectives who investigated safe crackings and big breaking and entry jobs.

Before Brian could blink, the two lackeys took hold of the

A brush with corruption

fellow they had apprehended and led him out. The boss looked at the safe and noted the damage. 'One of you will have to wait here until the safe is inspected,' he said.

It was impossible to tell if the safebreaker had added explosives to the safe mechanism yet, so the next step was to get someone from the Mines Department to come and examine it.

'I will, sir,' Brian said, keen as mustard, rapt that the Breakers had arrived on the scene. He and Ronnie Taylor were probably in for a commendation for catching the wanted man.

Taylor rode his bike back to the police station to tell the Breakers how the events had unfolded at the Post Office while Brian waited at the scene until a specialist from the Mines Department arrived and cleared the safe. It took over an hour, so he didn't get back to the police station until 3 a.m. Taylor had contacted the Post Master General's Department and someone arrived to lock up the premises.

Brian pedalled his bike as fast as he could back to the police station to bask in the glory of the arrest.

'What's going on?' he asked, when he met Taylor in the watch house.

'Mate, you know as much as me,' Taylor shrugged. The Breakers had taken the crook and that was the last he had seen of them.

'Jesus, that's a bit rough,' said Brian.

Footsteps down the corridor of the watch house heralded the arrival of the Breakers boss. 'Did you get the name of that bloke at the Post Office tonight?' he said in a gruff voice.

They both looked up at his aggressive countenance.

'We didn't have a chance,' Brian said. 'You blokes came straight in as we handcuffed him.'

'I don't give a fuck,' he said. 'You always get their name first.' The boss tossed Brian the handcuffs he'd earlier put on the safecracker.

'Did you lock him up?' Brian asked, puzzled.

'Nah. We took the handcuffs off him and he smashed one of my blokes in the face and got away. That's why you should always get their name first.'

Brian and Taylor stared at him, gobsmacked. They couldn't believe the Breakers had let their safe-cracker go.

'Well, we'd better be off looking for him.' The boss walked away.

Watching him go, Brian turned to the watch-house keeper and asked if he knew the detective.

'Yep,' he said. 'That's Wog Slater. Don't fuck with him. He's a dangerous bastard.'

'Something stinks here,' Brian said to Taylor.

'At least you got your handcuffs back.'

Most of the bosses were reasonable men and none had ever spoken to them like Slater had just done. Brian turned to Taylor and the watch-house keeper. 'I think there's a fair bit of bullshit in what he just said. I reckon he knows who that bloke is.'

Taylor agreed. It didn't add up. Now that they had time to think about it, *how did the Breaking Squad get there so quickly*? Were they watching the safe-cracker, trying to catch him in the act? But if they *were* watching the safe-cracker, why had they waited so long? From the damage to the safe, he had been there a while.

'And they didn't have their guns drawn,' said Taylor suddenly.

'They must have seen us go in,' Brian said. 'Were they sitting off the post office when we rode up?'

They pondered these questions and found no satisfactory answers. The only answers they could come up with were most *unsatisfactory*. Had Slater let the thief go on purpose? If he had, could the Breakers have been sitting off the Post Office giving the man cover? When Brian voiced his theory, Taylor was quick with his response.

'Mate, don't go down that road,' he said.

'He's right. Don't go there,' agreed the watch-house keeper.

Brian was beyond angry. What right did Slater have to do this?

A brush with corruption

What the hell was going on? And more importantly, who would believe this could happen? Even if he reported it to his bosses, he could hear their voices: *you've got no proof… keep talking like this and you'll be in more shit than a Werribee duck.*

For the next couple of weeks, Brian worried about what had happened. He didn't miss an opportunity to ask other cops casual questions about Wog Slater and the Breakers. The consensus was that Slater was not to be fucked with and the Breakers did whatever they pleased.

A couple of months later, another incident made Brian see red. There was an old recluse who lived in Nelson Street, South Melbourne. Brian's father used to organise a regular delivery of firewood to him through St Vinnie's. One day at work, Brian heard talk that the old man had died—and that his house was a virtual goldmine.

After tea, he walked into the muster room and saw a huge pile of gold sovereign coins on the table; the mountain would have been worth a fortune.

'Get out of here!' growled one of the senior constables.

Brian withdrew.

A moment later, the senior constable came out and looked apologetic. 'Sorry son,' he said, 'we're all just a bit busy in here. Do you wear cufflinks?'

'No,' said Brian, suspiciously.

The senior constable leaned forward conspiratorially. He held out four gold sovereigns. 'Take these and buy yourself some nice cufflinks.'

'Don't wear 'em, don't need 'em,' Brian said, backing away. *Evil bastards!* he thought. *They're all thieves.* And they were trying to involve him.

The senior constable looked perplexed and was about to say something when Brian interrupted.

'I don't know what's going on anyway, okay.' He walked away.

When he got home that night, Brian told his dad the old recluse had died. Reg organised for St Vinnie's to go round to the man's house to see if they could find contact details for his family, if he had any. By the time they got there, the front door was wide open and the place had been stripped.

Brian found out later, that a couple of senior constables had borrowed a furniture van and gone there the night the man had died. They backed up the truck and loaded it with his belongings. The sovereigns would have been his, too.

As a young copper at the bottom of the policing pecking order, there was nothing Brian could do about it formally, so he decided to get the senior constables back in the only way a powerless junior police officer could. And they would never know it was him. From that moment, he swore an oath to be a thorn in their sides. Every time one of them nicked off to the pub, Brian would go to a phone box and make an anonymous call to police headquarters. 'There's a policeman in full uniform drinking in the London Tavern,' he'd say, disguising his voice. The local inspector would have to check it out because the phone call ostensibly came from a member of the public. The guilty cop would come back to the police station grumbling about the sanctimonious inspector who'd given them a serve after catching them at the pub.

If Brian knew any of those coppers had a girlfriend on the side, he'd make sure he rang their wives. 'Is Senior Constable So-and-So there?' he'd ask the wife.

'He's at work,' she'd reply.

'No he's not,' he'd say. 'I'm a mate of his and I just rang the police station and they said he knocked off hours ago.'

Big blue that night. Guaranteed.

In the 1950s and 60s, it was easy for some coppers to go on the take because the police wage was barely enough to support a family. Some cops supplemented it with honest labouring work, while others chose a quicker and more lucrative way to line their pockets. The most trustworthy cops were the married non-drinkers who were faithful to their wives. Brian reasoned that any bloke who

A brush with corruption

could drink up a storm and support a wife with a mistress on the side on a police wage had to be getting money from somewhere no good.

Throughout his policing career, Brian took on a lot of extra jobs to earn a crust. Once, his boss Mick Miller got him a job transporting coal. Brian would arrive at the docks and watch the huge machines funnel mountains of Newcastle coal into the back of a truck. Because of the way it was funnelled, the load of coal sat in the truck with a peak in the middle while the load was lower at the sides.

Brian would drive the truck very slowly until he got to the bend where City Road becomes Bay Street. Then, he always seemed to take the corner too sharply. The truck would tilt and a scattering of coal would go flying off the side of the tray. As he innocently drove off, the old ladies waiting patiently pushing tattered prams that hadn't seen babies for decades, waved in gratitude. Then they filled their prams with spilt coal and went home to warm their hearths.

That was Brian's version of skimming a little off the top.

10

CLEARING THE ALLEYWAYS

When Brian was stationed in South Melbourne, his superiors formed a taskforce and allocated half a dozen coppers to clean the streets of Starting Price (SP) bookmakers. After months on the job, their arrest tally was zero. That was when Superintendent Thompson approached Brian.

Brian was secretly pleased. The lack of arrests by the taskforce had made him suspicious. SP bookies were everywhere—how could the taskforce not find them? Brian agreed to take on the job, but asked for one thing: he wanted to choose his partner. He needed an officer he could trust; Constable Harry Gooden and Brian had gone through the Depot together. Harry came from a long line of fearless policemen. He was also built like a brick shithouse and no one would take him on. At this stage, Brian did a lot of manual labour to supplement his income and had a strapping pair of broad shoulders of his own.

SP bookies were part of the landscape. When Brian was a kid, his father would send him to a bookie called Mr Drew, with thruppence for a bet each way. The coins were wrapped in a piece of paper with the name of the horse written in Reg's neat handwriting. There was an SP bookmaker in nearly every lane around South Melbourne. A lot of people became bookies to make ends meet. Mr Drew was a pensioner now and Reg knew him. Brian had gone to school with his daughters.

A lot had changed since the innocent days of Reg's three-penny bets. While the bookies were harmless enough, corruption swirled

Clearing the alleyways

around them like moths to a flame.

The word around the traps was that coppers were on the take and it was bad for the Force's reputation; dishonesty tainted them all. Brian told Superintendent Thompson that he wanted to warn the bookies first, and give them a fair chance to close up shop. Thompson agreed. Brian figured if he warned the bookies that he was going to arrest them, they might stop paying protection money to coppers who could no longer protect them.

The bookies laughed in his face.

The first week, Brian developed a wily plan. SP bookies operated in the middle of long cobblestone lanes with a lookout posted on each end. If coppers approached, the lookout would whistle a warning, giving the bookie time to push his betting slips into a hidey-hole and pretend he was in the lane to take a leak.

Being a local, Brian knew this arrangement like the back of his hand. That was why he decided that he wouldn't approach the lanes from the streets, but rather get to them by going through houses and through back gates. Brian approached the ladies of the houses during the day—many were friends of his mother. The women were usually happy to be rid of the rowdy dealings that made their lanes unsafe. Harry and Brian would creep up their side paths and slip through back gates, straight into the centre of the alleyways. They quickly made a dent in the numbers of bookies, arresting fourteen in the first week.

After the arrests, the bookies, and the cops who made a fat living from their protection money, weren't going to take this lying down. Brian's mother got so many harassing phone calls, she rang Russell Street and made a formal complaint, so they sent a detective senior sergeant, called Jack Matthews, around to interview her.

Maggie was sweeping the veranda when he arrived; she did not invite Matthews into the house, though.

'The calls are coming from police stations,' she told him.

'How do you know that?' Jack Matthews asked in a smooth voice.

'I can recognise the buzzing sound of the switchboard from when my son calls me from work.'

Detective Senior Sergeant Jack Matthews looked her up and down, a slow smile spreading across his face. 'How many children have you got?' he asked Maggie.

'Six,' she replied, eyes narrow with suspicion.

'And are you married?' He smirked.

Without warning, Maggie raised her broom and swiped at the senior sergeant. 'Get off my veranda,' she yelled, 'or I'll belt you over the head!'

Matthews knew the best part of valour was retreat—especially when a broom-wielding mother was trying to knock his block off. He scrambled out the front gate. When he got back to the police station, he told anyone who would listen: 'I know where that imbecile gets it from—his mother's just as bad.'

The next thing Brian knew, his car was firebombed.

His little soft-top coupé had cost forty quid, but after his esteemed colleagues were finished with it, it was worthless.

Most of the time, he left the car parked outside the family home because he usually walked to work. Maggie hadn't realised the car was on fire until the fire brigade screamed into their street, bells and whistles. Drawn outside by the noise, Maggie saw the smouldering ruin. She sent Brian's brother around to the police station to tell him what had happened.

Weak bastards, Brian thought. *They won't come to me face-to-face.*

In the burning of his car, a line had been drawn in the sand. Some of his colleagues were not on the same side as he was.

'Pack of mongrels,' said Maggie.

Even though the consequences of his work had literally come to the Murphys' front door, Brian didn't offer to back down from the fight because he knew Maggie wouldn't want him to. In fact, to have offered, would have grossly insulted her.

'Go harder,' was Maggie's last word on the subject. She knew human nature: bullies only back down in the face of superior force.

Reg shook his head in disgust. The torching of his son's car by coppers simply reinforced his dislike of police in general.

The next day at work, one copper, who Brian knew was a decent person said, 'Heard you had your car burnt.'

'Yeah,' Brian said. 'And I've got a fair idea who did it.'

'Close to home, close to here,' the bloke said with a worried look. The identity of the culprit, it seemed, was an open secret.

Bosses buried their heads in the sand and the burning of Brian's car was never solved.

When he replaced the car, he announced it at the station: 'I've bought another car. Wonder if they'll torch this one.'

While his new car stayed untorched, his dishonest colleagues tried to get their revenge in other ways. But every time they did it, he got closer to knowing for certain who his enemies were. Their hatred no doubt grew because he continued to arrest bookies.

One night, he was working the counter on watch-house duty, when a prostitute tottered in on high heels. 'Is Brian Murphy here?' she asked, fluttering her eyelashes. 'I was with him last night and I left my purse in his room.'

'Hmmm,' Brian said thoughtfully. 'Tall bloke, red hair?' He described a cop on duty that night who he suspected was involved in the car fire.

'Yes,' she said eagerly, 'That's him!'

'Well, he's not in at the moment.' As Brian spoke, the cop with red hair came in. 'There he is!' he said. 'There's Brian Murphy.'

The prostitute ran over to him and continued her ruse. 'Brian! Brian!' she cooed, clearly not the sharpest tool in the shed.

'Shhh,' he said urgently.

The woman came back to the counter. 'That's him. That's Brian Murphy.'

Fury bubbled inside the real Brian Murphy at the clear attempt to set him up. He picked up the heavy watch-house book and donged her over the head. She went down like a ragdoll.

'That's for using my name,' he said to her as she scrambled to her feet and gave the red-headed copper a dirty look.

The cop stared at Brian, rabbit in the headlights.

'I'm beginning to understand who torched my car,' Brian said.

A long look passed between them.

The next attempt to get Brian failed, too. He was on foot patrol in South Melbourne when an old knock-about mate of Reg's called him over.

'Are you Snowy Murphy's son?' he asked.

Brian nodded.

The old guy, leaned over and said, 'I know your dad and he's a good bloke so I'm going to tell you this. They're going to put something in your locker at the police station.'

'What do you mean?' Brian asked.

'Listen carefully. They're going to stitch you up. But there's a way around it. Case law Donnelly v Devenish means that if you don't have keys to your locker, you don't have dominion and control over it. Ditch your keys and make it known that your locker is open.'

Brian laughed. The old guy sounded crazy.

The man looked at him closely. 'You can laugh, mate, but they are going to stitch you up. You won't be around for much longer. I've heard it from the bookies. Your copper mates have told them everything is going to be all right.'

That was a sobering thought. 'Thanks, mate,' Brian said, shaking his hand.

'That's all right,' he said. 'I've got no love for the coppers, but I know your dad and I want fair play.'

Brian did a bit of research on Donnelly v Devenish. In 1926, Peter Devenish was convicted of having tins of stolen kerosene in his car. When he appealed his conviction, the Appeals Court recognised that while the stolen tins were found in his car, Devenish was at the beach and had other people with him. The judges concluded that: 'the defendant was not shown to be in actual possession of the kerosene when apprehended. There was no complete physical control of it to the exclusion of others; nor did the defendant have it where he alone had the exclusive right or power to place his hands on it …' In other words, if Brian's esteemed colleagues put something in his locker—something like stolen property—if he was the only one with access to his locker, he would be in strife. On the other hand, if his locker was open to all, it would be a different matter. Good to know.

The next day, having a cup of tea in the crowded police muster room, Brian fished some keys from his pocket and made a show as if they were uncomfortable and jabbing into him. In a loud voice, he announced they were driving him mad and he was going to leave his locker open. In front of a bunch of coppers, he chucked his keys into the fireplace where they slowly melted.

'What did you do that for?' asked a colleague. 'You're mad!'

'I don't need to be carrying so many keys around in my pocket,' Brian said with a shrug.

Things were quiet for a while and he made a great show of opening his locker and telling everyone that he never locked it.

A couple of weeks later, the key-burning paid off. Two inspectors—Winterton and Healy—arrived at the station for a surprise inspection. All police officers were ordered to stand in front of their lockers. Even though Brian was prepared, his heart still beat a little faster; the arrival of the inspectors was further proof of the vendetta against him by men who wore the same uniform. While the others unlocked their lockers ready to be searched, he pulled his open in front of them.

Ignoring all the other police officers, Winterton went straight to Brian's locker. He reached inside and pulled out a double-barrelled Hollis shotgun hidden under some clothes at the bottom. Even though he had expected this, Brian couldn't quite believe the audacity.

'Who owns this?' asked Winterton.

'Wouldn't have a clue,' Brian said. 'Never seen it before and never put it there.'

'But it's in your locker.' Winterton's tone was arrogant.

'It doesn't belong to me, sir.'

'Well how can you account for it being there?'

'I've never seen that gun before. I don't have a key to the locker. Somebody must have put it in there.'

This clearly wasn't what Winterton was expecting. To throw the inspector further off kilter, Brian reminded him of the principles of Donnelly v Devenish. 'I have no dominion and control over my locker,' he said loftily, quoting Reg's knock-about mate.

'Wait here,' said Winterton. He went over to speak to the other inspector.

Brian saw Healy look over at him and raise his eyebrows. They both knew they'd been trumped.

'I think we have to give him the benefit of the doubt,' said Healy, who was known as a fair man. 'Donnelly and Devenish have got us.'

The two inspectors left without checking anyone else's locker.

The copper who Brian suspected of putting the gun in his locker was a likeable bastard at first glance, but once Brian got to know him, the man was nothing but a brazen thief. It turned out that the Hollis shotgun had been reported stolen from a house in South Melbourne. Whether it was stolen by actual thieves then purloined by cops, or stolen directly by cops, was never made clear. What was clear was that the cop Brian suspected was well-known to be light-fingered. Not long after that incident, a piece of evidence—a knife used in a murder—went missing from the property room at the police station. When it came time to go to trial, locating the missing murder weapon became a source of panic.

'It's in the property book,' Brian told his inspector. 'I logged it in and put it in the property room.'

They both realised that the solution was obvious. Without much discussion, the inspector and Brian drove to their light-fingered colleague's house.

'Yeah, it's in the drawer,' said the cop-thief without a shadow of guilt.

'How the hell could you take a *murder weapon* home to carve the roast for your kids?' Brian asked incredulously.

'Forget about it,' said the inspector, who was a friend of the thief. 'You've got it now, just forget about it.'

Later that day, Brian produced the knife in court and the legal fraternity was none the wiser.

11

YOU'VE GOT MAIL

In the 1950s, informers were known as fizzes. Brian thinks they were called that because it's the sound you make when you whisper something. In his job, fizzes certainly whispered some interesting intel; the police called it 'getting good mail'. Fizzes were like manure: nobody liked to handle it because of the stench, but it gave you good results. Cops ran the gauntlet when dealing with fizzes from the criminal world who would trade information for a future favour; it might be to say a good word for them in court, or help out a mate. But at the same time, if a fizz gave you any bullshit, you had to come down on them like a ton of bricks. A cop had to remember which side he was on, and the crook had to know it too; even good informers had to understand that you would also lock them up.

Not all fizzes were from the criminal world. Some were members of the community who informed simply because it was the right thing to do.

When Brian was a constable in South Melbourne, he could see the true value of a police informer and listened to anybody willing to give him information.

One morning, a milko waved Brian over and told him he'd seen a blonde woman in her 40s carrying a big plaster statue of Jesus in St Vincent's Place around 2 a.m. The two men spent a moment pondering what she could possibly have been doing with Jesus in the small hours. They came up blank.

The next week, Brian spent all his off-duty hours sitting in the St Vincent's Gardens at night watching for her. He hadn't told his bosses that he was staking out the park because he knew they'd grumble about overtime or manpower. His chilly night vigil was rewarded at 2.30 a.m. The blonde woman appeared. She wasn't carrying a Jesus statue this time, but her very presence in St Vincent's Place at that hour suggested she was up to no good. Brian followed behind at a safe distance, walking on the grass nature-strips to silence his footsteps. He watched her go through a number of front gates to check windows and doors and then leave one front yard and continue onto the next. In most houses, the front rooms were lounge rooms. Brian guessed that if she was the thief he suspected she was, she would climb in an unlocked front window, grab the nearest valuables, and be outside before anyone knew she'd been there.

When she finally got to a house that was clearly hers—she opened the door with a key—Brian ran back to South Melbourne police station and got the local divvy van crew to go to her house. He jumped in with them.

When they knocked on the door and Brian got a good look at the woman; she looked like a desolate soul. Life had beaten her down. If he hadn't been so excited about his pinch, he might have felt sorry for her. But one of the skills you had to develop as a copper, was to remove yourself emotionally from people who commit crimes. Millions of people have sob stories, but to Brian, a good sob story is not a licence to break into someone else's house.

Her house was a veritable Aladdin's cave and Brian knew he had caught a very active thief. The place was closed up and musty. You couldn't take more than a couple of steps in any direction before tripping over stuff. Royal Doulton figurines, clothing, fur coats, suits, clocks, even a preserving pan. You name it, she had it. And among the treasure trove, they found Jesus.

He was wearing a Stetson hat.

'What right have you got to be here?' the woman shrilled. 'I've got a 14-year-old son! I don't want him woken up!'

'Your place is full of stolen property,' said a senior constable in a firm voice.

And that was all it took. The woman's shoulders slumped and then she followed the police officers meekly as they went through her house. Occasionally, the senior constable would point out an item and ask where she got it from. She had a remarkable memory for houses and addresses.

'I took him from the boys' hostel up the road,' she said, pointing to Stetson Jesus.

Later when they were loading the stolen property into a big van for an audit, Brian found the Jesus statue was so heavy that he wondered how she could have carried it. The constables at the station did a door knock in the area and were able to return most of the stolen goods to their rightful owners.

The woman had no reason for what she had done; she'd never sold anything she stole. From the wisdom of current understanding, she was a kleptomaniac and had psychological problems. But in the 1950s, they didn't know much about criminal motivation. All they knew was that she was a crook and her life was buggered.

Listening to the milko's story about a woman carrying Jesus, led to a good arrest. For coppers who listened hard enough, there was valuable information on the streets. Ironically, if he had followed protocol, he would have written the milko's story in the CIB information book and it may or may not have been followed up—depending on the conscientiousness and sobriety of the detectives.

In Brian's day, keen coppers would chat to bakers, milkmen, and rent and gas collectors who moved around the community. They were honest hard-working men, by and large, and if they saw a woman with a black eye, they would not hesitate to report it to the police. These unassuming men did their best to keep an eye on things. One such man was the watchman at St Vincent's Gardens who was employed by the council to watch out for perverts. This man was the best source of information that Brian had ever met. He knew every paedophile by sight and, if he saw a man in the

You've got mail

park with a bag of lollies, he'd ring the police immediately. Brian arrested one of these men with the obligatory bag of lollies. He kept the bag in his desk drawer as evidence until the magistrates' court hearing came up. When he went to retrieve it, the bag was empty.

'Who's eaten those friggin' lollies?' he hollered around the office.

Not me, came the chorus.

'They came from a pervert!' Brian said, angrily.

A couple of colleagues looked horrified at that thought, so he knew they were guilty.

Luckily, across the road from the South Melbourne police station was a little milkbar where Brian headed to get the bag refilled. He figured the *exact* lollies didn't matter. No one would examine them and he would be careful not to claim they were the *actual* sweets carried by the offender. His heart was in his throat, though, when he saw the pervert's barrister at the counter, buying a packet of Benson and Hedges cigarettes.

'Mr Murphy,' he nodded.

'Mr Vernon,' Brian replied, nodding back.

Brian waited till the barrister left the shop before making his purchase. The defendant ended up pleading guilty, so Brian just had to explain how he had come to arrest him.

After the trial, Brian left the new bag of lollies on the table in the police station and sure enough, they were gone an hour later. Sometimes he wondered if there were more thieves *inside* police stations than on the outside.

On patrol one night, he pulled over a couple of thieves driving an old ute which was choc-a-block full of stolen women's apparel that had been reported stolen from a tailor shop. Brian arrested the occupants of the ute and arranged for all the goods to be brought back to the police station. When the shop owner came in the next morning, she looked over the recovered pile of items and narrowed her eyes. 'Did you recover everything?' she asked.

'Yes,' he said, embarrassment rising in his cheeks as he realised that the pile she was looking at was distinctly smaller than the pile he had stacked the night before.

Brian quickly led her into one of the nearby offices and shut the door, then stormed back to the muster room, furious. He roared to anyone within earshot: 'I have a full inventory of what was on this table. The owner knows exactly what should be here. In fifteen minutes, I'm going to ring the duty officer and make sure he searches every locker and every car in the building.'

After taking her statement, he led the woman back into the muster room. The pile had grown substantially. 'Some of the goods had been put somewhere else,' he said vaguely.

She looked over the pile and declared the only things missing were a couple of packets of pantyhose.

In Brian's thinking, real thieves were low enough on the scale of scumbags, but the bastards in uniforms who stole from the thieves were rock bottom.

Not all cops were bad, of course. Some of Brian's colleagues were really dedicated coppers who were terrified of the rogues among them. Fear kept them from saying or doing anything. Brian had a voice and, right from the start, he felt obliged to use it on behalf of those who remained silent.

Staying silent was a skill he did not possess.

12

MEETING MARGARET

The week before Brian met Margaret, he had broken up with a girl who he had been dating for a couple of years. To get himself on his feet again, he decided to attend a dance at the St Kilda Town Hall with his brother. He was 23 and had been in the police force for about 18 months. His mother Maggie warned him before he went out.

'Don't you go off and pick up a tart!' she said.

'I won't,' he promised.

Brian noticed Margaret as soon as she walked into the room; she was wearing a black dress with a full skirt, and her red hair was neatly curled. He and his brother discussed the merits of the girls on the dance floor and Brian pointed out the girl in the black dress.

'She's got red hair,' warned his brother. 'Mum hates red hair.'

He was right; Maggie had a thing about red-heads; for some unfathomable reason, she thought they couldn't be trusted.

Despite the warning, Brian headed straight for Margaret. 'G'day. Howya going?' he asked in his smoothest voice. 'Would you like the next dance?'

He swirled around with Margaret for a couple of dances before she mentioned the YCW badge that he wore on his lapel.

'Is that a blood donor's badge?' she asked innocently.

'No,' Brian said, 'it's a Young Christian Workers' badge.'

'Of course it is!' she exclaimed. 'My brother has one just like it.'

Aha! That meant she was Catholic, too. After a couple of dances, he knew that he was going to marry her.

At the end of the night, Brian left his brother and escorted Margaret safely home on the tram. When his brother arrived home without him, Maggie demanded to know where he was. By the time Brian crossed the threshold, she had the full story—her son had taken home a red-head.

'What did I tell you about picking up the first girl you met?' Maggie demanded.

'I haven't picked up anyone yet.' Brian tried to sound innocent.

'She's a red-head. You won't have any luck with her!'

'What time Mass are you going to?' he asked to change the subject.

'You'll find out in the morning,' snapped Maggie.

'Goodnight, Mum.' Brian smiled to himself and went to bed thinking about Margaret and her red hair. She was a bit of all right.

One night, Brian took Margaret to the Glen Huntly picture theatre and there were some young hooligans in the audience swearing—f-this and f-that. In the film, a woman died and a male character asked another male character what they should do with the body.

'Fuck her while she's warm!' one of the idiots in the audience called out.

At interval, Brian popped out to the foyer to get Margaret an ice cream and noticed the two hooligans. He wandered over to them and asked in a polite voice, 'Mate, can you tone down your language?'

In reply, one of the youths swung a punch at him. Brian ducked, returned the gesture, and knocked him flying. He smashed into the window nook display of film posters. Then his mate leapt in. Brian knocked him flying too. Leaving the two sprawled in the foyer, he headed back into the theatre and told the usher at the door not to let them back in—he needed time to get Margaret out.

The usher grinned at the two prone men. 'They're regulars and they're trouble.'

Brian escaped with Margaret through the exit next to the screen.

Meeting Margaret

By day, Brian was investigating sly-grog shops which, on occasion, was more dangerous than taking Margaret to the pictures. Drinkers of Melbourne who wanted to drink after the mandated pub closing time of 6 p.m. were happy to pay double the price at sly grog shops which were often set up in houses close to pubs. Most thought these establishments were a harmless way of challenging a silly law, but the truth was that sly groggers were magnets for crime. Their patrons often paid in stolen property, exchanging a watch or jewellery for a dozen bottles of beer. And any visit by the constabulary to such an establishment would reveal people wanted by the police.

One police target was a sly grogger who ran an illegal establishment opposite the Argo Hotel in Prahran. It was handy for patrons; they would leave the pub at closing time, stagger across the road, and continue drinking. One night, Brian and his boss waited in the shadows outside. It was a house with a driveway down the side and a fence out the front. An electronic gate locked shut behind customers—until one bloke went in and slammed the electronic gate so hard, it bounced off the catch. Brian stepped out of the shadows and grabbed the gate.

The lookout got such a fright when he opened the front door to two uniformed coppers, that he scrambled away, dropping the gun he'd had in his hand, before disappearing out the back. The gun clunked onto the floor and came to rest by Brian's feet. As he picked it up, his boss spotted a crime figure called Jimmy Doyle having a quiet ale on the other side of the room.

'Give the gun to him,' said the boss, pointing at Doyle.

'What for?' Brian asked. There was no way he was going to plant a gun on anyone.

'Jimmy Doyle broke a copper's finger last week,' said the boss with a smirk. 'Let's load him up.'

It was a defining moment. Brian had a choice to make.

'No!' he said, adamantly. He pointed to the bloke who had actually dropped the gun. 'It was that guy over there who had the gun. If you want Jimmy Doyle to have a gun, fucken give him yours, but I'm not giving him this one!'

It was a stupid suggestion anyway; if Brian had done what he was told, there were four or five witnesses who would testify in court that he had fitted Jimmy Doyle up with a gun.

Jimmy Doyle watched this exchange with great interest. 'Thank you, Mr Murphy!' he said, grinning like Brian's new best friend.

Grumbling all the while, the boss nodded his head towards the fellow who'd answered the door and whose gun it actually was. Brian arrested him and took him back to the police station where he was fingerprinted.

Once they were finished, the boss grabbed Brian's arm in front of a room full of coppers. 'Don't you ever disobey a direct order in front of a room full of crims!' He spat the words out, his face livid.

Anger roiled in Brian's gut and he wrenched himself from his boss's grip. 'And don't you ever ask me to do anything like that again whether there's a room full of witnesses or not!'

The next morning, someone from the fingerprint branch rang Brian. The fellow they had picked up was wanted for murder. Brian's insistence that they didn't load up Jimmy Doyle for breaking a cop's finger meant they caught a murderer, instead.

Brian had no idea his actions that night at the sly grog shop would save his life.

A couple of days later, he was on patrol in South Melbourne with two other cops. Mid-afternoon, they stopped into the Golden Fleece Hotel for a routine check to see who was consorting with who. Jack Twist, a notorious member of the Painters and Dockers, was drinking at the pub with Harold Nugent, Freddie 'The Frog' Harrison, and Jimmy Doyle.

The Federated Ship Painters and Dockers Union was an affiliation of dock workers that became infamous for standover rackets, theft, extortion, and murder. Dock workers were bound by a code of silence that left most members untouchable as far as the police were concerned. Factions emerged, and greedy, dangerous men scrambled like rats to get to the top of the pile.

Rule number one in checking pubs for consorting criminals was never question anyone in the pub; if things turned pear-shaped, police officers were outnumbered.

'C'mon fellas,' Brian said to the four men. 'Let's talk outside.' Blinking against the brightness after the dim interior of the pub, he opened his notebook and asked them for their names and addresses. Nugent, Twist and Doyle cooperated. Then he came to Freddie Harrison, the most aggressive of the lot. When Brian asked him to state his name, the thug's jaw tightened with fury. Some men thought their names should be so well known that a copper shouldn't have to ask.

But coppers asked anyway. It was part of the game.

'You fucken know who I am,' sneered Harrison who quickly slid his hand into his overcoat pocket and pointed something shaped like a gun through the fabric at Brian. 'I'll give it to you!'

Brian's pen slipped down the page of his notebook making a black streak. Harrison had mad eyes and for a moment, Brian wondered if he would walk away from this encounter. Before he had time to further consider the perils facing him, a voice cried out.

'Hang on! Hang on!' It was Jimmy Doyle. He had seen what happened and stepped up and said, 'Leave him alone. He could have loaded me up with a gun the other night, but he didn't.'

Reluctantly, Harrison pulled his hands out of his pockets, raised them to show they were empty.

Jack Twist pushed Harrison back towards the pub and he disappeared into the dimness. Brian looked around, trying to locate the two coppers who had accompanied him into the bar.

Jack Twist laughed. 'Mate, you're by yourself. Your two mates have just locked themselves in the police car.'

Brian stormed over to the car. 'What the fuck! Why did you leave me for dead?'

'We were trying to get in touch with D24 to get help,' one of them said.

'What? Both of you?' Brian seethed all the way back to the police station. As soon as they parked the car, he got out and went straight home. It wasn't the first time he'd been left for dead by someone who should have had his back.

And he suspected it wouldn't be the last.

Jack Twist knocked on the Murphys' door that night. Because Brian was local, everyone knew where he lived. When Maggie answered the door; she happened to be holding a knife from carving the roast.

'What do you want, John Eric Twist?' Maggie knew him well from stories in the newspapers. She supplemented her knowledge by quizzing Brian about the gangsters, many of whom originated from their neighbourhood.

Twist was taken aback. 'Um,' he said, eyeing the knife. 'I just wanted to talk to Brian.'

'You do it at the bloody police station. He starts at 7 o'clock in the morning. See him at Russell Street. Now, get off my veranda.'

'I-I just wanted to apologise,' he stammered.

Brian heard his voice and came up behind her. 'Mum, I'll look after this.'

'You look after this at work. This is not a police station; this is my house.'

'Just give me a minute, Mum. Please.'

She huffed her retreat, but her look left both men in no doubt that she and the knife would return if anything untoward happened on her neatly swept porch.

'Jesus Christ,' said Twist, looking after Brian's disappearing mother. 'I just wanted to apologise for Harrison. He won't be around for long.'

Brian looked at Twist and figured that Jimmy Doyle must've repeated the story about how Brian had refused to fit him up with the gun. Twist was either a big fan of peace, or he didn't want the coppers to come down on them like a ton of bricks.

'I reckon you've done the right thing by coming here to apologise and I won't forget it,' Brian told him sincerely.

As Jack Twist walked down the veranda steps, Brian suspected a bridge had just been built. He also reckoned that if he was ever in trouble, Twist would intervene, just like Jimmy Doyle had.

He had no doubt that Jimmy Doyle had saved his life. And that's a powerful feeling.

A camaraderie formed between these tough men that transcended the crim-copper dynamic. It was further deepened the next day when Brian went to work to find his colleagues had forgotten to mention their cowards' dash to the car in their official recording of the incident.

About three months after the encounter, on Thursday, 6 February 1958, Freddie 'The Frog' Harrison spent five hours drinking with Jimmy Doyle at a hotel before heading off to the docks to collect his pay packet and return a borrowed trailer. As he was removing the trailer from his car, a gunman appeared out of nowhere and shot Harrison in the head. There were 30 men there that day. No one saw anything. Twelve said they were in the two-man toilet when the shooting happened.

Jack Twist remained a strong suspect in the shooting.

Luckily Maggie and Reg became very fond of Margaret. Maggie wasn't the type to admit she was wrong, but Margaret's warm and friendly presence was quickly accepted in the Murphy household. In due course, Brian and Margaret got engaged, but all was not rosy. Brian worried that the life of a policeman was a big thing to inflict on a wife. The consequences of his job—the blowing up of his car and criminals coming to visit—never worried his tough-as-nails mother, but a wife was different. He worried about how having a wife and kids might hold him back: would he hesitate before arresting a violent person? Would he stop to consider the dangers of the job? Up until now, he jumped into the fray without hesitation. Would he do the same if he had little ones who could become fatherless as a result?

Six months into the engagement, when the worries got the better of him, Brian broke it off. Margaret was stunned and upset, but acted with dignity and handed back the ring.

Like a lot of Catholic men did in those days, Brian took his concerns to the local priest.

'She comes from good stock,' the priest advised. 'Marry her and get her pregnant and that'll give her something to worry about.'

Brian's boss, Mick Miller, a man he greatly admired, weighed in on the matter. Miller had combined a police career with a marriage and was confident Brian could too.

Two weeks after ending the engagement, and loaded with advice, Brian headed straight around to see Margaret to make things right again. When he arrived at her house, she wasn't there; she had gone to the pictures with her sister. Now that he had made his decision, he wasn't going anywhere until he spoke to her. Perched like a gargoyle on her front fence, Brian waited. After what seemed like ages, Margaret and her sister came walking up the street. They both saw him and kept walking straight past.

Brian scrambled to his feet. 'Margaret!' he called after her. 'I've made a big mistake!'

Margaret turned and smiled. 'I know that,' she said generously, waiting for him to catch up with her.

He put the engagement ring back on her finger where it belonged.

The wedding was held on the same day as the Caulfield Cup in 1958. Father Paddy Gleeson from St Anthony's in Glen Huntly hurried through the service because he was also the chaplain at the races. A police photographer took an album full of beautiful coloured photographs.

After the service, the guests went to a party at Margaret's family home in Glen Huntly where a chef cooked goulash—a culinary

Meeting Margaret

delight which was all the rage at the time—for all the guests.

They honeymooned in Mildura.

Soon after, Margaret and Brian bought a house in Middle Park which was a semi-slum suburb then, but a step above South Melbourne and Albert Park. It was known as a boarding house area that attracted transients. The area was hard to police because people skipped out on rent, then vanished into the wind.

As a young married man, Brian would work his regular police shifts and, in his spare time, work as a labourer carting grain or splitting logs. The labouring jobs gave him a good workout for his job as a copper.

A year after the wedding, their first son, Reg, was born in 1959. As he suspected it would, becoming a father made Brian even more protective of his family, and more determined to provide well for them. He tried to save a penny whenever he could. Lunches were four pieces of cold Vegemite toast. Margaret would make soup and he would heat up leftovers at work. These sacrifices were easy because he knew they were for the good of his family. He never had two bob in his pocket and he couldn't understand how colleagues could go to the pub or put a bet on. He could only imagine that those coppers were keeping most of their wages and giving their wives very little. Some even questioned him on the wisdom of letting Margaret control the family finances. Brian thought those men were ridiculous. They might have been having a good time, but it was at the expense of their wife and kids. He never would have considered keeping the money he earned. Margaret controlled the lot and she was much better at it than he was.

But it wasn't all plain sailing.

One day, Brian came home after four days away doing surveillance work. He hadn't showered or shaved, and stunk like a pole cat. Margaret was upset and in tears after managing without him day and night, and being pregnant with their second child. Brian was tired himself and unused to discord, so instead of gently trying to find out what was wrong, he yelled at her. Afterwards, he felt incredibly ashamed; he couldn't believe he had further distressed his wife.

Brian didn't understand her behaviour nor did he understand his own. But he knew he had to fix things up: he loaded the baby into the pram, and he and Margaret walked around to the local doctor. After the doctor checked Margaret over, he called Brian in.

'I've got a prescription,' he said.

'For her?' Brian asked.

'No, for you,' he said. 'You have to give her a pound and a half of TLC.' He proceeded to lecture Brian on looking after Margaret. He ended with a sound piece of advice: good husbands took their wives out to parties every now and again. This made them feel appreciated and loved.

On the way home, the two were pushing Reg in the pram and—although they could ill afford it—they stopped for a coffee and some fruit toast in a café in St Kilda. The doctor's advice rang in Brian's ears. He needed to pull his head in. He had come home thinking: *poor me*, rather than thinking about what she had been through—pregnant and unwell, and home all day with a baby.

Through the window of the café, Brian saw a woman he knew. He had charged her with prostitution offences in the past. Just a couple of weeks earlier, she had told him that she had just terminated a pregnancy. Brian had felt so sorry for her. She was Catholic and abortion was condemned by the Church. He knew the weight of religious guilt would be significant. When she spotted them through the window, she burst into tears. Brian gestured for her to come inside.

'Will the baby be all right?' asked Margaret, a little concerned.

'Certainly,' he assured his wife. 'She's just had an abortion. She probably just wants to look at him.'

When the woman approached, without hesitating, Margaret lifted Reg out of the pram and handed him to her. She sat down at the table and nursed the baby lovingly. Her shining eyes told them how grateful she was for Margaret's kindness.

She stared down at Reg and said wistfully, 'I could've had a baby like this'.

There were a lot of prostitutes working the streets in St Kilda in those days. One night on patrol, Brian saw a woman with a little dog on a lead.

'She's a crow,' he told his partner, using the slang word for prostitute.

'How can you tell?' he asked; he was new to the job.

Brian shrugged. 'I've seen her a couple of times tonight.' When they saw her, again, she was putting the little dog over the low fence of a notorious boarding house. That meant she was ready for business. They pulled over to talk to her.

'What are you doing here so late at night?' Brian asked in a friendly voice through the open window of the police car.

'I-I-I'm just taking my dog for a walk,' she stammered.

'If you're going to do this kind of work,' Brian said to her, 'you need to be careful or you're going to get arrested.'

He took in her features. The woman had the demeanour of a housewife not of the street workers he saw on the beat. She also looked very new at the game, and hadn't yet developed the necessary guile to dodge coppers effectively.

Even so, she gave it a shot. 'Doing what?' she asked.

'You're chaining your dog up when you get a customer, the dog lets them know that you'll be back soon.'

She didn't reply.

'You've gotta have a really good reason for doing this, for taking this kind of risk.'

That did the trick.

With tears in her eyes, the woman explained that her husband was in the Painters and Dockers and he rarely gave her money for their three kids. 'I'm doing this to keep the family together, to feed the kids and send them to school.'

When she mentioned her husband's name, Brian recognised it immediately. He was a bad bloke, the type who would have no qualms about killing her if she tried to leave. Brian could see her desperation. He also knew there was no law that made men support their families, nor a pension for a wife who chose to leave.

'You won't have a problem with me,' he told her, 'but you need to be careful because I can't guarantee no other copper will arrest you and lock you up.'

Driving away from her, Brian remembered a story his dad had told him. Reg had stolen food during the Depression to feed his family. In the Confessional, he told the priest what he had done and the priest said, 'What did you do with the food you stole?'

Reg told him he had used it to feed his family, then gave the rest away to others in need.

'My son, this confessional is to hear sins, not to hear about the necessities of life,' said the priest.

No one in the Murphy family had ever forgotten this story. As a copper, Brian saw this every day: it was his job to listen to people and judge the difference between sins and necessity.

13

THE FIRST SHOT

One Friday night in the late 1950s, Brian and a fellow officer, Peter Morris, were called to a break-in at a commercial garage on the corner of Pickles and Crockford Streets in Port Melbourne. A neighbour had reported a light on inside after the owners had left. In those days, garages had petrol pumps out the front and a garage area inside where mechanics fixed cars. They closed at 6 p.m. and any lights on after that suggested someone might be up to no good. The way these robberies usually worked was that one man would break in alone, then whistle to his mates to come and loot the place. Robbing a garage was not a one-man job.

When Brian and Morris arrived, they had a look around outside. While everything seemed secure, they noticed some suspicious scuff marks on the drain pipe. Peter Morris scaled the pipe to gain entry, and when he was inside, he let Brian in the easy way—through the front door.

To flush the intruder out, the two coppers made enough noise to let him know they were there, then waited at the entrance. It wasn't long before a shadow came their way; the shadow was armed with an iron bar. When the man got closer, they told him to drop the weapon and come out with his hands up. The intruder made it clear he wasn't going to do that.

They each knew where they stood.

Brian aimed his gun.

The man suddenly emerged from the shadows wielding the iron bar and rushed at the two cops. Adrenaline flooded Brian's body and slowed everything down for a moment. He fired. The iron bar clanged to the concrete as the burglar fell to the floor, screaming and clutching at his shoulder.

'Who else is with you?' Brian shouted, fearful that any minute, he and Morris could be outnumbered by thugs.

'I'm not telling you,' the man wailed. 'I'm dying. You've shot me.'

Brian turned to Morris and said, 'Handcuff him to that pipe over there and we'll leave him here for the weekend.'

The man looked terror-stricken. 'No! I'll die.' His voice was pleading. Sweat dripped from his brow.

The two cops shrugged in a well-rehearsed way. 'We'll just say we were never here,' said Morris.

Still hyped from the shooting, Brian guarded the wounded man while Morris searched the garage. There was no one else there.

When the bird in the hand still refused to give up the ones in the bush, Brian rang an ambulance. When it arrived, the burglar was loaded in, and Brian hopped in for the ride. He would use the time to persuade him to give up his cronies. When the man again refused, Brian called for the ambo to slow down the trip to the hospital so that he could chat to his groaning passenger. The ambo pulled over and hopped out for a smoke.

'I'm dying! I'm dying!' shrieked the burglar.

Brian examined the bullet wound; the hole the .32 had made was smaller than the width of a pencil. It wasn't a bad wound—but he didn't tell him that.

Brian creased his forehead with mock concern. 'Yep, you *are* dying.' Luckily, the man was bleeding like a stuck pig which helped the impression. 'You might as well give up your mates because you won't be around much longer. Probably wasn't even your job, and they've left you for dead.'

Staring down the barrel of eternity, the crook's tongue loosened and he sang like a bleeding canary. Brian took notes. Got names.

The ambo jumped back in his seat and drove them to the

The first shot

hospital. They unloaded the man and Brian followed the stretcher into emergency. As soon as a doctor appeared at his side, the burglar cried in deep gulping breaths. 'I'm dying, doc!'

'Who told you that?' said the doctor, stifling a grin.

'He did!' With his good arm, the burglar pointed at Brian.

'He's no doctor. I'm the doctor and I'm telling you, you're not dying. In fact, by the looks of this, we can patch you up and you can go home tonight.'

A look of outrage crossed the man's face when he knew that he'd been duped. It was quickly replaced by a look of relief when he realised he'd live to burgle another day.

When Brian got back to the station, one of his colleagues said, 'You're a fucken idiot! You'll get the boot for this.'

While the copper might have thought this would put the fear of God into him, he was wrong; Brian already had the fear of God put into him a couple of hours earlier when the bloke was coming at him with an iron bar. That was the real fear. Fear of repercussions doesn't hold a candle to fear of death. An old saying sprang to mind: *better to be judged by twelve than carried out by six.*

Before Brian shot the burglar, he'd had the words 'mad bastard' thrown in his direction more times than he'd had hot dinners. Afterwards, this growing reputation served him well. Crims were wary of him, but more importantly, so were cops. If a crim ever sidled up to a crooked copper and asked him to intervene in a matter that Brian Murphy was involved in, the cop would shake his head.

Nothing he could do if that mad bastard, Murphy, was involved.

14

BRIANY AND THE BIG BLOKE

It was a fine St Kilda day in 1959 when Brian and a couple of uniformed police officers were doing a job in St Leonards Avenue. They were surprised and chuffed in equal measure when they bumped into two detectives from the Breakers Squad. It had been a couple of years since Brian's brush with Wog Slater, and in the intervening time, he had heard many stories of the legendary antics of the Breakers.

'We're sitting off this address,' one of the detectives said, nodding at a block of flats. 'We're waiting for a bloke from interstate; we've been told he has explosives in the joint.'

Since the detectives were from the Breakers, Brian assumed the explosives would be used for cracking safes.

'We can't wait any longer,' said the detective, looking at his watch. 'Can you blokes keep an eye out and when he gets home, grab him and search his joint?'

They eagerly agreed, honoured to be given such a task. The detectives headed back to the city, leaving Brian and his fellow officers sitting off the suspect's house. They waited until a man built like a brick dunny approached. It figured he would be the one they were waiting for.

When Brian and his colleagues leapt out of the car and formed a rough circle around the man, the man stacked on a turn which left all of them with a shirtful of sore ribs, including the suspect. After he'd quietened down, they took him inside his flat and he watched angrily as the police officers searched his room. Sparsely furnished with only a bed, a dresser and a wardrobe, it didn't take long to have a look around. They found nothing.

Brian looked closely at the bed frame which was made of tubular steel. The legs had rubber stoppers on them. One of the officers suggested taking the stoppers off the bed legs. Once Brian twisted them off, he found gelignite tucked inside the hollow tube on one side, and detonators in the tube on the other. At this point, the big bloke fired up again and it was on for young and old. He was a violent bastard and they were lucky he didn't kill one of them.

They left the flat and bundled the big guy into the police car and took him to the South Melbourne police station.

'I've been fucken loaded up! It's not my gear,' he snarled over and over all the way there.

In Brian's experience, the average villain went off a bit and then quietened down, knowing when they're beat. The fact that this bloke had fired up twice was either because the big bastard thought he could take them on—or he might have genuinely been set up. When he fired up a third time as they got to the police station, Brian began to have doubts about what they were dealing with. The big guy was handcuffed, but it didn't stop him. He was like a wild thing. He head-butted and kicked and slammed himself into anyone who got close.

Once they subdued him, he kept repeating, 'It's not my fucken gear! I've been loaded up.'

'Bullshit,' Brian said. 'We hear this every day. You had it and we're going to charge you with it.'

This clearly wasn't what the big bloke wanted to hear but Brian didn't have time to argue. Time was against him that afternoon. Margaret had to go out so he was on babysitting duty. Brian begged a lift home with one of the cops, leaving the other two at the station with the suspect. Aside from the angry giant, things were quiet at the end of shift. Brian got home around six, and when Margaret told him her meeting had been cancelled, he decided to enjoy an evening at home with her. Back at the station, the other three cops would charge the big bloke and put him in the cells and that would be the end of that.

But it wasn't.

He'd been home less than an hour when there was a knock at the door. It was the officer who had dropped him off. Brian was needed back at work, urgently. In the privacy of the police car, his colleague told him a sorry tale. They had taken the handcuffs off the prisoner to fingerprint him, and he had fired up again.

'We had to give him another biffing and now we can't bring him around.' The cop's voice was strained. 'He's unconscious.'

'Have you put him in the shower?' Brian asked.

'Yep, we tried everything, but he's hardly breathing.'

Fuck, he thought.

But at least the man was still alive.

When they got to the station, Brian saw the big bloke lying in the shower cubical, unconscious. Sure enough, he was breathing in a shallow kind of way, but he didn't look good. By this time, Brian had a plan. He rang his brother who was a plumber and lived close by.

'Bring your ute to the police station and park out the back,' he instructed. 'And leave a tarp in the back.'

Brian's brother asked no questions and promised to bring the ute as soon as he could.

No one else knew the big guy was at the police station—he'd been playing up so much when they had brought him in, it took all of them to restrain him and they hadn't had time to enter him into the arrest register. The sergeants were out on the piss, so the coast was clear.

In due course, Brian's brother left the ute with the keys in it in the back alley. As soon as he walked off, Brian went out and grabbed the tarp. They wrapped the unconscious man in it and loaded him into the ute. Before they left, Brian rang the woman who owned the milk bar near the police station. Cops were her best customers and she was very police-friendly. Brian asked her

Briany and the big bloke

to anonymously ring D24 at 7.45 p.m. and tell them that she had seen two men dumping what she thought was a body at Albert Park Lake near the rowing sheds. She agreed and didn't ask any questions.

The plan was afoot.

Taking both a police car and his brother's ute, they all drove around to the rowing sheds and unloaded the bloke. Brian told one of the cops to take the ute back to his brother's house and leave the keys in the letter box.

Once the ute left, Brian drove the two other cops in the police car straight to the George Hotel in Fitzroy Street as fast as they could. He left the driver in the car while he and the other cop went into the hotel and started a fight—which was easy to do at the George. All they had to do was look at a certain minority group and it was on for young and old. And just as he knew there would be, in minutes there was an almighty brawl.

In front of witnesses.

At the George Hotel.

And not dropping off a body.

Over the sounds of the brawl, Brian heard the police car sound its horn. They left the punch-up, and the cop in the car told them an ambulance had been dispatched to Albert Park Lake and they had been called to attend.

'We're at the George Hotel,' Brian told D24 breathlessly over the radio. 'There's just been a big blue. We'll get there as fast as we can.' He knew that every car in the area would hear their location and their alibi. They drove down Aughtie Drive and arrived at the same time as the ambulance. Once they examined him, the ambos shook their heads and declared that the bloke probably wouldn't make it.

You're joking! Brian thought in horror. The reality hit him as they loaded the guy onto the ambulance. They could all go down for murder. He was terrified. The other cops were standing there like stunned goslings. They weren't saying a word either.

They followed the ambulance to the hospital.

'Right,' said Brian once they were safely inside the police car. 'We don't know who he is and how he came to be there.' Part of this was true. They didn't know who he was—that was why they needed to fingerprint him and that was when he had arced up for the last time.

There was a lot of nodding from his scared colleagues.

'I'll go into the hospital and you two stay in the car,' Brian said.

From the looks of the two he left in the car, he sensed they didn't have the capacity to think long-term. They were all the same rank and all had a similar policing experience. But at that moment Brian knew he had something that they didn't—a survival instinct. He guessed they knew it too because that was why one of them had said, 'Get Murphy', when they couldn't revive the bloke in the first place.

Inside the hospital, Brian saw a doctor he knew called Dr John Coldbeck. He was one of the most gentlemanly and professional doctors he'd ever met. Police and hospitals were like toast and jam—their paths crossed often. Dr Coldbeck approached the stretcher and nodded to Brian.

'Good evening, Briany,' he said. For some reason from the moment they met, he called him Briany. In his cultured educated voice, it sounded old-world and charming.

Brian listened as the ambos told the doctor where they'd found him.

'Thank you, chaps,' said the doctor. 'We'll have a look at him.'

'He looks pretty crook,' Brian said.

'He does indeed,' agreed Coldbeck, 'but we'll see what we can do for him, Briany.'

Brian followed the stretcher and the doctor into the cubicle in the emergency section in Prince Henry's Hospital. He wanted to see if the bloke woke up, and had a vested interest in what he might say if he did.

Dr Coldbeck bent over the patient with a stethoscope. 'His

Briany and the big bloke

heart seems okay,' he said.

Brian stayed a while but there was no change. The man was still deeply unconscious. He asked Dr Coldbeck to let him know as soon as he woke up.

If he woke up.

Back at the police station, Brian sat at the mess table with the three other cops. Two of the blokes were okay but the third had the potential to crack under the pressure of what had happened.

'Here's how it has to be,' he instructed. 'You don't tell anyone. Don't ring anyone. None of us can say anything to anyone. We were at the George Hotel when the bloke was found. No one knows he was here.'

At the end of the conversation, all agreed. The stakes were high. If the bloke died, they could all be locked up. Even though Brian hadn't been there for the final beating, a good silk could argue in court that a punch he'd delivered at the man's flat might have been the fatal one.

If he died that was.

That Sunday at Mass, Brian sat by Margaret and their baby in his bassinet, knowing what he would lose if the man died. He prayed and made lots of promises to God. After Mass, he rang the hospital, but there was no change.

On Monday morning, Brian was about to leave the office to go to the hospital when the phone rang. 'Detective Murphy speaking,' he said.

'Oh, I'm glad about that Briany,' came the genteel voice of Dr Coldbeck. 'I think our friend is playing possum.'

'Oh?'

'I saw him close his eyes as I came into the room.'

'Did you?' Brian said, his mind ticking over.

At the hospital, he met with Dr Coldbeck who said that in his professional opinion, the big bloke was more awake than he wanted anyone to know.

They both made their way to his bedside. Brian gave Dr

Coldbeck a big stage wink and said in a loud voice, 'Do you think he is going to die?'

'I don't hold out a lot of hope,' said the doctor in a grave voice.

Brian nodded towards the door and the doctor took the hint and left. On his way out, he said that he would be down the hall having a cup of tea and asked Brian to join him when he was ready.

Brian waited until the coast was clear and then bent over the big bloke and spoke in a low voice: 'Mate, in just a moment, I'm gonna grab you by the nuts to see if you're awake or not. It's going to hurt a whole lot. Just letting you know.'

'No need,' came a gravelly voice from the bed.

'Here's what I'm gonna do,' Brian told him. 'I don't know who you are and I don't want to know who you are. I'm going to put 40 quid on your bedside table. All your clothes are in your locker by the bed. I'm going down to see the doctor and have a nice cup of tea. If you're still here when I come back in ten minutes, I will have to charge you for those explosives we found.'

There was no answer, just a nod. Brian went to have a cuppa with Dr Coldbeck. He told him that he had been right; the man was not unconscious.

'The bloke said he felt tired so I'd let him sleep.'

'Good idea, Briany,' said the doctor, raising his cup to his lips.

After they finished their tea, the two stopped back to look in on the man.

The hospital bed was empty.

'I hope he's okay,' said Dr Coldbeck.

'Me, too,' said Brian, deep in thought.

A week after the big bloke disappeared, the head of the CIB at Russell Street, Superintendent Hughie Clugston, called Brian to his office. He headed straight into town and was ushered into the superintendent's office. The door was shut behind him.

Hughie Clugston opened with: 'In the CIB, we want brave courageous and thinking men.'

Briany and the big bloke

If this was a fishing expedition, Brian didn't know what the catch was. His mind raced with all his actions over the last six months to see what Clugston could have been referring to.

'I think you've got the potential of at least being one of them. But anything you do in the future, don't do with people who drink too much.'

What was he talking about?

Hughie Clugston himself was well-known for sitting in the Police Club and getting a continuous refill of red wine. Mid-drink, his head would droop, and he would fall asleep.

'I'll tell you what I heard in the club,' he said. 'Three young detectives like you from South Melbourne were talking about a man being found by the side of Albert Park Lake. Your name was mentioned continuously. No doubt you know nothing of it.'

'You're quite right, Mr Clugston,' Brian said, 'I know nothing about it.'

Clugston looked thoughtful. 'Don't jump in too quickly to help people who drink too much, especially in the Police Club.'

Brian nodded. 'Yes, boss.' He stood up to leave. But Clugston wasn't finished.

'For a bloke who wasn't there, you did a good job,' he said with a wink.

Brian made his escape as quickly as was polite. Doing his best to walk rather than run out of the Russell Street CIB, who should he bump into but the Breaking Squad detective who had asked him to search the big bloke's flat in the first place.

'Did you end up seeing him?' the detective asked.

Brian's mind was so full of what had happened over the last week that he was momentarily stunned. 'No, he never turned up. Never saw him.'

'Did you find the explosives in the bed?' he asked.

'Never saw him. Never went into the house.'

And in that small exchange, all was revealed.

How could the detective have known where the explosives were if they didn't put them there? Suddenly the big bloke's aggression made sense; he had indeed been fitted up by the Breakers. Brian had never forgotten his encounter with Wog Slater. The potential for junior police officers to be stooged by detectives was always in the back of his mind.

He now needed to move it to the front of his mind. And keep it there.

Brian headed back to South Melbourne, wanting to biff the Breaking Squad detectives as well as his loose-lipped mates. He gathered the three and told them that they had been overheard at the Police Club.

'That's bullshit!' they said. 'We've told nobody. We just talked about it among ourselves.'

'Was Hughie Clugston there?' Brian asked.

'Yeah, but he was pissed out of his brain.'

'Not so pissed that he didn't hear every word you said!'

Afterwards, Brian thought about what happened from every angle. The whole incident showed him what a strong survival instinct he had. It also brought home that things were not always as they seem. The big bloke looked like a villain but he wasn't guilty. The cops on the other hand, were. Brian was glad that the big bloke walked out of the hospital knowing one of the cops believed him.

Brian's actions had saved a lot of people a lot of grief and Superintendent Hughie Clugston's words made it all seem okay.

Of course, others might argue that getting away with something like this made Brian more brazen.

15

THE TROUBLE WITH HARRY MAC

One day in 1959, Brian was on the corner of Russell Street and Little Bourke when he spotted a thief by the name of Emanuel Kronopolus. Brian had seen him hanging around the card games; the guy was a real smart alec. He dressed like some kind of Greek urban cowboy with white shoes, a long linen coat, and a Mexican band around his hat. This flamboyance stood out like dog's balls among the cardigans of his compatriots.

Kronopolus was loitering on the corner when Brian and a fellow detective approached.

'Good afternoon, Mr Kronopolus,' Brian said, looking him up and down, wishing he could charge him with crimes against fashion.

Some blokes get their hackles up without the slightest provocation. Kronopolus was one of them. Came out fighting. 'Don't you talk to me,' he spat. 'I know Mr Mac.'

'Who's Mr Mac?' Brian said, playing dumb. While he had never met Superintendent Harry McMenamin, he knew the senior officer was in cahoots with Wog Slater. This meant he wouldn't trust him as far as he could throw him.

'He's your boss and I can get you sacked,' Kronopolus said, arrogance dripping from his voice.

Brian took his arrogance and raised it with anger. 'Fuck you and fuck Mr Mac,' he told him. 'You're going in.'

Arresting Kronopolus was a safe bet. There would be warrants—there always were with gamblers. As soon as Brian snapped the handcuffs on him, Kronopolus started grandstanding, swearing and struggling, threatening to get Brian fired.

Undaunted, Brian frogmarched Kronopolus up Russell Street to the city watch house and had him locked up for offensive behaviour. Across the road at the Russell Street CIB, Brian checked Kronopolus's name for warrants and as he suspected there were a couple outstanding; the man would spend the next 24 hours in the lock-up cooling his white heels.

In front of the magistrate the next day, Brian gave evidence that Kronopolus had threatened to get him sacked because he knew Superintendent Harry McMenamin. The magistrate was unimpressed.

'So the fact that you know a senior policeman, you can carry on like this in the street?'

Kronopolus hung his head and said nothing.

The magistrate found him guilty and fined him a couple of quid for his trouble.

As soon as Kronopolus was released, he made a beeline to Harry Mac's office. Brian knew this because not long after, he was summoned there himself.

Superintendent Harry McMenamin was not a man to beat around the bush. 'Tell me to get fucked?' he challenged.

'I wouldn't tell you to get fucked, sir.' Feigned innocence.

'You know what I'm talking about!'

'He's telling you lies,' said Brian. 'I told him that I didn't give a fuck *who he knew*. I certainly didn't tell you to get fucked.' Brian was lying through his teeth of course, but this forced Harry McMenamin to take sides.

McMenamin took the criminal's side. Brian was transferred to the Broadmeadows CIB.

Broadmeadows was a long way away from the Murphys' house in Middle Park, nearly twenty miles. The transfer was most inconvenient, but like all other decisions made by the vagaries of the bosses, the street copper is powerless to protest.

On the first day of his new placement, Brian made the long train ride north. He alighted and began the walk from the train station to the police station. Along the way, he bumped into an old mate he hadn't seen for ages. The guy was stepping out of a phone box.

'G'day, Murph!' he said, big grin on his face. 'Howya going?'

'Good,' Brian said.

'Where are you headed?' he asked.

'I'm headed off to work,' Brian told him. He was dressed in the plain-clothes suit required of a detective.

'You don't need a new suit do you?'

Brian glanced at his mate's vagrant-like attire. The whole time Brian had known him, the bloke always had the backside out of his trousers; it looked as if nothing much had changed.

'Where did you get suits to sell?' he asked.

'Mate, I've got a house full of 'em. We knocked over the Roger David store in the city.'

'Whereabouts are they?' Brian asked casually.

'At my house down the road,' grinned the light-fingered fellow, eager for a sale.

On the way to his house, they chatted about mutual friends. A crim mate of his met them both at the door.

'What's he doing here?!' he asked in horror, staring at Brian.

'He's my mate, Brian,' said the ragtag friend.

'He's a copper!'

At this point, the friend turned to Brian, slack-jawed. 'You really a copper?'

'Yes I am,' Brian said, shrugging.

There followed that awkward moment when you realise that you've just invited a copper in to look at your stolen goods.

The ragtag friend's voice was suddenly uncertain. 'But he's all right. He won't say anything.'

Brian slowly shook his head. 'It doesn't work that way,' he said, getting out the handcuffs.

Brian arrested them both and walked them to the phone box where he had originally bumped into his mate. A quick telephone call to the station had a divvy van arrive minutes later to collect the two men, and a second divvy van to pick up the suits.

Brian continued his walk to work, and arrived whistling a tune of satisfaction. He was in a good mood, but his new Broadmeadows boss was not. He hauled Brian over the coals. Half an hour late! What kind of copper was he?

Brian let him vent. 'Sorry boss,' he said when he could get a word in edgeways. 'I was late because I made an arrest on the way here.'

He looked at Brian suspiciously. 'What?' he said. 'A drunk and disorderly?'

'No, I just located all the suits that were knocked off from the Roger David store last night. Caught the two blokes who did it.'

Lips pursed angrily, the boss picked up the phone and rang Russell Street to ask if the Roger David store had been robbed. Brian saw him nodding, face relaxing. Then, he asked to be put through to Harry McMenamin at the Russell Street CIB and told him that Broadmeadows had located the suits from the robbery.

'We've cleaned it up,' he said. 'We're processing two heads now.'

Brian waited for the boss to mention his name but he didn't. He knew then that his new boss was a Harry Mac man and that his reputation had preceded him. Brian caught the crooks, the boss took the glory.

Lucky for Brian, catching crooks was its own reward.

That same boss at the Broadmeadows CIB, turned out to be a weak bludger who niggled and complained constantly. He was a stickler for paperwork. He didn't ask the other detectives, but he asked Brian every day: *is your diary up to date?* Paperwork was not one of Brian's strong suits, but he realised pretty quickly that if his diary wasn't up to date, the boss would use it as a breach of discipline. No matter what he did at Broadmeadows, he would be under the microscope.

It didn't take him long to find a chink in the boss's armour, though. The boss constantly complained about his firewood going missing. He suspected his next door neighbour was jumping over his fence and pinching it.

Brian began to exploit his boss's paranoia.

He overheard the boss talking on the phone to his wife: 'Have you checked the wood pile?' He waited for her answer. 'No, there should be another four pieces than that.' The voice rose loudly enough to be heard around the office. He sounded a little nutty.

When he got off the phone, Brian said, 'Boss, I heard about the firewood missing from your joint'.

'How did you hear that?' Face intense.

'I couldn't help overhearing your conversation.'

The boss's face reddened with anger and his story spilled out. 'The bloke next door is pinching my firewood. He hops over the fence every night and steals it.'

'You might have to sit up all night and—'

'What!?' the boss screeched, clearly the thought of actually policing his woodpile was beneath him.

Brian changed tack. 'Or get some of the coppers to sit up all night.'

His anger flowed from the alleged firewood thief to Brian. 'I don't live in this area! I can't use my own men. And anyway, coppers aren't paid for that kind of thing.'

'We get paid to catch thieves.' Brian reasoned.

'Don't you worry about it!'

Brian shrugged and walked off, satisfied. The pot was stirred.

Every day after that, Brian would inquire about the firewood. And every day, the boss would give him a version of: 'Don't you worry about my firewood. Let me take care of it.' But every day, the boss looked more rattled.

One day, Brian upped the ante: 'You have to be careful—he

might start pinching your wife's linen …' He let the thought hang in the air. 'Or her underclothes …'

Brian watched his eyes narrow. The boss hurried to the nearest telephone and rang his wife. 'What are you doing today?' he barked. Then listened for a moment. 'Well cancel your plans! You have to stay at home to guard the backyard.'

At that moment, Brian knew he had him. From then on, he would wait until the boss was approaching the muster room, and start talking about cases where people had broken into other people's backyards.

'If someone was stealing my firewood, this is what I would do,' Brian said. 'I'd get some firecrackers and hide them in the firewood.'

'Hmmm?' said the boss, reeled in like a Murray cod.

Brian nodded. 'When he lights it, the crackers'll go off in his fireplace. Scare the shit out of him.'

'Where would you get the crackers?' the boss asked shrewdly.

The other cops knew what Brian was up to and did their best not to crack up laughing.

All's fair in love and war … and workplace bullying. While his boss was paranoid about his backyard woodpile … he had less energy to focus on Brian.

After a couple of months, Brian was transferred over to Coburg where one day, he was called to a backyard shooting; a man had been shot in the stomach. In those days, forensic work was in its infancy and police mostly relied on common sense. At the scene, Brian located a bullet hole in the fence and had an idea. He grabbed a bit of straw and lined it up. It seemed to point to the block of flats across the road.

When he walked across the road and knocked on the door of the front flat, a woman answered. 'Are you coming to arrest my husband for shooting that bloke?' she asked.

'Yes,' Brian said, trying to hide his surprise.

'The gun's in the rubbish bin where he put it and he's hiding in the bedroom,' she said. 'He didn't mean to do it. He was just mucking around with it.'

Once Brian had arrested the man, he had an idea that might counter the negativity that Harry McMenamin was spreading about him. If Brian's name was in the paper for making an arrest, it might make others stop and think that maybe he wasn't such a nutcase after all. Back at the office, Brian put on a different voice and rang the newspapers. He told them that he'd heard that the detectives in Coburg had done a great job and arrested a man over a shooting. Minutes later, the phone rang and Brian used his normal voice to answer.

'Coburg CIB.'

Sure enough, the media was onto it like a dieter to a cupcake. The story of the shooting and arrest made the papers the next morning. Detective Brian Murphy had arrested a gunman.

From his throne at Russell Street, Harry McMenamin rang Brian to haul him over the coals for speaking to the press.

Brian played dumb. 'I couldn't help it boss; they rang me.'

Which technically was true.

Brian ended up with a great boss when he moved from Coburg to Brunswick. Senior Sergeant Eric Duffy wasn't threatened by a detective with an idea. Brunswick was a melting pot, a rich breeding ground for a variety of good criminals. Brian did the same work, but there was no tension; sometimes you don't understand what tension does to you until it's not there.

Every morning, Duffy would gather his troops and ask what they had on for the day. He'd listen and then list jobs that had come up overnight. When the detectives were finished, they were free to pursue their ongoing cases. Duffy taught Brian the value of listening and giving people a loose rein, and when necessary, backing them up with whatever they needed.

In one case, a girl had been attacked and raped in a park on Melville Road, West Brunswick. The victim had worked with a police artist, and together they had come up with a sketch of the suspect; he looked Middle Eastern or Italian as far as Brian could tell. The girl gave a solid description of the clothes he was wearing, right down to a pair of sandshoes.

To Brian's way of thinking, the perpetrator was probably a local and probably frequented the park. That gave him an idea.

'I know a bloke who has a car yard,' he told his boss. 'I could borrow a car and we could sit close to the park where he grabbed the girl and watch for him.'

Duffy mulled it over, nodding. 'Don't drive it,' he said, 'because our insurance won't cover it. Get your mate to drop the car off and you can sit in it doing surveillance. I'll give you a week.'

After sitting in the borrowed car for four days, Brian and his colleagues saw a man who could have walked straight out of the sketch. They jumped out of the car and arrested him on the spot then drove him to his house where they found the clothing and sandshoes that the victim had described. The rapist got three years in prison.

If it hadn't been for Duffy allowing Brian's idea, they never would have caught him.

Although a lot of cops had heard Harry McMenamin's version of Brian Murphy, the more arrests Brian made, the more people believed in what they saw rather than what they heard. From the time his boss picked on him back when he was an apprentice watchmaker, to the trouble with Harry, Brian began to see the pattern. He was slowly learning to keep his mouth shut and fly under the radar. Well, occasionally, anyway.

16

GLAZEBROOKS PAINTS

At 4 p.m. one Friday afternoon in 1959, at the South Melbourne CIB, Brian and his partner Peter Morris got called to a job at Glazebrooks Paints. When they arrived, it became apparent that the paint factory itself was no advertisement for the company's products—it was a huge ugly post-war building with rusted window frames and walls blackened by fumes from Williamstown Road traffic.

'Are you the coppers?' asked the girl at the counter in a nasal voice, before slouching off to get the manager.

The middle-aged manager, wearing a wrinkled, grey dust coat, appeared and invited the detectives into his office. After introductions, Brian asked him what the problem was.

'We've had a stocktake and it seems that a lot of paint is missing,' he said. 'Thousands of pounds' worth.'

'Really?' Brian asked, wondering how huge quantities of paint could vanish right under his nose.

The manager nodded. 'It's definitely been stolen and we don't know where it's gone.'

Brian got the distinct impression that the manager was only reporting it missing because he would eventually have to account for it and his job might be on the line. A glance at Morris, told him his partner was thinking the same thing.

Brian asked to see the storeman, truck driver and forklift driver. He figured that if significant quantities of anything had gone missing, all three would have to be in cahoots.

As soon as the manager returned with the three men, Brian and Morris took the forklift driver and left the others to stew. He was a little man. He scratched a match against a matchbook and lit a thin hand-rolled cigarette, blinking nervously at the two coppers.

'Gees, the jacks,' he said, using the street slang for cops, snorting in between words and dragging on his cigarette like some wannabe movie gangster.

'Mate, you're in deep shit,' said Brian. 'Missing paint. We know what you've all been up to and I bet you're getting nothing compared to what they've made.' He nodded towards the adjacent offices where the others were waiting. 'You're going down.'

The forklift driver looked jumpy and upset—the desired attributes in a weak link. He put the cigarette in his mouth and didn't draw on it. 'You don't know what ya talking about.'

'We do fucken know what we're talking about,' Brian said as if he really did. At this stage, all they knew was that paint had gone missing, and lots of paint needed a forklift to move it. Brian went with his gut. 'And we're going to lock you up.'

The man's shoulders slumped. 'Aw fuck. Who gave me up?'

Bingo! 'Mate, it doesn't matter who gave you up. We know everything.' Brian always enjoyed this bit.

'Are you going to search my joint?' he whined.

Thanks for that. 'Why? What have you got at your joint?' Brian asked the question in a way that suggested he already knew.

'Couple of tins of paint.'

Brian nodded. 'Here's how it's gonna be. We're going to take you back to the South Melbourne CIB and we'll have someone search your house and find out what you've got hidden.'

The bloke physically trembled. Then Morris had a turn.

'You know the two blokes you came up here with—would you say they're the main offenders?'

The forklift driver nodded. 'But there're others as well.'

Brian called for a divvy van and another CIB car so they could transport the three men separately.

Glazebrooks paints

Back at the CIB, the forklift driver told them the whole story. He would use the forklift to load up the truck at the direction of the foreman. Stolen paint was always put in a crate which was how the forklift driver recognised it. He was getting an extra five quid a day to help out—an amount that effectively doubled his wages. As an extra lark, the forklift driver would also load drums of paint out the back of the premises into a huge rubbish pile. Municipal workers from the tip were in on the whole operation and took the paint drums and filled orders for paint just like a little side business. The whole operation had been going on for a couple of years.

Even though it had been years, Brian offered the forklift driver a deal. 'These other bastards are earning a fortune,' he said, 'and you're getting a measly five quid a day.'

'Yeah,' the forklift driver agreed eagerly.

'We'll look after you. We'll only charge you with a year.'

'Thanks!'

'But if I find out anything else,' Brian warned, 'we're going to come back.'

It was always better to leave them nervous.

A month later, the CIB got an anonymous tip that a bloke called Wilson who owned a pub in Port Melbourne had painted his whole place with stolen paint.

'Prove it,' Wilson said when Brian and Morris confronted him.

Cops love it when smug crooks say that. Proving stuff was their *raison d'être*.

Around the back of the pub were some discarded paint tins with the Glazebrooks logo. They were the same large tins that the forklift driver had reported carting out the back of the factory and leaving on the rubbish dump. The pub owner was shifty when Brian asked him for receipts; he didn't have any. Considering he could have claimed the cost on his tax, the lack of receipts for paint that would have cost a fortune, was damning.

They collected the empty paint tins and took them to

Glazebrooks Paints. The tins had a code on them that told the company what the paint was and when it was produced. They took batch samples kept by the company, and after consultation with the techs at Glazebrooks, Brian went back to the pub and scraped samples off the pub's walls. The case was easier to prove than it looked; Glazebrooks told the detectives that particular colour hadn't been released yet.

Brian had heard someone at the CIB talking about some new technology at Melbourne University—an electro-spectrographic machine that could scientifically identify and match colours. Brian took three samples to a scientist there who was very excited to help the police.

'We can prove whether or not these samples come from the same paint source,' the scientist said.

'That would be fantastic!' Brian enthused. If he could match the paint from the tins behind the pub and the wall scrapings with the samples from Glazebrooks Paints, that would give the police enough evidence to charge the pub owner with receiving stolen paint. It wasn't often that a copper got to use science in crime investigations in those days.

'We will expedite this immediately for you, Mr Murphy.'

Immediately took ten days.

When the scientist sent word his report was ready, Brian read it eagerly; in a nutshell, the three paint samples came from the same source. That meant the paint was stolen.

It also meant that the forklift driver had lied. He had sold enough drums of the stolen paint for Wilson to paint his entire pub. With a little digging, Brian and Morris soon saw the size of the operation. They reckoned every house in South Melbourne had been painted with stolen Glazebrooks paints.

As soon as Brian knocked on the forklift driver's door, the man said, 'I know what you're here for.'

'Mate, I gave you the opportunity to tell the truth and you lied

Glazebrooks paints

to us.'

The forklift driver ended up doing jail time. Ironically, the other two received heavy fines but remained free. The day Brian arrested him, he declared, 'I'm only a small fish in all of this.'

'What are you talking about?' said Brian, not willing to trust the shifty forklift driver.

'Once a fortnight, a semi-trailer loaded with 44-gallon drums goes to Western Australia and it's not accounted for. It's going from the very top.'

This is going to be a ball-tearer, Brian thought. He knew the security officer at Glazebrooks Paints, a guy called Hanlon whose brother was a cop. Brian rang him and arranged to meet at the police station with Brian's senior sergeant, Jimmy Ryan.

Jimmy Ryan didn't like Hanlon's cop brother—reckoned he was sanctimonious.

'The brother's a good bloke,' Brian said. 'So is this guy. I don't want him upset. I think I can get to the truth.'

As soon as Hanlon sat down, he told the two coppers he could check the paperwork for the truck, which meant that police could investigate the destination points to see where the truck was taking the stolen paint.

As soon as Hanlon left, Jimmy Ryan told Brian to take leave immediately.

Brian was puzzled. 'Why? I don't want to go on leave.'

'You're going on leave for three weeks,' Ryan said. 'Do as you're fucken told.'

The manager of Glazebrooks Paints resigned that week and was made an Australian trade commissioner overseas so conveniently left the country. If Brian was a suspicious man, he might have suspected that Jimmy Ryan saw the potential to make a quid and took his information, hat in hand—with the other hand held out—to Glazebrooks Paints.

When Brian came back from leave, he visited Glazebrooks Paints and spoke to Hanlon. 'You wouldn't believe what happened,'

Hanlon said. 'I gave your sergeant the information and nothing happened. The big boss resigned and went overseas.'

'I think my boss got a quid out of it,' Brian said.

Hanlon nodded in disgust. 'I spoke to my brother and he reckons the same thing.'

Not willing to forget it, Brian approached Jimmy Ryan. 'What happened with the arrest?' His tone made the accusation clear.

Ryan shook his head. 'We were a couple of days too late.' He shrugged. 'We missed our opportunity.'

Yeah right.

In a strange twist of fate, Brian would run into the forklift driver 30 years later when he was visiting a sick mate in hospital. During the visit, he noticed the man in the next bed glaring at him.

'Who's that?' Brian asked his mate in a low voice.

The mate mistook Brian's query for a desire to be introduced.

'This is my mate, Brian Murphy,' he said in a chipper voice.

'I know who you are,' snarled the little bloke, 'you fucken sent me to jail and I never fucken got over it.'

'What are you talking about?' Brian said. 'I don't remember your face.' These kinds of encounters, thankfully rare, were always a possibility when you locked up a lot of people.

'From Glazebrooks.'

Brian started laughing. Of course he remembered. The forklift driver.

'I've been laying here thinking about what I was going to say to you.'

'If you're going to say something, say it,' Brian said, squarely.

'The number of times I've thought about bashing the shit out of you—'

'You should have tried it then,' Brian deadpanned. 'You've lost the fucken chance—you're in hospital on a bloody oxygen machine.'

The man's face softened. 'When I got out of the can, my life changed. My wife gave me a second chance and the next 20 years were the best of my life.' The man's wife had visited him faithfully in jail.

'That was good of her,' Brian said.

The old man looked wistful. 'At first, I thought she was doing it to keep up appearances, you know, so that people would think she was being a good wife. But after a long time, I realised she was doing it out of loyalty to me.' He wiped a tear from his eye.

So did Brian.

In the end, they had a good laugh and he declared that Brian mustn't be such a bad bloke, after all.

From then on, every time Brian visited his mate, he always took the former forklift driver some magazines and had a nice visit.

17

BILLY 'THE TEXAN' LONGLEY

Back in June 1958 when Billy 'The Texan' Longley was just plain Billy, he married a woman named Pat McGowan at the Wesley Church in Lonsdale Street in the city. He said he loved her, but it would only be a couple of years before Brian stood guarding the scene of her murder and Billy was on the run.

It was early January in the summer of 1961 when detectives at the South Melbourne CIB were called to the crime scene in Coventry Street. By the time Brian got there with a uniform copper called Noel Boyd, Pat McGowan's body had been taken to the morgue. It was their job to guard the house in case Billy Longley returned.

A gaggle of press pushed microphones in the faces of the Homicide Squad detectives as Brian and Boyd drove up. They parked further up the street and skirted around the media scrum.

The Homicide detectives at the scene that night were as arrogant as the rest of their ilk. Given the mutual dislike, the detectives skipped the pleasantries and fired off a summary. 'Longley has shot his missus and scarpered. Bunch of drunks here when we arrived. None of 'em knew where Longley went, and none of 'em saw anything. You two are to guard the scene till 8 o'clock in the morning.'

Brian and Boyd would wait in the dark house overnight, and if Longley came back, they were to arrest him. Questioning him was off the table—that would be the job of the Homicide Squad who would swoop in and claim the glory for themselves.

There was a long list of don'ts: don't use the phone, answer the phone, turn on any lights, and most importantly, don't drink anything. Brian and Boyd didn't need a warning for that one. A year earlier, a detective guarding a murder scene in Brighton made the mistake of helping himself to a bottle of milk in the fridge. Unbeknownst to the detective, the milk had been laced with some deadly poison and the detective had spent months in hospital at death's door.

The parting words of the Homicide detectives: 'Don't go near the fucken fridge and keep your fucken hands off everything'.

Brian always carried a gun, but on this day, he had been caught on the hop and didn't have one. He wondered what would happen if Billy Longley returned. While Brian had never met the infamous member of the Painters and Dockers, Longley was well-known for carrying a .45. Boyd didn't have a gun either. Brian knew him from the station and he was one of the politest blokes he'd ever met—not the ideal quality to confront a man who had allegedly just shot his missus.

Left to their own devices, Brian and Boyd had a bit of a stickybeak around the house. The cottage Billy lived in with his bride of two years was neat and nicely kept—aside from the blood. Pat McGowan had died in the front bedroom. Brian was careful not to touch anything because the fingerprint branch hadn't been there yet. The front window had had an obvious bullet hole in the centre with spider-web cracks emanating from it. A lace curtain moved languidly in the faint breeze. As a detective, Brian could read the scene well enough. Pat had been standing in her bedroom when someone fired the fatal shot from the outside.

'Reckon she bled to death,' Brian told Boyd as they looked down at the pool of congealing blood on the linoleum. Freshly-spilled blood has an odour that is hard to describe: butcher shop? slaughterhouse? sorrow? Tomorrow, it would turn rancid in the heat and attract flies.

A small hole in the opposite wall showed the trajectory of the bullet. It had travelled through Pat and lodged itself into the plaster.

A wedding photo on the sideboard showed Mr and Mrs Longley looking like Hollywood movie stars—him in a neat suit and tie, and her in a three-quarter-length satin wedding frock, holding a small posy of flowers. Hours earlier, the bride had been carried back over the threshold, by morgue attendants who left scuff marks in her blood.

'How did it get from that to this?' Boyd said, looking from the photo to the blood.

Brian's best guess was that Billy Longley must've gone off his nut and shot her. He had seen a lot of violence perpetrated on women. Mix alcohol and aggression and it always came home to roost. There were signs of a party—bottles of grog and glasses littered around. Because neither of them had a gun, Brian made his way into the kitchen to look for a weapon. The kitchen cupboards were Harlequin—all different colours. The Murphys had similar ones in their house.

Brian ferreted around in the utility drawer and found a rolling pin; it would make a good weapon if Billy surprised them in his lounge room in the middle of the night. Boyd chose not to have a weapon. From what Brian knew of him, he might not use it anyway. Even so, he was a big strong man and would make good back-up.

Brian and Boyd settled into armchairs in the lounge room in the small hours of the morning, and drifted off to sleep.

Around 4 a.m., a loud banging noise woke them. Brian scrambled for the rolling pin but couldn't find it in the dark. He sensed Boyd moving too. The next minute, in the pitch dark, a figure loomed towards Brian. He swung a punch and connected with a jaw. There was an *ooomphh* sound and then the sound of someone collapsing onto the couch. Brian's eyes adjusted to the dark and he could see the outline of a man on the couch, clutching at his jaw.

'I think I've got a broken jaw,' came a muffled voice from the couch. It was Boyd.

Brian's adrenaline levels dropped from 100 to guilty immediately.

'Mate!' He was horrified and hurried to the side of his fallen comrade. 'Jesus, I'm sorry.'

Boyd patted Brian's arm and said, 'It's all right.'

'I'll ring D24. We'll get someone here.'

Boyd spoke out of the corner of his mouth. 'Nah, we'll be in the shit if we use the phone.'

They were both stuck. Brian couldn't even open the fridge to see if the Longleys had some ice, because it could be booby-trapped. They passed the next four hours waiting to be relieved with no way to let anyone know they needed help. When the sun rose and the blackness in the lounge room turned to grey, Brian could see Boyd properly. His cheek was so swollen, it looked as if he had a golf ball in his mouth. His jaw was definitely broken.

'What was that bloody banging sound?' Brian said.

'Cat jumping on the roof?' Boyd slurred out of the good corner of his mouth.

When they heard the divvy van pull up outside, Brian helped Boyd to his feet and they made their way out of the house. Boyd clutched the side of his face, clearly in a lot of pain.

'Who the fuck did that?' one of the replacements asked.

'Me,' Brian said after an awkward moment. 'We heard a noise and we both were half asleep and jumped up together. I biffed him.'

Boyd nodded.

The replacements pissed themselves laughing. Brian and Boyd didn't see the funny side of it.

After he recovered, Boyd never said anything about his broken jaw. He would greet Brian with a cheery, 'G'day Murph!' and that was it.

Billy gave himself up on the following Monday with his solicitor in tow. Even though the solicitor told the Homicide detectives that he was handing Billy over unharmed, that didn't stop detectives from beating him so severely over the next four hours that it would be described in court as torture. Billy later told Brian that the beating was so bad he wanted to die that day.

Brian could only hope that the pain of what happened to his wife might have made Billy want to die that day, too. While Billy admitted to having a violent argument, during which he accused her of seeing another man, he denied firing the fatal shot. He claimed it was Pat's father who had the gun. He and Billy had fought on the veranda and the gun had gone off. The first jury did not believe Billy's story and the judge sentenced him to nine years in prison. An appeal granted a new trial and the second jury found Billy not guilty. All up, he spent a year in jail.

Pat McGowan left behind a son who was ten when she met Billy and barely a teenager when his mother died in her own bedroom.

As for Brian and Billy Longley, they weren't destined to meet that night although later they would become friends—but that only happened after the world twisted in on itself, and Brian learnt that a copper can find allies in the most unlikely of places.

18

HELLO HELL'S ANGELS

Back in the early 1960s, an elderly woman approached Brian near the grocery shop in Armstrong Street, Albert Park. Brian was stationed at Port Melbourne, but was off-duty when he greeted the woman and asked how she was. She immediately burst into tears.

'What's wrong?' he asked, taken aback by her distress.

'Mr Murphy, I can't be seen talking to you,' she wailed.

'Let's take a walk.' Brian took her by the elbow and led her away from the shops. After a bit of prompting, she told him her story.

'We live in Nimmo Street and next door some terrible people have moved in. They steal our bread and our milk.'

'Really?'

'Ask Old Bob at the newsagent. He'll tell you. The paperboys deliver the paper every day and the neighbours steal that, too.' The elderly woman explained that she and her sister lived in adjoining cottages, and the new neighbours urinated on her fence, causing a disgusting stench. When she tried to talk to her sister over their connecting fence, the men would shout and swear at her from their yard next door. 'They use disgraceful language,' she told Brian in a quivering voice, 'and they even take God's name in vain.'

While Brian himself was known to use disgraceful language when the situation called for it, he would never use it in front of ladies. 'Who *are* they?' he asked.

'I don't know who they are,' she said. 'They are dirty and they all have motorbikes,'

Brian considered this. Since very few people had more than one motorbike, it sounded like a bikie gang. 'Go home,' Brian told her. 'Lock your front door and forget about it.'

She smiled gratefully and took his hand. 'God bless you,' she said as tears glistened in her eyes.

Brian went down to the newsagent and spoke to Old Bob.

'Those old sheilas complaining again?' Old Bob muttered. 'They need to keep their mouths shut or they'll be in strife.'

'No,' Brian said. 'They should not keep their mouths shut. Who are these blokes?'

Bob looked from side to side as if he was in a spy movie. 'I don't want to say,' he said.

'Just bloody tell me who they are,' Brian snapped. He couldn't believe Old Bob knew there was a problem and was prepared to let the elderly sisters suffer.

'Hell's Angels,' he whispered.

As soon as Brian got to work that afternoon, he made a couple of phone calls to colleagues in South Melbourne, Port Melbourne, Prahran and St Kilda. His heart was beating a little faster as he shared his cunning plan. First, the bikies would be asked nicely to leave and, if they refused—which they were sure to—a couple of dozen police officers might help change their minds.

There were a lot of excited cops around that afternoon.

As soon as they arrived at the house, a big double-storey affair, Brian could see the problem. It looked as if the bikies had arrived one day and simply set up shop. Squatters, by the looks of things. The front door was wide open and the police could hear yelling and carrying on upstairs. Since they didn't want to be accused of using standover techniques—not this early in the game, at least—Brian went in alone. Drawn to the noise upstairs, he headed in that direction. The whole place stank of cigarettes, stale beer and filth. Jim Beam bottles fought for supremacy with beer bottles as the main decorating item.

'Go! Go! Go!' A chorus of about fifteen blokes chanting and clapping.

Brian had a fair suspicion of what might be going on—an initiation ceremony. These usually involved a new bikie doing the horizontal limbo with a female groupie while being cheered on in front of their bikie mates.

The bloke guarding the top of the stairs was about six foot tall, wearing black boots and leather pants topped with a black jacket.

'Good evening,' Brian said in the posh voice he liked to use for such occasions.

'I'll give you "good evening" you fucken poofter,' the bikie snarled.

'How dare you!' Brian said in mock dismay.

'I'll give you "how dare you!" I'll chuck you out the fucken door.'

'My good man, I've come here to ask you to quieten things down.' Brian raised his hands in mock innocence.

By this time, the six-footer was joined by another couple of blokes.

'I'm so sorry to have bothered you,' Brian said politely, backing down the stairs, knowing that they'd no doubt follow him down.

A couple of them laughed: threatening laughter, not mirth.

Without turning his back on them, he edged down the stairs and out the front door which he shut behind him. Once he was out, police reinforcements arrived. There were cop cars everywhere, silent, lights off, blocking off the whole street. It was a sight to behold.

Eighteen coppers stormed in like lunatics, swearing like troopers, heading up the stairs.

'Just fucken chuck 'em down the stairs,' Brian yelled.

Soon, there were Hell's Angels rolling down the stairs like nine-pins, to the waiting coppers at the bottom.

It took them about three minutes to empty the whole house.

Bikies were thrown into divvy vans. The woman who was the subject of the cheering, followed the police out, screaming, 'I'm sorry! I'm sorry!' She begged to be allowed to leave with her boyfriend.

In the confusion, someone agreed for her to leave. As soon as she jumped on the back of a waiting motorcycle, another cop who didn't know that she had permission to go, chucked a baton towards the bike. It hit the wheel and she plopped off on her arse. The bikie turned around to see where she'd gone and rode straight into a big tree, much to the amusement of the gathered law enforcers.

Some of the bikies took off like shit from a slingshot, while another dozen ended up at the police station for a bit of a mind-change. One by one, they were led into the watch-house—one of them with a half-dozen cops, who wanted to give them a taste of their own medicine. It turned out that bikie bravado doesn't last long when the tables are turned. Each bikie was charged and locked up.

The next day, Brian and a colleague went round to visit the old ladies. They put on crisp uniforms and arrived in a police car to make the ladies feel better. The sisters had an argument about whose house the two police officers would go into for a cup of tea and cake. The one who had spoken to Brian at the shops won. The ladies were tickled pink. The house next door was quiet and there wasn't a motorbike in sight.

'You lovely boys,' said the sister. 'We are so lucky to have such a wonderful police force.'

They had a nice visit, and Brian and his partner walked out of the house, full of cake and praise. It felt good to help people like that. They came into contact with so many arseholes, it was nice to be reminded who they were doing the job for.

19

THE GIRL IN THE TIP

The night watchman couldn't believe his eyes. Stumbling out the gate of the Port Melbourne tip, was a girl. A teenager, as far as he could tell. By the light of his torch, he could see she was injured; her clothes were filthy. She wore no shoes, and her bare legs were covered with blood and mud. He ran over to her and she backed away in terror.

'It's all right, missy,' he said in a kind voice. 'I'm not going to hurt you.'

The girl was distraught: shaking, crying, terrorised. Finally, she let him come closer and he took her arm and pointed to his car. 'I'll take you to the police station,' he said.

She nodded, tears spilling down her dirt-streaked face.

Brian was working the nightshift at the Port Melbourne police station when the two came through the front door. The night watchman explained how he had found the girl coming out of the tip onto Williamstown Road.

The girl was badly beaten. Looking into her eyes, Brian could see that whatever she had faced that night had hurt her profoundly. She shivered uncontrollably. Her nose ran and she wiped it with a dirty sleeve. He fought his natural inclination to offer her a handkerchief because she would be taken to the Royal Women's Hospital to be examined for evidence and he needed to leave her how he found her.

Brian led the girl to an interview room and sat her down. A cop came in with a blanket and wrapped it around her shoulders to get her warm and quell the shaking. Another brought her a hot cup of sweetened tea. Brian was the senior member on duty that night, so it fell to him to supervise. He began the questioning gently.

The girl wrapped her shaking hands around the mug of tea as if to extract its warmth. She was so traumatised, Brian had to repeat each question several times to get an answer. Under the dirt and the horror, the girl reminded Brian of a wounded baby bird.

In a halting voice, she told the police her name and address. Then, bit by bit, she told her story. She had gone into the city to meet a friend to go to the pictures. In the early evening, she had been waiting at the lights near Flinders Street Station to cross the road when a car pulled up at the red light. There were three men in the car and one had opened the door, jumped out, grabbed her, and dragged her into the back seat.

Brian couldn't believe the audacity of the offenders. The girl had literally been plucked off the street.

She continued her horror story. The men had driven her to the tip in Port Melbourne and each man took turns to rape her. When they had finished with her, they simply opened the door of the car and threw her out like rubbish.

Once Brian had taken down the basic details, his work was done and he could get the investigation started by alerting D24 so that all cops could be on the lookout for the three men. He rang Russell Street and asked for a policewoman to come in to talk to the girl further and take her statement. The wisdom of the day dictated that men didn't talk to women about specific details of a sexual assault. Brian and a couple of colleagues waited with the girl; the presence of uniformed police around her seemed to help. She was safe now.

As soon as the policewoman arrived, Brian stepped outside the interview room to brief her. The policewoman was someone he knew by sight. As he spoke to her, however, he felt something was off. While all the male police officers had been moved by the girl's distress, the policewoman seemed a little too cavalier. He and his

The girl in the tip

colleagues decided to wait in the corridor outside the room.

At first, it was okay. The policewoman asked the girl her name and address. But when she heard the girl's date of birth—which made her seventeen—the policewoman turned nasty.

'What are you doing out at this time of night at your age?' she said in a loud, intimidating voice. 'At your age, you should be home! You've gone out and looked for this and now you're here!'

Brian's blood boiled and before he knew it, he raced in. The poor girl was wide-eyed in shock.

The policewoman took one look at Brian and her face turned tomato red—embarrassment, anger? He didn't care. He grabbed her roughly and dragged her out of the room.

'You're a bloody disgrace!' Brian snarled at her. 'And don't open your mouth or I'll knock you out!' He gestured to one of the blokes to go in and sit with the girl.

'I'll report you!' cried the policewoman.

'Don't you worry about that!' Brian said, grabbing the nearest phone and calling for one of the bosses to attend. 'A policewoman's gone off her nut,' he told him.

When the officer turned up, Brian explained the situation. 'She's not going anywhere near that girl.'

'I wouldn't want to,' she sniffed indignantly and left the station in a huff.

Another policewoman was summoned who was the picture of kindness. Brian was glad he'd intervened so that the night wouldn't get any worse for the girl.

But it did.

As soon as she had given her details, Brian had asked one of the coppers to contact her parents and get them to come to the police station to be with her. Brian waited for them outside so he could talk to them before they saw their daughter. They needed to be prepared. The parents arrived at the police station and the mother came up to Brian while the father parked the car.

The mother quickly—and urgently—told Brian that the

girl's father wouldn't understand. Sure enough, the father strutted around the corner and Brian could see the reason the wife had warned him. The man looked down his nose at Brian and curled his lip with disdain.

'I've just been speaking with your wife,' Brian said. 'Your daughter has been grabbed by a couple of men and dragged into a car. She's in a pretty bad state and has been raped at the Port Melbourne tip.'

'I told her not to go out,' said the father, ice in his voice. 'Her mother said it was fine.' The father looked at the mother as if she was dirt.

'Listen, you've both been given the facts now. I'm going to take you in to see your daughter.' Despite the man's attitude, Brian still expected the father to act as a father should.

He was wrong.

As soon as the man saw his daughter, he snarled, 'Look at you! You brought this on yourself!'

The father was the second person to be dragged out of the room that night.

'You should be ashamed of yourself!' Brian roared at the father. 'What's happened to her is no fault of her own. You're not going into that room again, and you're not having anything to do with her until this is all over. You might as well go and sit in your car.'

The father gave Brian a look that he couldn't read, then turned and left the police station.

The mother was lovely. She stayed with her daughter while the second policewoman questioned her. Around 4 a.m., the girl was loaded into the police car along with her mother and taken to the Women's Hospital to be examined by the police surgeon.

Ordinarily, Brian wouldn't have heard anything more about the case once the girl had left the building. They would be called only if the offenders were caught, but no suspects were picked up in the days following the attack.

A couple of months later, a cop from Northcote mentioned the

The girl in the tip

case to Brian. 'You had the young girl who was raped at the tip?'

'Yeah, I remember that,' Brian told him—as if he would ever forget her.

'That was the night you gave it to the policewoman.' He grinned. Word had got around. Then his face turned serious. 'You know she's dead?' he said.

'*What?*'

'The girl had a music lesson after school and the teacher was late. When she got home, her father accused her of being out late with her new boyfriend.'

Brian pictured the shaking, wounded girl wrapped in a blanket at the police station.

'The girl said nothing and went into her father's study where he kept a gun. She put the gun to her head and blew her brains out.'

Brian was shaken to the core, and it took all of his restraint not to cry for her.

20

ROGUES AND SCOUNDRELS

Around 1963, Brian worked with a cop—let's call him the Weasel—who was quite possibly the greediest man for a quid Brian had ever met. He was athletic and charismatic—everyone noticed when he walked into the room; and a psychopath, before the term became fashionable.

One day, a woman came in to the police station and handed in a stray Persian cat. The coppers decided to keep it for a station cat but it would need to be neutered. The Weasel offered to take the cat to the Lort Smith Animal Hospital, and passed around the hat to pay for the surgery. The next shift, the Weasel arrived and told everyone that when he picked up the cat, it escaped out of his car. No one thought much of it, until one of the officers from work went to the Weasel's house and saw the cat.

'That's not the same cat. We've had this one for years,' the Weasel protested when the colleague called him on it.

But the upshot was that he ended up with a free Persian cat and the money for the surgery. The problem with charismatic blokes like Weasel was that they can get a big following of acolytes if they play their cards right—which he did. A big following was essential because when the Weasel wanted to cause trouble, he automatically had a lot of support behind him.

More about him later.

One night, Brian was partnered with a young policeman driving around on patrol in Port Melbourne when a pair of Victoria Dock plainclothes police pulled their unmarked police car up alongside Brian's marked police vehicle. One of the detectives wound down his window and called across.

'Murph, can you do us a favour? You might get a good pinch out of it.'

'Sure,' he said, affably.

'We just saw a bloke'—the detective named a notorious member of the Painters and Dockers—'loading an outboard motor into his car outside the London Hotel in Port Melbourne.'

'Is your arse stuck to the seat?' Brian asked, wondering why they didn't nab the guy themselves.

'Nah, we have to get into the city.' And with that, they drove off.

Brian drove down to the London Hotel and went into the bar. The pub was a watering hole for the Painters and Dockers. Brian suspected the Dock cops were too scared to go inside.

There's a psychology to walking into a pub when you're a cop. Even though you're outnumbered, you always have to look as if you're the one in control. They had a quick look around. In their neatly-pressed uniforms, highly-polished shoes and white hats, they stood out like sore toes. All talking stopped. The threatening silence lasted a moment, then a murmur rose up and conversation came back. Brian spied his target—a big bloke who worked as a standover man, throwing his considerable weight around. 'I want to see you,' he said, grabbing him by his meaty arm.

'What do you fucken want?' the man growled, struggling.

'You know what I want!' Brian nodded towards the men's room. 'In here.'

The cloying stench of stale urine was almost overwhelming but they needed to isolate the bloke from his herd. Once inside the room, the man broke Brian's grip on his arm and took a swing at him. This gave Brian a good excuse to take a swing back. He clipped the big bloke on the edge of the jaw and he went sprawling through the door of one of the cubicles. He tried to scramble back up but his hands slipped on the terrazzo floor, which was wet because while some of his mates might have had a good aim with a gun, they weren't so good in the gents.

The man grabbed the toilet bowl, trying to lever himself up. When his head dipped into the bowl, the temptation was too great. Brian flushed the toilet. There was much yelling and screaming and spitting and questioning of the marital status of Brian's parents. They dragged him upright and searched his pockets.

'Where's your keys?'

'The barman's got 'em,' he spluttered.

As they walked back into the bar to retrieve his keys, one wag called out, 'Hey, I thought you already took a shower this morning.'

'Mate, you're looking a little flushed!' called another.

They walked the wet man through the pub, creating much mirth.

Outside in the parking lot, Brian found the stolen motor in the man's car and drove him back to the police station. On the way there, the damp Painter and Docker offered Brian a small fortune to let him go—five thousand pounds.

'Have you got it on you?' Brian asked, as if he was considering his offer. If he did, Brian would confiscate it and charge him with attempting to bribe a police officer.

'No, but I can get it,' the man said eagerly.

'Sorry mate,' Brian shrugged. 'I don't work on promises.'

They walked him past the counter on the way to the interview room in full view of the Weasel who acknowledged the suspect with a nod of the head. The suspect nodded back. About fifteen minutes into the interview, the suspect was in the middle of telling Brian how he had come about the outboard motor when there was a knock on the door.

'Mate,' said a young constable in a low voice. 'This isn't from me, but there's a grand in it if you let him go.' He nodded towards the suspect. Brian could see the young cop was clearly uncomfortable with what he had been asked to do.

Rogues and scoundrels

'I know who made the offer,' Brian told him, looking him directly in the eye. 'Funny. I've just been offered five thousand. What's he going to do with the other four?' The young cop looked as if he wanted to melt into the ground.

Brian stared him down. 'Six months ago, you would never have made me this offer. Don't listen to him—you'll end up in jail.'

He knew exactly who Brian was talking about. The young man backed away, his face the colour of a red-brick wall. As he left, Brian called after him. 'That's the end of this.' He didn't want the young policeman tainted; he was a good kid and when he first joined, Brian had invited him around for dinner with Margaret and the kids. It made him wonder at the power of the Weasel to turn a decent young bloke into someone who would try and talk a fellow officer into taking a bribe.

Brian finished the interview and charged the Painter and Docker with theft. He was locked up, and bailed out that night.

Early the following morning, Brian saw the Weasel at the police station, bright as a button and congratulating him on a good job.

What bullshit! Brian thought. 'Yeah, it was a good pinch,' he agreed. 'And how are you going?'

'Bonzer!' he said and walked off.

Sometimes it is not about the words spoken. In this brief exchange, Brian knew that he had made an enemy. From that moment on, a whispering campaign began. And the results proved dangerous. Brian would ask an officer to accompany him on a job and the response would be: 'Do I have to?' If Brian entered a room, a bunch of blokes would walk out. It was schoolyard stuff, but annoying nonetheless. Brian reasoned that the most important thing when faced with a situation like that was not to let the aggressors know it's affecting you. They win when you're crushed. These colleagues had no idea who they were dealing with.

One day, Brian was in the muster room when the phone rang. A young cop whose job it was to answer it, ignored the ringing and drank his cup of tea instead.

'Go and answer the phone,' Brian told him.

'I'm having my tea.' He looked at Brian with contempt.

'Go and answer the phone!' Brian ordered him.

A couple of minutes later, the sullen man returned to his seat.

'Who was on the phone?' Brian asked.

'It was D24 ringing about a half-pie domestic down in Garden City.'

'And?' Brian asked, eyebrows raised. Even a half-pie—non-serious domestic—was potentially dangerous to the wife and children involved.

'I'm having my tea break.'

Brian was furious. 'Get off your arse and go to the call. If there's a murder, I'll be the first to give evidence in court to say you refused to take the call because you were having tea.'

As Brian spoke, a new bloke at the table, got up quickly and grabbed his hat. The other bloke followed, grumbling. As it turned out, the assault was a very serious one—the offender had beaten his wife and children so badly they were all taken to hospital. It could have been much worse if the lazy bastard had ignored the call.

It wasn't long before the undercurrent against Brian rose like a flood. He kept turning up to work and doing his job, despite the whispers and sidewards glances when he walked into the room. Brian had never doubted his own ability to outwit the wiliest of crooks, and now he had to use these same skills to deal with his own police colleagues—all because he wouldn't take a bribe. Ironically, the only one who remained polite to him was the Weasel. Maybe he expected Brian to ask him what was wrong with all the other young blokes. But Brian didn't need to ask.

One Saturday, Brian got into work about 1.30 p.m.—half an hour early for his afternoon shift. The boss, Marty Coughlin, was in his office, which was odd because he didn't usually work on a Saturday.

'G'day boss,' Brian said. 'Why are you working today?'

'It's about you,' Coughlin said. 'You'd better come in and close the door.'

Coughlin was a good, hard-working copper who Brian had a lot of respect for.

His agitation was clear. He rolled a cigarette and then put it aside, then rolled a second one without smoking the first.

'What's the trouble?' Brian asked, feeling a bit sorry for him. 'What have I done?'

'Well … ah…' Coughlin hesitated.

Brian decided to help him out. 'Have you ever given me an instruction that I haven't carried out to the letter of the law?'

Coughlin shook his head. 'Nope.'

'Have I ever let a bloke down on the street?'

'Nope.'

'Or in court?'

'Nope.' Coughlin looked embarrassed, then blurted: 'They've held a meeting this morning and there's been a vote of no confidence in you.'

Brian laughed. 'Mate, what do they reckon I've done wrong?'

'One of them had a complaint that you fart in the kitchen.'

'So does everyone. What else?'

'Do you have a water pistol that you fill with dishwashing liquid?'

Brian nodded.

'Do you squirt it at drunk drivers and take their keys?'

'Yes.'

'Well?'

'Dishwashing liquid irritates their eyes and they can't drive. At least they haven't killed themselves and they still have their licence the next morning. A lot of them thank me afterwards.'

Marty Coughlin sighed. 'All I want is a happy station,' he said.

'I'll talk to them,' Brian offered.

Coughlin looked relieved. He ran a good station and didn't want to get bogged down in what he called domestic issues.

Brian had a strategy. Most of the blokes were young and didn't have the guts to confront him so he figured he would confront them all one by one, man to man. And that's what he did. He opened with: 'Do you want to work with me?' and then would follow with: 'If there's something wrong, tell me to my face. Don't go running to the senior sergeant.'

Not one colleague, individually, told Brian that he didn't want to work with him.

An older cop at the station was a bit more cunning. So Brian became more overt. Every day as soon as he got to work, Brian would say loudly, 'Mate! Have you got any complaints about me? If so, I'll come to the boss with you so you can make them.'

Two younger coppers, who Brian knew had attended the no-confidence meeting, were also slow to let go of whatever it was they were bugged about. One day, Brian asked them to go on a job with him.

'Go and get the car. We're going to pick up a crook. He's got a gun in his room.' The man was a well-known criminal called Ray.

'We've got correspondence to do,' one of them said.

Brian pulled rank. 'Get the car!'

Once they got to the address in Bay Street, the two young coppers refused to go inside. Brian took off alone and snuck over the fence into the boarding house where Ray lived in a rented room upstairs. Luckily, the door was unlocked, so Brian was able to surprise Ray in his bed by aiming a gun at him and ordering him to his feet. While the handcuffed suspect looked on, Brian searched the room, annoyed because this was a job for more than one cop and there were two perfectly good ones polishing seat leather with their arses in the police car. He found the gun under Ray's pillow, and an idea formed.

Out of the dusty window of Ray's room, Brian could see the police car parked in the street below. He fired his gun though the window, sending broken glass raining down onto its roof. Meanwhile, he led Ray down the back stairs and out the back gate. They hailed a taxi a little further up Bay Street.

Back at the police station, Brian put Ray in the cells and told the watch-house keeper that the two young cops would be back shortly. 'When they come in,' he told him, 'ask them where Murphy is.'

Brian waited behind a door of the watch house and a couple of minutes later, the two arrived.

'Where's Murphy?' said the watch-house keeper, dutifully.

'We don't know where he is,' said one of the cops, looking a little pale and shamefaced.

Brian stepped out from behind the door. 'I should shoot the both of you for not doing your job. Ray's in the cells without any help from you.' Both officers studied their shoes. Brian's disappearing act had no doubt reminded them of what could happen when cops did not back each other up.

After that, things returned to normal.

Of all who got caught in the Weasel's vortex to discredit him, Brian was most surprised by the young cop who had originally offered him the thousand pounds at the door of the interview room. Even though they were mates, the police officer had voted against Brian in the no-confidence vote, then transferred to another police station. Three months later, he returned to Port Melbourne and made a big entrance. The muster room was full of cops not just locals, but cops from other stations who were scheduled to give evidence in the courthouse next door. Brian was there enjoying a cup of coffee.

'Excuse me, gents,' the young policeman said. 'Can I have a bit of silence?'

Everyone stopped and looked at him.

'Three months ago, I was here and joined in the vote of no confidence against Brian Murphy. I would just like to say I was wrong and I would like to apologise. I hope he'll accept my apology.'

'Good onya,' Brian said. 'Thank you, very much.'

A bunch of other cops asked later what had happened. 'It's all over now,' Brian said, himself not really sure what it had all been about. And that was the end of that.

21

RONALD RYAN AND PETER WALKER

Mid-afternoon on Sunday 19 December 1965, one of the tower guards at Pentridge Prison had been watching prisoners in the yard below and then had turned to see prisoner Ronald Ryan standing behind him. Armed with a pipe, Ryan grabbed the guard's rifle from a rack. With the rifle pointed at him, the guard was forced to open the gate below. He pulled the wrong lever and instead, opened the door below, but not the gate. Ryan marched the guard down the flight of stairs at gunpoint, and it was then the guard realised that Ronald Ryan was not escaping alone. Hiding at the bottom of the stairs was Peter Walker. When Ryan found the gate was still locked, he jabbed the rifle into the guard's kidneys and marched him back up the stairs.

As soon as the gate was unlocked, Ryan and Walker fled, leaving the guard to raise the alarm. On the way out, Ryan threatened a prison chaplain with the rifle. Warder, George Hodson, raced after the fleeing pair. As the scene played out, guards watched helplessly from the tower above. One saw the escapees try to hold up a car in Bell Street but the car sped off, leaving them behind. As George Hodson chased them, Ryan lifted the rifle and aimed. Hodson raised his arms above his head, then fell to the ground as the sound of a gunshot exploded.

He died on the tram tracks on Sydney Road.

Of the two escapees, Ryan was the older, at 41. He had been serving nine years for shop breaking, possession of explosives, and armed burglary. At just 24 years of age, Peter Walker was serving 12 years for armed robbery. As their escape hit the headlines, Victoria Police described the pair as 'desperate and highly dangerous'.

In the days following the prison break, almost a thousand police were called in to join the search. They weren't taking any chances; the rifle Ryan had stolen from the prison was a high-powered 30-calibre US marine carbine, and so every high-powered rifle and pistol available was brought out, cleaned, and given to coppers. Sightings in those early days were rife. A ute found in North Melbourne believed to be used in the escape, had police rushing into the area.

On Thursday 23 December, Ryan and Walker robbed an ANZ Bank in Ormond, menacing staff with the carbine used to shoot George Hodson. During the hold-up, Ryan shouted: 'This gun shot a man a few days ago and I'll use it again!' The two made off with £4,500.

During the hold-up, Ryan shouted: 'This gun shot a man a few days ago and I'll use it again!' The two made off with £4,500.

The Victorian Government offered a £5,000 reward[2] for their capture.

The following day was Christmas Eve. Tensions were high. Ryan and Walker had been on the run for five days and every copper in Melbourne wanted to be the one to nab them. Brian was on duty and attended a car accident in Pickles Street, South Melbourne. By the time he got there, three or four tow-trucks had already arrived, and he knew things could get nasty; tow-truck drivers were a bit like carrion birds—they swooped at the first sign of colliding vehicles and would occasionally come to blows with rivals at the scene of an accident.

Brian stepped in between burley towies. 'All right, fellas,' he said. 'Who was here first?'

---

2   Equivalent to $10,000 at the time–a huge sum then considering the census the following year gave the average salary, post decimal currency, as $57 per week, and the cost of an average house was under $10,000.

A young fellow by the name of Arthur James Henderson from Melbourne Towing Services said he was the first there, and the other towies grudgingly agreed. Coppers got to know tow-truck drivers since they often attended the same accidents scenes. Brian knew Arthur Henderson—known affectionately as 'Boofhead'. He was a bit of a scallywag, but he was a hard worker and a good bloke. He was really grateful when Brian sent the other towies away.

'Are you going to be home in the morning?' Boofhead asked.

'I'll be at work, mate. Why do you ask?' Brian looked at the young man closely.

'Right,' he said, 'I'll come by and give you the best Christmas present ever.'

'What would that be?'

'Walker and Ryan!' Boofhead looked very pleased with himself.

'If you know where they are, tell me and I'll let the Homicide Squad know,' Brian said sharply.

Henderson grinned. 'Nah, I won't tell you now because I don't know for sure, but I know that they'll be at a place that I'm going to at 10.30 in the morning. I'll ring you as soon as I get Chrissy and the baby out.' Chrissy was his girlfriend and she had a two-year-old daughter.

Once the reward was offered, sightings were coming in thick and fast, so Brian left, unsure of whether the young man was bluffing or not.

Arthur Henderson didn't ring the next morning. By then, he was dead.

Sometime between when Brian spoke to him on Christmas Eve and Christmas morning, Henderson was shot in the back of the head at point-blank range. His body was left in a toilet block on Beaconsfield Parade in Albert Park. He was just 26 years old.

On Christmas morning, when Ryan and Walker left the flat where they had all been staying, Henderson's girlfriend, Chrissy—Christina Evelyn Aitken—took her two-year-old daughter to a police station. When questioned, she admitted that Ryan and Walker had come to her flat the day after they escaped. To the 22-year-old woman, no doubt there was a thrill to helping the escapees. Chrissy also admitted buying hair dye for Peter Walker, and had even accompanied him to a hairdresser in Prahran. For her troubles, Walker had given her money which she used to trade in her car and buy a newer one, as well as pay a deposit on a house in Frankston, where the escapees were going to stay.

Chrissy said that Ryan and Walker got the idea—the correct idea as it turned out—that Henderson was going to turn them in for the reward. Chrissy had pleaded with the two fugitives, saying that her boyfriend was harmless. But Walker had gone out to buy beer and had taken Henderson with him, returning to the house alone. A short time later, Chrissy overheard Ryan ask if Henderson was dead.

'There was a pool of blood. His pulse had stopped,' Walker said.

That was when Chrissy decided to go to the police at the first opportunity, even though she would be charged with harbouring the fugitives. The heat from Henderson's murder on top of the heat for killing the prison warden made Ryan and Walker head north.

Ronald Ryan and Peter Walker were captured on Wednesday 5 January. They were free for 18 days and had left two dead men in their wake. Ryan was hanged, but Walker managed to convince a jury that he had killed Arthur Henderson in self-defence.

He got 12 years tacked onto his sentence.

Brian harboured strong doubts as to Walker's plea of self-defence. Henderson was going to turn Ryan and Walker in for the reward money; he knew that for sure. Why would Henderson attack the cash cow the night before? But it wasn't the weak sentence for Henderson's death that riled Brian, rather it was the fact that Walker wasn't charged with acting in concert with Ryan in the death of George Hodson. The law stated that if you act in concert with someone and one commits a crime, all are guilty.

Walker acted with Ryan in the prison escape and Hodson was shot dead as a result.

At the end of the day, Walker's relatively light sentence in the wake of Ryan's hanging, meant little. Brian knew that someone like Walker would eventually be released and because of his nature, would quickly re-offend and probably spend most of his life behind bars. Which turned out to be the case.

22

THE PUSS

In the time between Brian's run-in years earlier with crooked Breakers Squad detectives, the squad's corruption had been exposed in a tell-all book by a Mr X-type informer. The squad had been disbanded and re-formed and Inspector Keith Plattfuss was put in charge of the new Breakers Squad.

Brian first laid squinting eyes on Inspector Keith Plattfuss while lying on the ground outside Government House. Moments earlier, a woman in the crowd protesting a visit by Lyndon B Johnston, had kneed Brian in the unmentionables and down he went. Plattfuss, a huge man, grabbed the woman and drove her headfirst into the rear-end of a police horse, then held a large hand out to Brian, who took it and climbed painfully to his feet.

Later, Brian appeared at the inspector's office with a gift. He'd asked around and found out Plattfuss was fond of fishing and bought him a Mitchell fishing reel.

'What the fuck is this?' said the cantankerous inspector as Brian held it out to him.

'It's a thank-you gift for helping me out at the LBJ protest,' said Brian. To his surprise, Plattfuss's eyes welled with tears.

And thus began a friendship of sorts.

When Plattfuss asked him to come on board, Brian jumped at the chance—everyone knew Breakers detectives got the best jobs. As a boss, Plattfuss—who quickly became the Puss—was blunt and cranky but as honest as the day was long—and days at the Breakers were very long indeed. Sometimes he would work his officers three days straight. When he did this, Brian developed a strategy. He would go into the Puss's office and tell him he had sent everyone home.

'What did you fucken do that for?' the Puss would roar.

'They've all got wives and kids who need to see them,' Brian would say in a low calm voice. And that would get the Puss every time—the thought of wives and kids missing their husbands and fathers. Then he would nod and go on with what he was doing.

Brian would return to the main area and wave his arms at the crew. 'Go! Go!' he would whisper. They would all scramble out the door.

In June 1970, there was an operation that needed the help of the Breakers. Surveillance cops—known as 'the dogs'—had been following some crims who were set to do a robbery. The problem was that the dogs had to stay undercover and could only enter the game if things got rough. A surveillance operative called the Mongrel put in an urgent call; a robbery was underway at an electrical goods store on Glenferrie Road in Kew. Brian and his crew sped to the scene, lights and bells.

They screeched to a halt in the middle of the road, and Brian and his colleagues jumped out of the car. The robbers' vehicle was pulling out of the laneway behind the store. For a moment, Brian felt a bit like a TV cop standing in the middle of the road, gun in one hand and waving them down with the other hand. But instead of stopping, the driver of the getaway car put his foot down and drove straight at him.

As the car bore down on him, Brian watched in horror as it swerved past so closely, he could have touched it. Quickly recovering from the shock, he fired two shots into the passenger's door at close range and two into the boot, then jumped into the back seat of the Breakers car and set off in hot pursuit. The villains were doing 70 or 80 miles an hour (110-130 kmph) along Victoria Street, heading toward the city.

The Puss

'Go faster!' Brian yelled gun in hand.

Mostly on the wrong side of the road and weaving past trams, the chase lasted all the way to Fitzroy. It was a hairy ride. Meanwhile, in his own car, the Mongrel headed around the opposite side of an overpass to close in on the bandits, boxing them in. The getaway car came to a grinding halt and two of the occupants took off, running, leaving another man in the back seat. He wasn't running anywhere. Brian's bullets had hit a target. He'd been shot in the leg and from the looks of things, the bullet had hit an artery, spilling a lot of blood.

Brian ran straight over to the wounded man, adrenaline running stronger than compassion. 'You bastard,' he yelled. 'You could have killed me!'

When the ambulance arrived, the ambos showed great restraint towards the crim riding in the car that tried to run down coppers; he only fell off the stretcher once.

When Brian examined the vehicle, he found a bullet in the back seat. It had gone right through the crim and come out the other side. 'Have a look at what I found!' he called out to his colleagues as he held the bullet aloft. He promptly pocketed it as a souvenir.

Taking a look in the boot, Brian found another two bullets. One of them was stuck in the metal, and one of them had gone through the boot and had come to rest in a leather strap in the back seat right where the man who was shot had been sitting. If the bullet had not stopped, it would have got him right in the back. Brian pocketed those two bullets for souvenirs, too.

Meanwhile, the Mongrel had cornered one of the crims who made the mistake of charging towards the giant copper. The Mongrel gave him a biff in the breadbasket and the crim doubled over, collapsing to the ground with an *oooomph* sound. Some blokes can take a blow to the middle, others have an immediate and unsavoury response like this guy who soiled his trousers. A third accomplice was rounded up as well. The driver was his brother— the notorious Delany brothers.

They took them off to Russell Street.

As always, there was a lot of bluster from colleagues and the brass about what if the injured man died, but Brian's attitude had never changed. The fear of a consequence could never be as bad as the fear a cop felt, staring death in the face—at the end of a gun or in the approach of a fast-moving car. Decisions made in milliseconds could always be pondered at length later, but the truth was, if he had his time over, he would have done the same thing.

In the wake of the shooting, Inspector 'Thunderfoot' Mitchell demanded to speak to the Delany brothers. Brian watched with interest as he entered the interview room where the still-soiled Delany brother was ensconced. Thunderfoot barely lasted a minute before he was back, nose wrinkled in disgust.

'Er, I think I'll talk to him tomorrow,' he said.

The interviews between Brian, his colleagues and their bosses over the car chase and the use of the firearm took till 4 a.m. Brian was castigated by Mitchell for being, among other things, insolent and brash. He said he would bring the matters to Brian's superiors at the Breakers. His tirade, however, was interrupted by a call at 4.10 a.m. It was a chief superintendent ordering Brian to collect him from his Brighton address. The chief super wanted to be taken to the scene of a big armed robbery in Clarke Street, South Melbourne. MSS Security—a big counting house, had been robbed.

When Brian and the chief superintendent arrived, the distressed security guard told them his story. Two men had buzzed the intercom from outside and announced themselves as police officers, there to return some keys that had been in a van stolen from the company the week before. Through a peephole, the security guard had seen one man in a police uniform and the other in a suit. He let the men inside, and the next minute, he was staring down the barrel of a gun. The thieves then proceeded to cut through the cages holding the cash, and helped themselves to an estimated $300,000.

It was an audacious robbery orchestrated, the investigation later

St Mary's West Melbourne Boxing troupe. Young Brian sits in the middle, under the letter M (1944).

Brian in his first year as a police officer in summer uniform, wearing the white pith helmet.

Morris Street, South Melbourne – Brian standing in front of the house he grew up in (1953).

The dashing young copper (1958).

Brian and Margaret marry at St Anthony's, Glenhuntly (1958).

Brian in his police uniform (1962).

Brian's father, Reg Murphy.

The Gaming Branch (1979) – photograph taken when the sergeant in charge, Mick Miller (front row, 3rd from right), was leaving to take a promotion. Journalist John Silvester's father, Fred, is in the front row, 3rd from left. Brian (2nd row, 2nd from left).

Brian receives the Valour Award (1976).

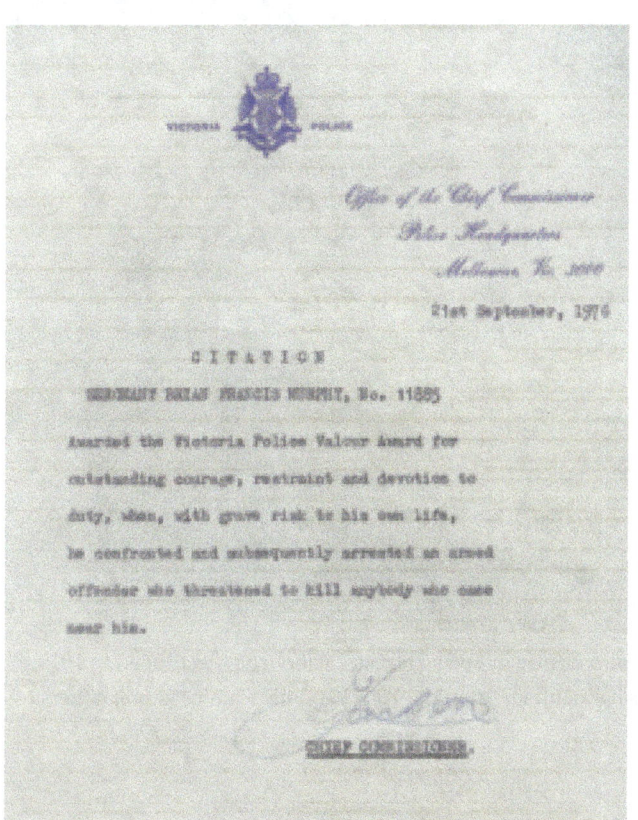

The Valour Award commendation awarded 'for outstanding courage, restraint and devotion to duty when, with grave risk to his own life, he confronted and subsequently arrested an armed offender who threatened to kill anybody who came near him.

Brian (centre) as a sergeant in the Consorting Squad offices in Russell Street.

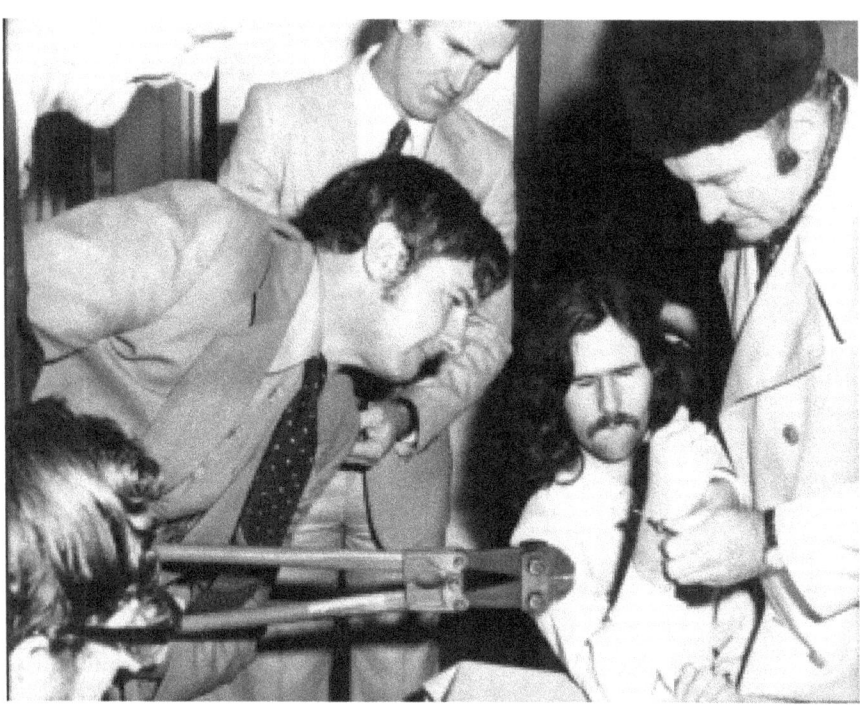

When the Commonwealth Centre in Spring Street, Melbourne was robbed in 1979, one of the workers was handcuffed. Brian (far right) and his team used bolt cutters to free him.

In his trademark hat, Brian hams it up for the camera.

Brian and his mother, Maggie (1997).

Brian (left) and Billy 'The Texan' Longley (1993).

Brian and his beloved wife, Margaret (1996).

The Puss

found out, by a member of the Painters and Dockers called Joey Turner. Using a guy he planted at the security company, Turner organised the theft of one of their vans that conveniently had a large set of keys inside it. In preparation for the heist, Turner's gang broke into a police station and stole some police uniforms. When the security guard at MSS answered the door in the small hours of the morning to two 'coppers' returning the stolen keys, he had no reason to suspect anything untoward. The guard was quickly overpowered and the foxes were in the henhouse.

In one of those coincidences that always seemed to happen to Brian—when Turner was caught and went to trial, he made a statement to his barrister that he had paid Brian Murphy to keep a lookout for him that night.

Brian was hauled in for an interview, but was happily able to tell the detectives that every minute of his day was accounted for in the pursuit and shooting at Fitzroy, and every part of his night was accounted for since he was being put through the ringer about the shooting in Fitzroy by Thunderfoot Mitchell.

23

CRIM, COPPER, CROSSOVER

Midnight shoppers was a term given to thieves who liked to frequent establishments at night, when they weren't open. Ivan Alfred Kane was one of the best midnight shoppers Brian had ever met. They first crossed paths when Ivan was shot in the backside by a cop as he clambered over a roof after robbing a warehouse. Brian interviewed Ivan afterwards at the Royal Melbourne Hospital. It was a stinking hot day and Ivan languished in the heat of the casualty ward.

Brian, and fellow detectives Harry and Jimmy made their way to Ivan's bedside. Ivan was a big bloke with a friendly face. At the same time the detectives arrived, so did his doctor. After checking the medical chart, the doc declared that Ivan could eat; he had been fasting in case his bullet wound required further surgery. When the hospital tray arrived, Ivan let the stench of boiled cabbage make the decision for him, and pushed it away without even lifting the aluminium lid.

'Don't suppose you happen to have a couple of cans on you?'

Brian considered his request for a moment, then nodded to Jimmy to pop over the road to the pub and get some beer. A bit of amber truth serum might loosen his tongue. Before they were through with the pleasantries, Jimmy was back with a bag of tall frosty cans. Everyone except Brian cracked the top off their beers. Sure enough, on an empty stomach, the beer took effect. While Ivan was unwilling to talk about the job that morning, he was keen to chat, and everybody got a mention—who was getting a quid and who wasn't. The trade in information was a crim's survival techniques. Ivan had the recipe down pat: drip-feed information to keen coppers and leave them wanting more.

'I don't think this can is going to numb the pain,' said Ivan cheekily once he'd drained his beer.

'You're not getting any more, mate,' Brian told him. 'If you finish up pissed, we're all in trouble.'

Ivan was happy to keep talking anyway, and Brian and his colleagues left the hospital knowing a lot more about a number of criminals than they did when they arrived.

The next time Brian saw Ivan Kane was when Breakers detectives did an early morning raid on his house. Ivan opened the door wearing nought but a pair of undies. His huge near-naked frame nearly filled the doorway; Brian hadn't realised how tall Ivan was since on the hospital visit, he'd been flat on his back. Ivan was even bigger than Plattfuss, who was huge.

'Looks like an official visit,' he said in his slow Queensland drawl.

'I fucken want to talk to you,' growled Plattfuss, never one for pleasantries.

'Sweet,' Ivan said, stepping back and inviting them all in.

They followed him into his kitchen, which was filled with piles of meat.

'What the fuck's this?' The Puss was in no mood for chitchat.

Ivan told them he was a butcher and that he was preparing meat. It wasn't an unlikely story; butchers started work in the small hours. But still, the Puss wasn't convinced until Ivan grabbed a knife and whipped on an apron. In minutes he sliced a bunch of thick steaks and offered to cook breakfast. There didn't seem to be anything untoward at Ivan's house, so they accepted his invitation and sat down at the table. He went all out with steak and eggs and bacon and snags.

'What going on here?' came a cultured woman's voice.

An awkward silence followed. There stood Ivan's wife, stark

naked, strangely unconcerned about appearing in front of a room of coppers in her birthday suit. Her nudity brought out the puritan in the Puss. 'Ivan, tell your wife to put some clothes on,' he snarled.

'It's my house, not his!' She was defiant. And very attractive.

'Do as you're told,' said Ivan to his wife. 'Go and put some clothes on.'

She strutted out of the room and they went back to eating. The Puss, however, seemed to be put off his food.

'Can you believe that?' he muttered to Brian.

The sun was peering over the horizon when they all finished breakfast and headed back to Russell Street. As they pulled into the car park, a report came over the radio of an overnight break-in at a suburban butcher shop in Dingley. Brian thought Plattfuss was going to explode. If he was a cartoon cop, there would have been whistles of steam shooting out his ears. Breaking lots of speed limits, the Breakers hightailed it back to Ivan Kane's house in Cheltenham. He opened the door and looked surprised and pleased to see them again. The Puss was like thunder. He stormed into the house, barrelling into the now spotless kitchen that held not a trace of the piles of meat they had all seen earlier.

'Where's the meat?' roared the Puss.

'What meat?' Ivan asked, innocently.

He had a ton of dash—to invite coppers to breakfast on stolen meat, then clear it out before they realised their complicity. He did turn to water a bit when the Puss threatened him with a fist to his considerable middle.

Brian had a bit of fun with Ivan on the way to the police station. He told him that Plattfuss's name was Platypus—he did that to a lot of crims, and to say the Puss enjoyed it would be an overstatement. He also told him that when the Puss sat on the edge of his desk smoking as he was talking to a suspect, it meant he was about to clock them. Sure enough, the Puss roared that his name was NOT Platypus and as he took a drag on his cigarette from the edge of his desk, Ivan took a dive to the floor and cowered. The Puss looked

Crim, copper, crossover

suspiciously in Brian's direction.

After all the fun was over, Ivan Kane confessed to a bunch of robberies and the Breakers locked him up. Ivan got bail and soon returned to his old ways. Thus began the cat and mouse game he enjoyed with the Breakers Squad. He'd steal and they'd catch him and lock him up. 'Not you again, Ivan,' Brian would say and he'd reply with a cheerful, 'G'day, Mr Murphy!'

One morning, early, Brian and fellow detective, Harry, got a call to go to Campbell's Gemstones in Moorabbin, opposite the Town Hall. A neighbour reported an alarm going off. When Brian inspected the premises, he could see that the daring raiders had broken the window and triggered the alarm, but stayed around long enough to cut the safe.

'Fired a couple of shots,' said one copper, first on the scene. 'But they got away.'

On the footpath outside the shop, there was a huge pair of size 14 moccasins, mustard in colour.

'Only one bloke I know with feet this big,' Brian said to Harry. 'It's got to be Ivan.' Harry nodded. He'd been thinking the same thing.

'He might cause you a bit of embarrassment one of these days.' Harry knew that Brian had grown fond of the thieving gentle giant.

They arranged for some local coppers to check Ivan's house, but they reported no one home. Brian was suspicious. He rang Ivan's phone three times and then he answered.

'Thought it might be you,' Ivan said.

'I've got your shoes here,' Brian said, looking down at the huge moccasins. 'Mate, I'm going to have to question you over this.' Brian hated having to arrest him again.

'How about we meet in the city at 2 o'clock?' Ivan said, naming a coffee shop.

Brian rang the Puss and told him about the meeting, but in case the fugitive had other plans, the Puss organised for the observation squad to also watch Ivan's house.

As the meeting time drew nearer, Brian tried to ring Ivan to check he was on his way. No answer. The Puss ordered a raid on his house. Ivan wasn't there even though surveillance hadn't seen him leave.

When Brian got to the coffee shop, Ivan was waiting.

'Mate! Where have you been? Everybody's been looking for you?' he cried.

'I've been here waiting for you.'

Brian hadn't noticed him going in; the guy was like a chameleon. They sat down to order. Brian was starving and ordered cake.

Suddenly the Puss appeared, furious. 'You're one smartarse! What are you doing here?'

'I said I'd meet Mr Murphy here, and here I am. I can't help it if your blokes were guarding an empty house.'

'How did you get out?' Plattfuss grumbled.

'Went over the back fence. Had my car out the back.'

Plattfuss shook his head and left them to their afternoon tea.

The problem with Ivan was that his size presented a generous target to anyone who cared to take a pot shot at him. One such person was the owner of an electrical goods store who chased him with a shotgun after the lumbering thief took off with a TV. For those unfamiliar with the effects of a shotgun blast, the closer the target, the bigger the wound. The further away, the more the shotgun pellets spread out into a starburst. That's what happened to Ivan. Brian heard about it on the police radio. A red ute was seen roaring away from the scene of the robbery with cops in pursuit. He suspected Ivan—who drove such a car—and hoped he wouldn't do anything silly. Aside from his rampant thieving, Ivan was an honest bugger. He was finally brought to a halt by a couple of bullets in his tyres, and coppers dragged him bleeding from his car.

Ivan had dozens of pellets in his back and one in his leg. The coppers loaded him into the back seat of the police car while Ivan wailed, 'Call Mr Murphy! I'll only confess to him.'

The arresting officers didn't want to share the glory so they gave their prisoner a biffing for good measure. In hindsight, they should have handcuffed Ivan's hands around his back rather than his front because he put his fingers down his throat and vomited all over them. They jumped from the car and called Brian. By the time he arrived in Seaford and settled the situation, Ivan was lying on the nature strip. Pieces of his shirt had been torn away by the shotgun blast, and he's spilt a lot of blood. Brian looked down with pity at the man he had grown rather fond of.

'I told them to ring you,' Ivan drawled.

'I'm here now,' Brian said. 'Looks like you'll have to go to the hospital.'

Naturally, the two coppers called an ambulance to take him because they refused to let Ivan back into their car. Brian laughed so hard at their vomit-stained clothes that they got a little shirty. He was just relieved his shirty was cleaner than theirs.

At the hospital, they removed a bunch of pellets from Ivan's back, but left about 60 pellets still there because to remove the tiny fragments would be too big a procedure When Brian visited, he came equipped with beer. Ivan was grateful and cracked open a cleansing ale. Soon, they were joined by a doctor who enjoyed a can himself.

'I did the wrong thing by those blokes,' said Ivan, taking a sip. 'I'll pay for their dry-cleaning.'

'Nah,' Brian said, appreciating his generosity, 'they get a clothing allowance. Let 'em spend it.'

When Ivan Kane finally fronted the judge, Brian gave evidence about all the crimes he had confessed to. Ivan got five years, but even so, he was good-natured about it and wrote Brian a letter from prison. He thanked him for the respectful way he'd been treated. Ivan bore no ill-feelings about going to jail. He was that kind of bloke.

24

MEETING NEIL STANLEY COLLINGBURN

Brian first met Neil Stanley Collingburn a couple of years before the young man died. Collingburn had been brought in to Russell Street for questioning—not by the Breakers, but by the Armed Robbery Squad.

Neil Collingburn was a member of the Painters and Dockers—one who collected a pay packet without doing much legitimate work. He was the kind of man who demanded to be treated with respect, but was not known for extending the same courtesy to others.

When the Armed Robbery Squad—known as the Robbers since their acronym was embarrassing—arrested Collingburn, they called the Breakers to see if they had a detective available to do a search of his house in Richmond. The job fell to Brian. Because squads were notoriously precious when it came to processing their own crims, as he walked upstairs to the Robbers, Brian wondered why they had outsourced the search.

Ostensibly, as it turned out, the detective from the Robbers who had arrested Collingburn, already had him up on charges and therefore didn't want to be involved in the search. Brian found out later that there was a bit of a smell around that first arrest.

But he knew none of this when he walked into their office and heard a commotion.

From the moment Brian laid eyes on Neil Collingburn, he quickly took his measure; he wasn't a bloke to be trifled with. He was aggro and he wasn't afraid to show it. Collingburn was chucking an absolute fit. Apparently, he objected to them trying to handcuff him, and was swearing like the wharfie he pretended to be. He stood in the Armed Robbery Squad office yelling abuse at the detectives who—curiously—weren't saying a word. Brian couldn't understand it—he'd never let a suspect talk to him like that because it meant that you lost control; they had *you* instead of you having *them*.

Two detectives wrestled Collingburn and grabbed his hands to shove them up his back to get the handcuffs on. The young crim was tall and thin with curly hair and plenty of muscle to put up a fight.

'Don't bother with the handcuffs,' Brian said stepping into the fray. 'If he tries to jump out of the car, I'll shoot him stone fucken dead.'

Threats of intense violence usually had a sobering effect on a suspect. Collingburn stopped struggling and gave Brian his full attention, eyeing him shrewdly. 'You wouldn't really shoot me dead?' It's a crim's business to know coppers by name and sight. He knew who Brian was.

'Fucken oath, I would!' Brian said looking him straight in the eye.

When Collingburn nodded that he understood, Brian led him out of the Armed Robbery Squad offices and downstairs to the police car. While Brian drove, he could see Collingburn in the rear-vision mirror. The closer they got to his house, the edgier he got. This often happens when a crim is on the way home with the coppers; for these ego-driven tough men, it was belittling to arrive home in the custody of police.

Brian sensed that he needed reassurance. He told Collingburn that they would search his house and if there was nothing there, he didn't need to worry. 'No one is going to plant anything there. You have my word.'

'Fair dinkum?' he said.

'Yep.'

'Thank you.' Collingburn was quiet for a moment, then spoke again. 'When we get to my joint,' he said, 'I want you to do me a favour.'

'What is it?' Brian asked, wary.

'The baby isn't well, and I don't want you to go in and upset her. If you do, my missus is going to go off her head. If the baby's asleep, will you promise me you won't disturb her?'

'No. I can't promise that,' Brian said. He knew some crims would put a gun in the baby's bassinet in the hope that no one would go near the baby.

'Look me in the eyes, mate. I'm telling you, man to man, there's nothing in the bassinet that would interest you except the baby.'

By the time they got to his place in Elizabeth Street, Richmond, Collingburn and Brian had established a rapport of sorts. Now it was time to meet the wife. Brian was used to dealing with wives of crims. Sometimes they were nice women who got more than they bargained for in their choice of husband. Others were on the same criminal level as their husbands.

On this day, Mrs Collingburn had a tonne of dash about her. 'What are you bringing these bastards here for?' she snarled at her husband. 'The baby's asleep!'

'Everything's going to be okay,' Collingburn assured her. 'They're okay.'

'Look, we're only here to search the house,' Brian said. 'If there's nothing here, we'll take him straight back to Russell Street.'

She quietened down after that. Brian and his partner started at the back and worked their way down to the front. The house was spick and span and Mrs Collingburn was obviously house proud. Once she had calmed down, she turned out to be a very nice woman. Brian always left a house exactly how he found it. A lot of cops made a mess, opening drawers and flinging things everywhere. He never did that. When all the other rooms had been searched, they came to the room with the closed door. The baby's room.

Like her husband, Mrs Collingburn pleaded, 'Please don't wake the baby. She hasn't been well. I assure you, there's nothing in there.'

Meeting Neil Stanley Collingburn

Brian was the father of several small children and could appreciate the vagaries of a fussing baby. 'I'll take your word for it,' he told the couple. They had found nothing untoward in the rest of the house and he decided not to go into the baby's room. Small courtesies like this went a long way.

Collingburn was really grateful but Brian gave him the same disclaimer he gave to all crooks he decided to trust. 'If any other police officer comes back here and discovers you've lied to me, I will make it my business to bring you both down.'

Collingburn nodded. So did his wife.

Back at the office, Brian told Plattfuss what he'd done. The Puss reckoned he was nuts to trust Collingburn because he was one of the best breakers in Victoria. He had a page of priors for breaking into factories and for assault.

Brian shrugged. 'He behaved himself, and I found him to be okay. I don't know what went on up at the Armed Robbery Squad to make him fire up like he did.' For most cops, keeping crims calm was something they were proud of—it meant that they could handle them. Brian was always careful with anyone in his charge. He usually came in strong at the beginning with a threat to shoot them if necessary to let them know where they stood. It took a rare villain to fire up after that.

In the end, the whole episode with Collingburn ended up being for nothing. Even though the Armed Robbery Squad had found stolen property on him when they picked him up, the detectives there had failed to caution him and so when the case finally came to trial it was kicked out for that reason. Brian reckoned the whole thing was bullshit. Giving cautions is something that every cop does in continuous practice; it was beyond his comprehension how a police officer could have forgotten to do it.

The next time Brian saw Collingburn, was just before he died.

25

THE COLLINGBURN AFFAIR

On Friday 26 March 1971, a theft was reported. Someone had stolen a hundred grand's worth of leather jackets from a leather goods shop in Collingwood called Palermo's. Neil Stanley Collingburn and Ray Chuck Bennett were suspects. Brian remembered Collingburn from the day he'd searched his house, but he had never met Bennett who was a bank robber and a member of the Painters and Dockers.

Brian and Detective Harry Kramme were tasked with the investigation. They were out and about when they heard a check over the car radio for Neil Collingburn. Crime Car cops had pulled Collingburn over near St Vincent's Hospital with two other crims: Ian Revell Carroll, and Thomas Joseph Connellan. Officers Carl Stillman and Max Gosney had searched Collingburn's car and found a set of golf clubs. There had been a break-in at the Kew Golf Club and the three were picked up as suspects.

'Speak of the devil,' Brian told Harry.

He remembered the cocky young Collingburn, wiry and ready for a fight, and unhooked the radio receiver to call officer Carl Stillman. 'It's Brian Murphy, here mate,' he said. 'They're all dangerous blokes. Be careful when you're dealing with them. If Collingburn gets you down, you won't get back up.'

He suspected from the tone of First Constable Stillman's voice he wasn't about to take any advice. Brian didn't really know Stillman, but whether he took the advice or not, didn't stop Brian from offering it.

The Collingburn affair

After he returned the radio handset to its cradle, he didn't give the matter another thought.

Not only did Carl Stillman not take Brian's advice, he got into Collingburn's car and told him to drive to Russell Street. Stillman rode shotgun while Ian Carroll sat in the back seat. The other arresting officer, Max Gosney, took Tom Connellan with him in the police car. It was not a wise move; they should have called for a divvy van and loaded all three into it.

On the drive to Russell Street, Collingburn, pulled an iron bar from the side of his seat and threatened Stillman with it. Travelling behind them, Max Gosney and Tom Connellan saw the whole thing but there wasn't much they could do about it. As this was happening, Collingburn stopped at a traffic light and Max Gosney pulled up behind him. Gosney was halfway out of his car to go to the aid of his colleague when he saw Collingburn put the bar away. Collingburn took off at the lights and Gosney jumped back in his car and followed. Stillman clearly had not searched Collingburn's car to ensure that his driver did not have access to such a weapon. It was the first of a string of decisions that day that would have a ripple effect for years to come.

Brian and Harry got called back to Russell Street to speak with fellow detective, Jimmy Keegan about their case. They pulled into the crowded police carpark around 2.30 p.m. Their designated parking space was taken so they took the first available spot, blocking in a couple of other cars but hoping it wouldn't matter because they didn't expect to be there for long.

Brian was still chatting with Harry and Jimmy at 3 p.m. when a call came over the speakers for them to move their car. Since Brian had the keys, he volunteered for the job. He took the lift to the first floor, crossed over the causeway between the two buildings, and headed toward the passageway that would take him down to the car park.

Walking past the Crime Car offices, Brian looked through the doorway into the small reception area and saw Max Gosney on the telephone. Curious to see how they went with Collingburn, he wandered in for a quick stickybeak—the car moving could wait a moment. Beyond the small reception area, Brian could see Neil Collingburn in the main muster room. He was sitting on a swivel chair, and police officer Carl Stillman sat at a typewriter, typing.

Considering Collingburn was a suspect in the job he was currently investigating, Brian strode into the room.

'G'day, Neil,' he said.

'G'day, Mr Murphy,' said Collingburn amiably.

Brian raised his eyebrows with a question. 'What are you doing here?'

'I'm in a bit of a shit.' Collingburn gestured towards Carl Stillman. 'He got me over some golf clubs.'

Brian ignored that and kept the chat away from Stillman's case. 'Where are you living now?'

'With my mum and dad.'

Word on the street was that Collingburn was setting himself up nicely with a new house. Brian didn't know if it was true or not. 'I heard you built yourself a house.'

Neil denied it. 'Turn it up! Where would I get that kind of cash? I'm only a labourer.' It was the kind of banter that had an undercurrent. They both knew Neil's 'labouring' was much more lucrative than the minimum-wage kind.

They traded chit chat for a moment longer and then Brian said goodbye.

'Are you sure you can't help me?' he said as Brian made to leave.

Brian stopped. 'What have you done?'

Collingburn nodded at Stillman. 'He said I was going to hit him over the head with an iron bar, but I didn't.'

'Sorry. I don't think I can help you out with that.'

On the way out, Brian said, g'day to Tommy Connellan who

The Collingburn affair

seemed calm. Then he passed the third man and asked his name. Ian Carroll said he was there because he was carrying a knife.

A young cop called Robinson stood in the outer office. Brian nodded back towards the muster room. 'Do you know who those men are? Rather stupid to have the three of them with only one copper.' Moments later, the sound of raised voices from the muster room sent them running.

'You fucken shit!' Collingburn's voice. 'I should've given it to you over the head before.'

Brian entered the muster room in time to see Collingburn swing a punch at Carl Stillman who was still seated. He saw Stillman's head snap back, then his chair toppled backwards with him in it.

Connellan jumped to his feet and Brian grabbed him and shoved him back down. The small muster room was crowded and Brian scrambled to get over to Collingburn who was attacking Stillman in his overturned chair. Using his feet, Stillman defended himself by kicking Collingburn in the stomach. The kick worked and Collingburn flew backwards into another chair which also toppled over.

Bloody hell! Brian knew this could happen.

His attention was diverted by Carroll and Connellan who both needed to be restrained. Stillman struggled out of the chair and was on his feet pretty quickly. He flew over to Collingburn who also got to his feet fast. Both men continued to wrestle but Brian knew if he left Carroll and Connellan, they would run to join Collingburn against Stillman. In the confined space, Collingburn and Stillman wrestled each other until they both fell over the upturned chair. As Stillman gained the upper hand in the scuffle, Connellan broke loose and ran across the room to join the fray.

Connellan threw a punch that connected to the back of Stillman's head. The cop toppled sideways and Connellan kicked out at him. Brian heard a gasp but didn't know who made it.

Young Robinson grabbed Carroll who was yelling and threatening to join in. Robinson held onto him while Brian grabbed

Connellan and pushed him down the length of the muster room, then shoved him back into his chair. Stillman and Collingburn got to their feet, fists flying. Then there was another crash and Collingburn went over backwards.

A moan came from the floor. Stillman backed off and Collingburn climbed to his feet. But any hopes that the fight was over were in vain. Collingburn came up swinging. Stillman went in headfirst and grabbed Collingburn around the middle. Max Gosney took over the guarding of Connellan, leaving Brian free to go and help Stillman.

Once he navigated the desks and upturned chairs, Brian grabbed Collingburn by the neck and wrestled him into a headlock. 'Settle down Neil! For God's sake! You're in enough strife as it is without this sort of thing!' Once his legs began to sag, Brian sat him down.

'You know me, Mr Murphy,' said Collingburn, voice shaking with anger, 'I hate young cunts trying to stand over me.'

'Fucken dogs!' hollered Connellan from his seat. 'What are you doing this to him for?'

Connellan was clearly trying to inflame the situation. Both crim onlookers leapt to their feet. Brian landed a punch on Connellan's chin which did the trick. He threatened the same to Carroll. Both men sat down and a potential all-in brawl was avoided.

'This will get you nowhere!' Brian yelled to all three. 'Just calm down!'

As quickly as it started, everything quietened down. Stillman looked as if he was in a lot of pain. The melee had knocked more than just the wind out of him. It had robbed him of the cockiness that Brian had heard when they spoke earlier on the radio. Other cops arrived, so Brian felt it was okay at this point to leave the room, knowing that he still needed to move the car.

When he returned to the Breakers office, his two colleagues asked what had taken so long.

'Collingburn's just gone berserk,' Brian told them. 'They had

The Collingburn affair

them all in the same room and there was a blue.'

'You've got to be joking,' said Harry. 'Three in the same room! You already warned them.'

Brian shrugged. It was over now.

For Brian, Harry and Jimmy, their most pressing job for the day was to do a search on Ray Chuck Bennett's house in Kensington. If he and Collingburn had done the Palermo's robbery, they might find evidence there.

Bennett's house was an immaculate terrace in a quiet street. Not a lot of villain's places are as nice and clean. The detectives introduced themselves when Bennett's wife Gail opened the door.

'Come in,' she said politely, opening the door wider.

'We're investigating some stolen goods,' Brian explained. 'Do you mind if we go through the house?'

Mrs Bennett was helpful. 'You can look at anything,' she said. 'There's nothing in the house we can't account for.'

Except her, perhaps.

She didn't look like Chuck Bennett's type. He'd been in trouble for violence and robbery in the past and was active enough now for police to make the connection with Palermo's robbery. She was nice and well spoken, and seemed to have a law-abider's respect for police.

Mrs Bennett was happy to have a chat. She led the way to the bedroom she shared with Ray. Brian followed. She gestured to the cupboards and he took a look inside. Everything was neatly arranged and there was no sign of the stolen haul of leather jackets.

Harry and Jimmy headed to the back of the house. Jimmy opened a door off the hallway which turned out to be the toilet door. Perched on the throne was a little fella, about five years old. He got such a fright that he grabbed his pants, pulled them up, and ran screaming, 'Mum!'

They heard the kid before he materialised. Brian stepped out into the passage way and the boy flew straight into his arms. 'Hey, it's okay,' he said in a soothing voice. Being the father of five, gave him certain skills at calming children. 'I think he's had a fright,' Brian told the mother.

She smiled ruefully, 'Give him to me.' She took the child from his arms, hugged him, and patted him on the back.

Most coppers hate to upset families. Brian reckoned that if some crims saw their wives and kids coping with police searches on their homes, they might re-think their profession. Although, most wouldn't. The three detectives left the Bennett house, confident that if Chuck had done the Palermo job, he hadn't hidden the goods there.

That night, Brian, Harry and Jimmy took their dinner break at a pizza parlour next to the Victoria Market. As they walked up to the pizza shop, two men appeared from the deserted market—they must've been hiding in there. Ray Chuck Bennett and an armed robber called Bobby Dunn. Brian recognised Dunn as a regular at a nearby pub. Dunn obviously knew that the pizza shop was a police hangout and led Bennett straight to them.

'How fucken good are you?' Bennett was spitting mad. 'It's a bit different now, isn't it?'

'What are you talking about?' Brian roared back, matching his level of aggression.

'Throwing my kid across the room for my wife to catch.' Bennett was off his nut.

What?

Brian realised this was a bad, bad situation. He pulled out his gun. Dunn saw it, grabbed Bennett's arm, and pulled him away. As the two disappeared, Brian took a deep breath. That was a close call. Ray Chuck Bennett was crazy.

Brian's two colleagues shared his relief as Bennett and Dunn walked away. But just because they left, didn't meant they couldn't come back. This presented a problem. While Brian was armed, Harry and Jimmy weren't. Harry jumped in the police car and headed back to Russell Street to get guns. Meanwhile, Brian used

The Collingburn affair

the restaurant phone to ring the Breakers and get the afternoon crew to meet him at the pizza shop. Soon, they were eating pizza with a second crew and all was calm. By then, each detective was armed and full of pepperoni and cheese.

While they ordered coffee, Brian told them he would wait outside in case Bennett returned and did something crazy like throwing a grenade through the window.

They all laughed. 'You've seen too many films, Murph.'

Brian shrugged and went outside. The truth was, the earlier confrontation had put him on edge and he needed some air. As he stood in the doorway, a Valiant Regal pulled up to the kerb outside the restaurant. There was a click and the boot lid popped up by itself. At the same moment, the passenger door flew open and Bennet leapt out.

With only seconds to act, Brian kicked at the door with his heel trying to get the attention of his trusty colleagues inside, as he reached for the gun inside his coat. Bennett covered the distance across the kerb in a flash and grabbed for Brian's gun. As the two men scuffled, Bennett called over his shoulder.

'Get the gun!'

Dunn jumped out of the driver's seat and rushed to the boot and reached in. When he straightened up, he was holding a pump-action shotgun and pumping a cartridge into the breach. The sound was deadly.

While Brian struggled with Bennett, he kept pounding his foot against the door hoping his colleagues would hear.

'Give me the gun!' hollered Bennett to Dunn. Bennett leapt back with the dexterity of a gymnast and grabbed the gun. As he swung around, finger on the trigger, ready to shoot, half a dozen Italian blokes appeared out of the market, laughing and talking, and stepped into the space between the two men. It was truly like something out of a movie. One minute, Brian was staring down the barrel of his impending doom, and the next minute, a crowd of blokes appeared out of nowhere and saved his life.

Dunn growled. 'Let's get out of here!'

By the time the Italians walked past into the pizza restaurant, Bennett and Dunn had jumped into the car and roared off into the night.

It took Brian a split second to burst into the pizza shop to call to his colleagues. They came scrambling over. The first police officer tripped on the doorstep and the keys to the car, which he had in his hand, went shooting across the dark footpath and slid into the gutter flowing with murky water from the rain. Next, three detectives squatted down in the gutter, fishing for the keys. By the time they found them, Bennett was long gone.

Inside the safety of the pizza shop, Brian told the others what had happened. While his crew believed him, the others looked sceptical; they had seen nothing and hadn't heard his frantic kicking over the sounds of the restaurant.

Back at Russell Street, Brian told the bosses what happened. Bennett was out there with a shotgun ready to point it at a copper and mad enough to pull the trigger. It was one of the only moments in his career when Brian feared for his life.

Brian worked that Friday night, and the Saturday afternoon shift and, even though he had a day off on Sunday, he needed to get his diary up to date, so he went into work. Brian's sister-in-law had the kids up in Ballarat for a stay because Margaret was in New Zealand on holidays.

In the Breakers Squad, the phone rang and Brian picked it up. The voice on the other end of the line said, 'You fucken dog! You've killed my best mate!'

'What are you talking about?' he said, crossly.

'Collingburn, you dog. You've killed him! He died!'

As soon as Brian hung up on the mystery caller, a cop came into the office and told him the bosses were looking for him. 'You'd better get out of here. There's a distinct possibility you could get charged for murder.'

The Collingburn affair

'What's this bullshit about?' Brian asked, bewildered.

'Collingburn died in hospital. In St Vincent's. About two hours ago.'

'What did he die from?' Brian couldn't understand. Last time he'd seen Collingburn, he was sitting in a chair after attacking Carl Stillman. *What the hell had happened to him?*

'I don't know, but he's dead and you should get out of here.'

'Mate, I did nothing to end that bloke's life.' It wasn't in Brian's nature to run. He stayed at work and found Stillman's phone number and Gosney's. He rang them both and told them to get into the city because Collingburn had died.

From the moment Brian learnt that Neil Collingburn had died, he treated it like any other case. He knew there would be an inquest and a police investigation. Everything needed to be spick and span. He knew that Ian Carroll and Tommy Connellan would either agree with the police story, or come up with their own. Either way, those involved needed to document what happened.

When Gosney and Stillman arrived, Brian suggested adjourning to his house and putting their statements together there. They left Russell Street and drove to Brian's house in Middle Park. When they had settled into the comfy chairs in the lounge room, Brian set up the typewriter on the coffee table and typed his statement. From beginning to end, it spanned a page and a quarter of double-spaced typing. He had put Collingburn in a headlock for probably ten seconds to stop him attacking Stillman. Then he sat him down on a chair and left. End of story.

Step by step, just like they'd done a thousand times with witnesses, they all wrote down exactly what had happened. Gosney and Stillman had included a second bout of fisticuffs that had occurred after Brian left. Collingburn had punched Stillman in the jaw and chipped a tooth. When Stillman said that, Brian rang the police photographer and organised for him to meet Stillman at the St Kilda police station to photograph his injuries. According to Gosney and Stillman, Neil Collingburn complained of a sore stomach later in the afternoon. He looked pale and unwell so they had taken him to the hospital. The autopsy showed that Neil Collingburn had died of a ruptured duodenum which had caused a condition called gas gangrene to spread through his system and poison him.

Throughout that Sunday, Brian received several anonymous phone calls at home. All similar in tone. All threatening him for killing Collingburn. If he hadn't known how well connected Collingburn was before his death, the phone calls certainly reminded him. Collingburn was a member of the Painters and Dockers and a lot of those blokes had the capacity to gun him down. Brian fetched two shotguns and put one near the front door and one at the back. He wasn't so much worried for himself, but for his family. Luckily Margaret wasn't due home for a week, but the kids would be home later that afternoon.

On the Monday, Brian went to work as normal and the kids went to school as normal. As soon as he walked into the office, he bumped into a senior officer.

'Don't talk to me!' he said. 'I'm up for promotion and I will make a statement saying I wasn't there and I didn't see anything.'

Brian realised this guy must have walked in when Collingburn had run amok, seen what was going on, panicked, then run away. So much for police fraternity.

'You dog!' Brian spat. 'Never talk to me again!'

'I'm not doing my promotion for you or Stillman or for anybody else.'

And that marked the beginning of the arse covering. Brian couldn't understand his attitude. What was the risk for him?

Brian discussed it with his senior sergeant who advised him to take a fortnight's leave. Brian refused to take leave, though, because he reckoned it would look like he was hiding.

In the Breakers office, there was a lot of Collingburn talk. Providing a welcome interruption, a detective from the Armed Robbery Squad came in and gestured for Brian to follow him. Once outside, he explained that they had picked up Ray Chuck Bennett, and were going to put him and his wife into a room together that was bugged. It took Brian a moment to focus back on Bennett. After hearing Neil Collingburn had died, the drama of facing Chuck Bennett down the barrel of a gun had almost slipped his mind.

The detective wanted Brian to listen to what they said about Friday night. On the record, Bennett denied ever owning a shotgun.

Brian followed the detective into an interview room and sat at a table next to a tape recording device. He recognised the voices—Ray Chuck Bennett and his wife, Gail.

'Are they treating you okay?' His voice was keyed up and anxious.

'Yes they are.' Her voice was composed.

'What did you do with the receipt for that fucken shotgun?'

'I've got it in my bra,' she said in a low voice.

'When you leave here, tell them you want to go to the toilet, and flush the receipt.'

The detective opposite Brian, put his mouth in an oval shape and said, 'Whoops!'

Brian curled an imaginary moustache. They had them.

After the chat with his wife, Bennett was brought into Brian's office. When detectives from the Robbers asked him to do the interview with Bennett about Friday night, Brian wondered if they hoped he would do his block and smash Bennett. It was a game he shouldn't have had to play. Especially not that day. For Bennett, seeing Brian was like a red rag to a bull.

'One day I'm going to blow your fucken brains out for what you did to my kid. You won't see me coming.' Chuck Bennett's eyes were cold and black.

'Mate—'

'I'm no fucken mate of yours!' he spat.

'Mate,' Brian said, refusing to be belittled by the likes of him. 'You shouldn't have told me that because now I'll be fucken waiting for you, but I'll get in first.' Brian needed him to know that he wasn't afraid. And that he'd fight fire with fire. A lot of men would cower in the face of mad Ray Chuck Bennett. Not Brian.

Nothing further was said. Brian filled out paper work and charged him with a string of offences including being a felon in possession of a firearm. Bennett sat sullenly and refused to say another word.

A year later, something odd happened to that paperwork. A superintendent sent for it, and then it mysteriously vanished. When Brian rang the superintendent to check how the charges against Bennett were going, the man denied any knowledge of having the paperwork and slammed down the phone. It always made Brian wonder if Bennett had friends in high places.

Chuck Bennett had been a pain in the arse to the police force for years. When he was released on bail after threatening Brian, Bennett and his crew did a bunch of robberies and then went overseas to spend the money. He would return, however, and commit a robbery that was so big, it became a blight on the Victoria Police and would make headlines around the world for its audacity and multi-million dollar haul.

Ironically, if those charges had've gone ahead, Bennett might not have been free to commit the Great Bookie Robbery.

But more about that later.

A week after Collingburn died, Brian and Stillman met with lawyer, Ray Dunn. They told him the whole story.

'Have you made a statement?' Dunn asked.

Brian showed him the statement. Dunn liked it and told him not to change a word. He read Stillman's statement and asked him to check a few details on his report.

'There's going to be a bun fight,' Dunn said. 'There's going to be a lot of negative publicity. I hope you blokes are up to it.'

It was an honest assessment and Brian appreciated his candour.

26

INQUIRY B-11

The inquiry into the events leading up to Collingburn's death was called B-11—named after the label on the door of the external investigation unit. It was headed by Superintendent Keith McTier McLeod. On the Thursday following Collingburn's death—fittingly, April Fool's Day, 1971—McLeod and two detectives from Homicide arrived at Brian's house after dinner. McLeod was as drunk as a lord. The other two made gestures with their fingers on their lips—*don't say anything*, they warned. McLeod was so drunk that he nearly knocked over the television.

Before they arrived, a couple of Brian's friends from the Observation Squad had come for a visit, but as soon as McLeod walked in the front door, they skipped out the back and waited in their car. As McLeod wobbled out on unsteady legs, the two Observation Squad guys reappeared. On an impulse, Brian asked them to follow the superintendent. The already-drunk McLeod did more drinking at the Police Club, then made the long drive to Geelong, swerving all over the road. Brian's mates watched him fall out of his car and go to sleep in the driveway. One of them crept over to the comatose superintendent, turned off the ignition, and tossed his keys into a bush.

Later in evidence, McLeod said he left Brian's place and went to Russell Street to take notes on the meeting. That was the only time Brian was questioned.

While Stillman and Brian were under investigation, there was nothing more to do but go on with the general business of policing. Brian knew he hadn't done anything wrong in relation to Collingburn, and he also knew that the wheels of justice would grind slowly. For the most part, he tried to put it out of his mind. Sometimes, that wasn't easy, though.

One day, Brian's boss told him to go home early because there was going to be a protest by trade unionists. They planned to march past the Russell Street police headquarters carrying a coffin bearing Collingburn's name. The boss suggested Brian sneak out the back, but that went against his nature. Instead, Brian walked out of the front door of Russell Street just as the thousand-strong crowd marched past.

'*Who killed Collingburn? The Police killed Collingburn!*' they chanted.

Brian waited on the front steps and waved at them, and a couple waved back good-naturedly. As they milled around outside the police station, Brian walked past them to a waiting police car and was driven home.

In the end, Brian decided to take leave to wait out the verdict of the inquiry. It was Easter and the kids were staying at his brother's in Orbost. On Thursday 8 April 1971, Brian hooked up his boat and he and Margaret headed up to Metung for a spot of fishing. They got there mid-afternoon and stayed at a friend's place.

At 7 p.m., there was a knock at the door. Brian grabbed his gun to see who had come calling. It was three detectives from his squad; grim-faced, they told Brian that Stillman had been charged with manslaughter.

'Is there anything I can do for him?' Brian asked, concerned.

'No. You need to look after yourself because we've come to charge you as well.'

'You're joking!' Brian said, never believing things would go this far.

'We wish we were.'

Brian could see it in their faces; there was no joy for any of them in this situation. He would have to go back to town.

Inquiry B-11

Connellan and Carroll had both made statements that Brian and Carl Stillman had viciously bashed Collingburn. Their statements were fanciful. According to them, Brian had yelled, 'The bash is on!' then pounded Collingburn's head into a filing cabinet and jumped onto his stomach.

Among the three detectives was Harry who had been with Brian on the day of the Collingburn incident; Harry was almost in tears. He knew the extent of Brian's involvement because Brian had told them exactly what happened right after the event. But despite how they all felt, things had to be done by the book. They told Brian they needed to take his gun. Brian handed it over along with another one he'd hidden in Margaret's handbag without telling her.

'Don't worry,' Harry said. 'You'll be bailed out and we'll drive you straight back here.'

But it wasn't the ruined holiday Brian was worried about—it was what he knew was sure to follow: accusations, an inquest, a trial and an outcome. It was into this quagmire that he was about to drag his family. Margaret insisted on travelling back with him. They both sat in the back seat of the police car with one of the detectives while the other two sat up front. Margaret couldn't believe Brian was about to be charged. To her, the drive back felt dangerous; as if they could have an accident. And in the horror of it all, she didn't care if they did.

At Russell Street, Inspector Frank Holland charged Brian with manslaughter. Fortunately, the officers who were dealing with Brian were good men which made things a bit easier.

After the arrest and bail, the detectives drove Brian to his mother's house—he needed to tell her what was going on before she heard it on the news. While he was telling Maggie that he'd been charged, colleagues arrived with his suspension notice.

Maggie was not happy. 'Doesn't the last 17 years mean anything?' she spat. As far as she was concerned, her son was innocent and she was feeling very dark on the coppers.

Finally, they all arrived back at the Murphys' house in Middle

Park. It had been a long day, but Brian, Margaret and the three detectives sat in the kitchen and drank coffee until just before dawn.

Brian and Margaret started their holiday over again on Good Friday in Metung. His arrest made newspapers all over the country, but luckily, the kids were staying with his brother who let them know what was happening. Reg was twelve and Bernadine was eleven at the time. The younger three were too little to understand.

For the next two weeks, Margaret and Brian enjoyed their escape at Metung. All Brian could do was assure Margaret that he had done nothing wrong. Although she believed him to be innocent, it didn't stop her from worrying. Brian had enough confidence in the system to believe he wouldn't be convicted, but he didn't know what the broader repercussions would be. Collingburn's association with the Painters and Dockers had serious implications; murders connected to the union were commonplace. He tried to push those thoughts from his mind as he enjoyed the autumn sun-filled days on the unspoilt coast of Eastern Victoria.

As soon as Brian arrived back in town, however, he had to think strategically. While he didn't think anyone would attack him at home, he took precautions, nonetheless, cancelling the milk delivery in case somebody poisoned it, and once again secreting a gun in Margaret's handbag, without her knowledge.

Then he arranged to see Billy 'The Texan' Longley.

Brian had heard on the grapevine that Billy held him in high regard. Years earlier, Brian had refused to commit perjury against him and Longley hadn't forgotten. Brian sent a message through a contact, asking Billy to come and see him. Before long, one of the Murphy kids ran in from the street and told Brian there was a man in a big white car parked outside wanting to talk to him.

Sure enough, it was the man himself. Brian leaned into Billy's window.

'What can I do for you, Chief?' Billy was a big man and the tank-like white Ford Fairlane suited him.

'I want a guarantee for my wife and the kids and the house.'

Inquiry B-11

Brian nodded towards the family home.

'You know you got a lot against you.' Billy said.

Brian nodded. 'That's why I want a guarantee for Margaret and the kids.'

'It mightn't be the easiest thing to get, but I'll give it a shot.' Billy leaned back against his seat. He gave Brian a wink.

'Thanks,' Brian said, gratefully.

'I'll sort it out.' Billy turned the key in the ignition and gunned the engine. 'I'll be at the Middle Park Hotel at 5 p.m. tomorrow night. Ring there and ask for me. I'll let you know what's going on.'

Brian watched as the big fella drove off. He really appreciated the fact that Billy was willing to stick his neck out when all the Painters and Dockers were baying for Brian's blood. Longley's own life was in constant danger from various faction leaders, but he had a lot of clout.

As the big white car vanished around a corner, Brian realised this man was the best shot he had. If he could get the Painters and Dockers out of the way, he only had to worry about a sneak-go—somebody who wanted to make a name for himself by shooting Brian Murphy.

Brian spent a tense 24 hours waiting to ring Billy the following afternoon. He dialled the number and soon heard the gravel of Billy's voice.

'I can guarantee the house, your wife and kids, but not you or your car,' said Longley.

'Fair enough,' said Brian, relieved. It was never himself he was worried about.

Brian told Margaret about Longley's guarantee. With that and the police protection provided by Brian's colleagues, she was relieved.

A couple of days later, Billy appeared outside the Murphy house again and told Brian how the meeting had gone down. Longley had attended, carrying an automatic shot gun and a .45. His offsider, Jimmy Bazley, carried a machine gun. They put the proposition to the Painters and Dockers that it wasn't in the best interest of the union to go shooting a copper or his family. If that happened, Longley told them, that would be the end of the union. And the police might take it upon themselves to wipe a few of them out in revenge. He suggested that the Painters and Dockers should wait out the court verdict and if there was a conviction, they could get their revenge in prison.

In other words, a conviction would be a death sentence.

After that, Billy Longley would often drive past Brian's house and stop for a chat. The kids would yell that the man in the big white car was there, and Brian would wander out and pass the time of day with him. A couple of months later, the two men exchanged telephone numbers. What Brian liked most about Billy was that he was upfront and never ever asked for anything in return. Brian reckoned they became pals of sorts because Billy kept coming back. Perhaps Brian provided a bit of respite from Longley's leadership bid at the Painters and Dockers. There were only a few blokes there who he could trust, and he was always walking on thin ice down on the docks.

'They're all at the pub talking bullshit,' Longley told Brian on one such visit, 'but you never know when someone is going to have a go. Be careful.'

Luckily for Brian, things didn't affect him the way they affected many others. While his family and friends worried about him, he didn't worry about himself. He refused to worry about things that hadn't already taken place.

The police suggested that the Murphy children should be driven to school in the morning and picked up in the afternoon. Brian disagreed. He wanted the kids to walk to school as they always had, and he didn't want them looking over their shoulders. The next time Billy visited, Brian told him that if any of the kids were so much as spoken to, he'd kill four Painters and Dockers.

'That sounds fair and reasonable, Chief,' Longley said.

The tactic worked because the kids went happily about their

Inquiry B-11

business during this time, undisturbed.

Brian had more pressing needs, however, because he was suspended without pay, so he had to find a job. Fortunately, a mate of his called John Selby-Link, who ran a pump company, offered him one which Brian was very grateful for. His new job was based in Clarendon Street, South Melbourne, and was about as far from being a detective as he could get—his duties included readying pumps for mechanics to service them.. The job also put Brian right in the middle of Painters and Dockers' territory—they all drank in pubs around the area.

One day, the foreman asked Brian to help repair a pump in the dry dock. While he was given the option of not going, Brian figured he was being paid, so he might as well go down there. Even so, he was a little apprehensive once he arrived at the docks. It was hard not to be when every man there hated him and wanted him dead.

Despite the danger to his life, Brian found the dry docks an interesting place. As soon as the ships were docked in place, a huge gate was closed and sealed around the ship, then water was pumped out leaving the bottom of the ship exposed for repairs. That morning, Brian worked in the cavernous space, accessed via a steel ladder down a shaft. He was up and down the ladder and back and forth to the work vehicle.

Around 1.30 p.m., Brian passed Neil Collingburn's father who was a member of the Painters and Dockers. He looked at Brian but kept walking. Not long afterwards, about 60 Painters and Dockers gathered along the edge of the dry dock. As the minutes ticked by, they grew more vocal.

The manager of the dry docks, a bloke by the name of Shorten, hurried over to Brian, accompanied by Putty Nose Nicholls, a union big wig.

'Are you Brian Francis Murphy?' Shorten said.

'You know I am.' Brian looked from Shorten to Putty Nose, then to the gathering dozens.

'Unless you get off the docks, there's going to be a national strike,' said Shorten, nervously.

Brian turned to Nicholls. 'I'm only trying to feed my family,' he said angrily. 'When you were in jail, the coppers ran around to St Vincent's getting food and clothes for your family, and my brother put in a new bathroom at your house for nothing.'

Nicholls looked down and mumbled something Brian couldn't hear.

Brian headed back to the work car amid a raucous chorus of jeering. However, despite their threatening behaviour, not one of them approached him. Resisting the urge to go quietly, Brian raised his cap to them as he went past. Not perhaps the brightest move, but it made him feel better.

That evening, the kids ran in and told Brian that the man in the big white car was out the front.

'Howya going, Chief?' Longley said. Billy was impressed that Brian had gone to the docks. In fact, he laughed his head off. 'I just left the pub,' Billy said, 'and they're all there talking about what they done and what they should have done, but they've got no fucken guts. I told them that if Murphy's guts were on the Stock Exchange, they wouldn't have enough money to buy them.'

If Billy was impressed with Brian's trip to the docks, Margaret definitely wasn't. 'For God's sake,' she said, 'why did you go?' When he told her that he'd doffed his cap to the Painters and Dockers, she said, 'Oh Brian, you didn't!'

'I can't pick and choose my jobs. They're paying me,' Brian protested. But in the end, he promised her he wouldn't go back.

After they were charged, Carl Stillman and Brian talked every night on the phone, connected by circumstance. In one such conversation, Brian told him he'd given away smoking.

'Why?' Stillman asked.

'Because if I go to jail, I want to be the fittest bastard in there.'

'Why?'

'The first bloke that comes at me, I'll kill. That's the only way we will survive.'

There was a dumbfounded silence on Stillman's end. 'I don't think it will come to that,' he said eventually.

'Let's hope not,' said Brian.

27

THE INQUEST

The inquest was slated for June 1971. Margaret and Brian had to stay strong for the kids who watched their parents like hawks. If they wavered, the kids would worry. Neighbours and friends were very supportive and kept them all sane. One neighbour would even go out in the small hours of the morning and bring cups of steaming hot cocoa to the cops guarding the Murphys' house.

Frank Galbally represented the Collingburn family at the inquest. Brian later found out that Galbally was the reason the police laid charges out of the blue. Galbally had threatened to take out a common-law warrant for murder against Murphy and Stillman. One of the detectives, Kevin Carton, went to the bosses and told them that if Murphy and Stillman were charged with murder, they would never get bail. Riots at Pentridge suggested two cops wouldn't survive a day in jail. Strategically, Carton figured that if Murphy and Stillman were charged with manslaughter, it would mean they could get bail. Most importantly for the police, charges would quieten down the media that was baying for police blood. Brian was grateful for this forward-thinking which kept him out of jail.

Brian suspected Galbally was going to play dirty, though. While he had been suspended, he had been approached by two police members on behalf of Galbally to change his statement to blame the whole thing on Stillman. Brian told them to get stuffed. And he wasn't just being altruistic. If he had changed his statement, he would have been charged with making a false statement in the

The inquest

first place. He wouldn't have changed it, anyway. Together, he and Stillman stood a good chance of beating the charges. As the senior officer, Brian would be the first to front the inquest and tell the court what happened, And he'd been giving evidence and squaring off against men in wigs for years.

Ironically, Galbally's people approached Brian a second time. A mate of Galbally's had been the victim of a break-in and lost some valuable family silver. Galbally wondered if Brian could make some inquiries for him. This was how the legal system worked. Galbally would soon stand flamboyantly in court, pointing the finger at Brian and accusing him of bashing a man to death, but was also happy for Brian to find his friend's silver.

Brian told him to get stuffed.

Ray Dunn represented Brian and Stillman at the inquest. He was a gravel-voiced solicitor and the president of the Richmond Football Club. Ray was a favourite of the police force because his dad had been a police superintendent, so Ray knew the ropes. If any copper was charged with even the most minor of things, Ray was the man for the job.

Brian was buoyed somewhat by a chance meeting. A couple of weeks before the inquest started, he ran into the pathologist who had performed the post-mortem examination on Neil Collingburn.

'How do you think I'll go?' Brian said to him.

'Murphy, I shouldn't be talking to you,' he said, 'but from what I've seen, they've gilded the lily to a great degree.'

Brian didn't dare question him further, but suspected that he was talking about Connellan and Carroll's statements. He had no doubt that they would put the blame firmly in the hands of the cops. Thank God evidence doesn't lie.

Finally, the day came and the inquest began. Once the seven jurors were sworn in and the evidence began, Brian and Stillman had to watch every witness carefully and note inconsistencies in their stories. At the end of the day, they would sit with Ray Dunn to discuss strategies for questioning each witness.

Thomas Joseph Connellan was called first. He told of how he, Collingburn and Carroll had lunched in Nicholson Street. 'Not just fish and chips, or anything like that,' he told the inquest. 'It was a first-class restaurant.' He described how they were pulled over by Gosney and Stillman as they drove off down Nicholson Street. The two police officers had searched the car and found two sets of golf clubs which they suspected were stolen. Arrangements were made for them all to go to Russell Street for questioning. Officer Stillman rode with Collingburn and Carroll in Collingburn's car, while Gosney drove him in the police car. Connellan admitted that when he was driving to Russell Street, he could see Collingburn in the car ahead pull out a metal bar and shake it at Stillman.

At Russell Street, the three men had been taken by Gosney and Stillman into the Crime Cars office. Gosney had questioned him while Stillman spoke to Collingburn. Connellan said he bought the golf clubs at Northland shopping centre so Gosney went into the reception area to ring the shop and check.

That was the moment when Brian had walked past the doorway of the Crime Cars office. The Crime Cars Squad was a big squad and their charter was to be first on the scene at major crimes.

Connellan told the court that Brian made an appearance in the Crime Cars office, and returned several times over the afternoon. Brian knew this could easily be disproven because he had only been at Russell Street for the short time it took him to meet with colleagues from his office and quieten things down with Collingburn.

According to Connellan, Stillman ordered Collingburn to stand up, then felled him with one blow. Collingburn sagged and Brian propped him up so that Stillman could run across the room and knee him in the groin. Connellan said that once Collingburn dropped to the floor, Stillman jumped on him.

Connellan told the court that he had run over to another police officer guarding Ian Carroll and beseeched him: 'Get them off! They'll kill him.' Incongruously, moments later, Connellan said

The inquest

that during this time, only he, Carroll, Collingburn, Stillman and Murphy were in the room at the time. No mention of another police officer.

According to Connellan, Murphy and Stillman had asked Collingburn to stand up and then they both attacked him. He said they all rolled around on the floor and knocked Collingburn out. Connellan said that Murphy had yelled, 'The bash is on!' over and over again.

'I can't recall at what stage, but he was picked up and then they rammed him into the lockers ... they were stomping on him, jumping on him. I say they were jumping on him. They were taking it in turns. Firstly, Stillman jumped on ... the deceased's stomach. He jumped off the ground with two feet onto his stomach and landed on him. Stillman did that ... once or twice. As to Murphy, he stomped on his head. He just kept lifting his shoe, or whatever he was wearing, and stomped on his face. That happened a few times.' Connellan stepped out of the witness box and stomped to show the jury the force he was describing.

Listening to all of this, Brian understood what the pathologist meant during their chance conversation. While Connellan described a vicious beating, he knew from the autopsy photographs that Collingburn's body had no such corresponding injuries. There was a boot-shaped bruise on Collingburn's torso on the left side at the base of his ribs. Aside from a small cut over his eye, and a couple of dots on his face—which the doctors concluded had come from resuscitation attempts—his face was undamaged. Pictures don't lie. If anyone had stomped 'a few times' on his face, his face would be smashed. And it wasn't.

'What do you say if it is suggested that the deceased attacked, or attempted to attack Stillman when he was sitting on a chair?' Frank Galbally asked Connellan.

'I would say that is not correct.' Connellan sounded sanctimonious.

'And that he, in fact, almost knocked the chair and Stillman over?'

'I would say it is not correct, again.'

After being questioned by several lawyers, Connellan admitted that he, Collingburn and Carroll had drunk three bottles of beer at lunch between them. He said the golf clubs found in his car during the initial search were his and if the police had've driven him to Northland, he could have pointed out the salesman who sold them to him.

Connellan said that he had received a black eye in all the fighting. When asked if he had joined the fray in the muster room, he said he didn't think he would attack police at Russell Street considering some of them had guns.

Ray Dunn took a turn. The man on the witness stand admitted that he had lied about where he was working when Stillman and Gosney first picked him up—he didn't, in fact, have a job. Connellan admitted to lying about being on a day off, and then he said he lied when they asked him how he had hurt his left knuckle, and he lied about how much trouble he'd been in before. Under questioning, Connellan admitted to a long criminal record.

'And in that criminal record, you have had numerous occasions when you have accused the police of telling lies, haven't you?'

'I forget. I wouldn't call them lies.'

'But you denied all they said, didn't you?'

'Yes.'

'Why? Were you always convicted wrongly?'

'On a few occasions.' Connellan's impatience was showing. One minute cocky, the next minute, looking like a goose. 'What has that got to do with this?'

Dunn read out Connellan's entire criminal record, beginning in 1953. Considering that Connellan was only 28 when he appeared at the inquest, he must've begun his criminal career when he was barely double digits in age. It wasn't pretty. Wilful damage, housebreaking, stealing, jail, unlawful possession of a sawn-off pea rifle, jail again. Connellan said he was innocent of some of the

The inquest

charges but didn't appeal.

'You did 12 months' jail as a purely innocent man?'

'That's right,' said Connellan, self-righteously.

'Tell me this, have you got a deep resentment against the police force for that?'

'No,' said Connellan.

Dunn pressed on with Connellan's criminal history: shop-breaking, stealing, 6 months in jail, many charges of illegally using a motor car, shoplifting, 12 months in jail, assaulting police by kicking, 2 months in jail. The list went on and on. It seemed the only times Connellan wasn't breaking the law was when he was in jail. Ray Dunn pushed Connellan into an untenable position. If he didn't admit to being guilty every time he had done something wrong, then the police must've got it wrong. And if they did get it wrong or frame him, he served prison time for nothing. Any normal person would be seething. Seething enough to give evidence against police whether it was true or not.

Connellan denied that he was guilty of kicking a police officer before being sentenced to two months in prison. 'So you were framed?' asked Dunn.

'That's right.'

'You bore no resentment whatever against the police on that?'

'That's right.'

Brian enjoyed this line of questioning. He could see the jury looking at each other and murmuring.

All up, Connellan's criminal record took over half an hour to get into evidence. Dunn then led straight into chipping away at his story that had Murphy and Stillman stomping and jumping on Collingburn's face.

'Have you seen the pictures of the deceased?'

'No.'

'Do you know that there were very few marks on his face indicating violence?'

'I only seen what I seen,' said Connellan sullenly.

Ray Dunn was insistent in drawing the witness out on just how much violence Murphy and Stillman had 'committed' knowing full well there was no supporting physical evidence. The more violence both Connellan and Carroll described, the more foolish their evidence would sound. Connellan finally agreed that Stillman stomped twice on Collingburn's face and Murphy stomped three times.

As solicitors do, Dunn swept the questioning back to when the three men were picked up on Nicholson Street. In an earlier statement, Connellan had said that he had seen Collingburn threaten Stillman with the iron bar while driving and said that Collingburn appeared to be yelling at Stillman who had his arms raised to ward off the threat of the bar. He said clearly that Stillman did not appear to be saying anything. It was a good point to make—without provocation, Collingburn threatened Stillman earlier. But Connellan was having none of it. Now, he claimed, both men were yelling. He turned belligerent when Dunn suggested he had changed his story. 'I seen him yelling and that's all I got to say.'

Ian Revell Carroll was 23 when he took the witness box at the Coroners Court. He was somewhat baby-faced in appearance, but looks can be deceiving. He had a long criminal record and would go on to join Ray Chuck Bennett in the Great Bookie Robbery in just a few years' time.

According to Carroll, the argument in the car between Stillman and Collingburn that ended with the waving of an iron bar began when Collingburn asked the police officer his name. Stillman refused to give it.

'Neil said, "What's the matter with telling me your name? I'm just as much a man as you are." Stillman said, "Do you think so?"' That was when Collingburn slammed on the brakes and pulled the weapon.

Carroll admitted that he asked to use the toilet when they all arrived at Russell Street.

He denied having a knife on him at the time. Denied trying

The inquest

to put it in the waste paper basket. Denied it was his when Max Gosney found it.

Carroll had his own account of the circus of violence. Unlike Connellan, he had the room full of other coppers. Murphy and Stillman beat Collingburn unconscious, then jumped up and down on him. Meanwhile, Murphy spun around the room like a pinwheel, belting everyone.

'Brian Murphy ran back along the Russell Street side of the room screaming out, "Tell them all the bash is on, the bash is on."' And then, according to Carroll, Brian threatened to kill several friends of his.

This was good stuff. At the beginning of the inquest, the jury had visited the tiny muster room and Brian hoped they could see how ridiculous this was. How could he run around a tiny room? Two or three strides *was* the room.

Carroll painted his own vivid picture of Collingburn: 'He was unconscious on the ground and gurgling … some blood ran down his mouth … the left-hand side of his face appeared to be all black and blue, bruised, and there was blood running out of his mouth.'

And while Murphy and Stillman were spinning around, bashing, whumping, and threatening to kill his friends, Carroll claimed that Collingburn never raised a hand to either of them. 'In the fight, I did not see the deceased hitting or doing anything to defend himself.'

Brian hoped the jury could draw their own conclusions— would a man who was so easily affronted when Stillman refused to give him his name that he threatened Stillman with an iron bar, really not raise a hand when he was being bashed, as was being alleged?

When asked about the knife, Carroll told the inquest that he couldn't have been carrying it because he was wearing tight jeans and he wouldn't have had anywhere to put it.

As they did with Connellan, the lawyers wanted Carroll's criminal record in evidence so the jury knew exactly the kind of man they were being asked to believe. He had begun his life of crime in 1959—barely out of short pants. Housebreaking, unlawfully on the premises, possession of housebreaking implements, indecent behaviour, driving without a licence, possession of an offensive weapon, giving a false name and address, larceny. Carroll agreed that he had been guilty of all the things he'd been charged with.

Unlike Connellan who told the inquest that it was just the three of them and Murphy and Stillman in the room, Carroll painted a picture of a bunch of coppers standing in the annex adjoining the muster room all watching and smiling.

Ray Dunn questioned Carroll about his previous charge of carrying a weapon. 'You were convicted at the Preston Court in 1968, what was the offensive weapon?'

'A pocket knife,' said Carroll.

'I see,' said Dunn. 'A knife—'

The Coroner interrupted. 'Just a moment. The witness said a pocket knife and you said a knife. There's a big difference between those two, Mr Dunn.'

Dunn was unperturbed. 'I agree, but it is still a knife so far as a charge of offensive weapon is concerned.' He turned straight back to Carroll and continued. 'You see, you told your counsel, did you not, that you pleaded guilty to being found with an offensive weapon?'

'Yes.'

'That is not true, is it? You pleaded not guilty to the charge of being found with an offensive weapon, didn't you?'

'Don't recall.'

Dunn did the lawyer thing, asking Carroll about swearing to things on oath when he didn't remember. It was all designed to undermine anything else he might say and to remind the jury what kind of crim he was. When Carroll caged again, Dunn went in for the kill. 'You don't recall.' Incredulous voice. The charges had sent Carroll to jail. 'Surely it would stick in your mind, wouldn't it?'

Carroll hedged and Dunn brought the questioning back to the

The inquest

levels of aggression shown by Collingburn on the day. Carroll finally admitted that Stillman had been courteous and it was Collingburn who had become aggressive, first in the car with the iron bar and again as they all arrived at Russell Street.

Dunn showed Carroll a picture of Carl Stillman—the one Brian had insisted he get taken by the police photographer of the cut on his lip. Carroll begrudgingly agreed that Stillman had been injured but claimed he hadn't seen how it had happened.

Carroll told the inquest under the scathing questioning of Dunn that Collingburn's face—after a severe beating from Stillman and Murphy had turned black and blue on the left side. The Coroner interrupted and said that Carroll's previous testimony had the damage to Collingburn's face on the right side. Carroll shrugged.

'Have you seen any photographs of the deceased's body?' asked Dunn, knowing full well that there was no evidence of either side of Collingburn's face being black and blue.

'No,' admitted Carroll.

Dunn asked Carroll to demonstrate a stomp for the jury and Carroll obliged. Then the lawyer got Carroll to describe the three stomps onto Collingburn's face he claimed were delivered by Stillman and then another two by Brian. All this was leading to the photos of Neil Collingburn's face taken after the autopsy. No bruises, no swelling. Carroll happily dug the hole deeper.

For the next hour or so, Dunn led Carroll through the events in the Crime Car office, step-by-step, careful to ask him what the resulting injuries would be from the punches and stomps he described. In Carroll's version of events, Brian ran around the room screaming and stomping, and Stillman 'continually' stood above Collingburn and dropped down, driving his knee into his chest and stomach. After that, Collingburn rolled over and then Stillman 'smashed' his face into the floor.

'Did you expect to see some big marks on his face as a result of this?'

'Yes,' said Carroll.

Ray Dunn questioned Carroll on every time his statement differed from Connellan's. Carroll shrugged it off with an 'I can't recall'.

The next witness was a bloke named Franklin. He had been picked up that day, too, and ended up sitting in a small ante-room with Collingburn after he had been injured.

'I heard something said about a hospital,' said Franklin. 'One of the detectives said they were going to take him to hospital … I saw the way he left the room. He just walked out very slowly, as if he had something wrong with his hip in the kidney region.'

At the inquest, Franklin said he had heard swearing from the muster room, despite this never being mentioned in any of the statements he had made. Dunn was onto him like a flash. Why didn't he tell Kevin Carton in a later interview?

'I was nervous,' said Franklin.

'Does that make you dishonest?' asked Dunn quickly.

'Not really.' Franklin blushed.

Max Gosney was up next. He read his statement to the court and waited patiently for the questions.

The main difference between the way he treated Neil Collingburn and the way Stillman treated him was quickly evident. Collingburn had fired up because Stillman refused to give him his name. Gosney had a catch-more-flies-with-honey approach.

'I said, "How are you going, Neil? It's been a long time since I've seen you. You've changed a bit with that hair." He said, "What's your name again?" I said, "Max Gosney." He said, "That's right. I remember you." … I said, "Is this your car?" He said, "Yes." I said, "Is it an ex-police car?" He said, "Oh, fair go!" and laughed at that.'

Gosney told the court that Collingburn admitted he'd moved out of the Richmond house he'd shared with his wife.

Once they were in the cars heading to Russell Street, Gosney

The inquest

described the two incidents. 'I saw Collingburn turn towards Stillman, and I heard him shouting out in a loud voice ... I said to Connellan, "It looks like Neil's upset." He said, "He'll be okay." Neil Collingburn appeared to become calm again.' But not long after, Collingburn fired up again. This time, he was armed with an iron bar.

The bar was produced for the court and Gosney nodded. That was the one.

He described how he was half way out of his car to go to Stillman's aid when Collingburn put the bar away. Gosney could see Stillman through the rear window of the car and when his colleague didn't beckon him, he returned to his own car.

At Russell Street, Gosney told the court that Carroll had asked to go to the toilet. When Gosney went in after him, he saw Carroll put a knife into the waste paper bin.

When all three men were positioned in separate corners of the muster room, Gosney left to go to the outer office to make phone calls while Stillman went to the Information Bureau to get a set of particulars on his suspects.

Stillman returned and sat down at the typewriter in the muster room. 'Senior Detective Brian Murphy entered the office and had a short conversation with Collingburn, Connellan, and Carroll, and left the office and had gone out into the outer office ... I heard a loud noise and heard Collingburn shouting out, and I looked to see First Constable Stillman on his back on the floor in the chair.'

Gosney indicated the position and the chair from some photographs of the office.

'Stillman was lying in the chair ... Collingburn, at this stage, was learning over him in a threatening manner. I saw Stillman kick him away with ... both feet, kicked him away in the stomach or upper chest ... It was a good kick ... sufficient to push him away. Collingburn reeled backwards towards the chair in the corner of the room and he fell backwards to the ground ... to me, it appeared that he struck the chair as he fell.'

Max Gosney told the court how both men had struggled to their feet, wrestled, then both went over the chair. 'Connellan ran down the room and punched him at this stage to the back of the neck or head … it was a violent punch. At this stage, Connellan kicked with his right foot and appeared to strike Collingburn in the back.' Gosney speculated that Connellan hadn't meant to kick his mate, but was aiming for the felled police officer, instead.

Brian listened as Gosney described how at this point, Brian came racing back into the room, grabbed Connellan and took him back to his seat. 'I saw Senior Detective Murphy … take hold of Collingburn from behind … Collingburn was again struggling with Stillman.

 'I saw Collingburn go limp and Murphy let him go. Collingburn sank to his knees. I say that I saw him sag and go limp, that is from an approximate standing position. Nothing happened at that time to make him sag and go limp, other than that Senior Detective Murphy had him from behind and round the neck. He sank down, he buckled at the knees and went limp and then Murphy let him go and he sank to his knees. After a very short time, Senior Detective Murphy and First Constable Stillman escorted him back to the chair which he had come from originally, which was righted, and he was seated in that chair … he sat in that chair himself and Murphy said something to him. He said, "What's wrong with you? You are in enough strife as it is without this sort of thing." … Collingburn said, "You know me, Mr Murphy. I'm mad. I hate young cunts trying to stand over me," and that was the full conversation to my knowledge.'

Max Gosney made a good witness: steady, concise and unruffled. When asked how long the scuffle took, he estimated a little over one minute. The only injuries Gosney noticed on Collingburn after the scuffle was a small abrasion above his left eye.

After things calmed down, Gosney spoke to Collingburn about the golf clubs. He cautioned the young man, then charged him. Up until that point, Collingburn looked fine and was behaving

The inquest

normally.

The longer they spoke, the paler Collingburn became.

Gosney asked him if he was okay. 'I questioned him regarding his paleness, and he said that he felt sore across the stomach.' Collingburn was taken to St Vincent's Hospital at 4.30 p.m.— an hour after his attack on Carl Stillman. Gosney described how Collingburn walked out of Russell Street unaided, and into the hospital unaided. He had told hospital staff that he felt sick and they directed him to lie on a trolley.

'Whilst he was laying down, he said to me, "Gee, I feel sick, Max." I did not comment. He appeared pale to me.' Gosney told the court how Collingburn asked how the other bloke was. Gosney thought he meant Stillman. '"He's all right," I told him. He (Collingburn) said, "There's a thousand in it for you both if I beat them." I said, "I don't work like that. It is as it stands."'

Gosney described how the doctor had come in and examined Collingburn, questioning both of them about the nature of the injuries. At the end of the examination, the doctor told Gosney that he suspected Collingburn had a ruptured spleen. Gosney left the hospital then, and returned to Russell Street to question Connellan and Carroll.

The pathologist was called as a witness. He described that Collingburn had died from a ruptured duodenum. A couple of marks on Collingburn's face, the pathologist said, were consistent with vigorous resuscitation.

After hearing that, Brian knew that they were pretty much home and hosed. It didn't matter what Connellan and Carroll said, the injuries were not consistent with a violent bashing. Ray Dunn had read the statements of Connellan and Carroll and questioned the pathologist carefully. If someone had jumped on someone's head or stomach, what injuries would you expect? Were they there? No.

In his summing up, the Coroner, Mr H W Pascoe, SM, addressed members of the jury for nearly half an hour. He gave a brief recap of how the three criminals were picked up by Stillman and Gosney.

'If you believe the story of the assault by Connellan and Carroll, the finding can only be murder against Stillman and Murphy,' he said. 'You have heard it alleged that the deceased was punched and kneed in the groin, had his stomach kneed and his face and head stomped. If you believe this you must believe it was done with the intention of doing wilful bodily harm to the victim. The appropriate finding is murder.'

Brian watched the jury for a hint of how they were feeling; they looked uneasy. The time was coming to put the whole thing in their hands.

The Coroner made a remark that buoyed his spirits. He said that if the alleged ferocity had indeed taken place, it was remarkable the deceased had so few marks on him.

He then turned his attention to the hospital. The jury had to be satisfied that the hospital did not aggravate the situation in their treatment of Collingburn. Brian hoped the jury read between the lines—Collingburn could have been saved if he had received the proper treatment promptly. The fact that they parked him at the back of the ward for a day, may well have contributed to his death.

'Another matter is the pool of blood on the muster room floor,' he said. 'I would have thought that if the area of blood had been associated with an assault of discreditable nature, it would have been cleaned up very quickly to get rid of incriminating evidence. But we have been told that as late as 10.30 p.m. it was still there.'

While the headlines called it 'a pool' of blood, the scuff mark was the size of a button.

Mr Pascoe told the jury that as far as the fight was concerned, they might feel it was not as violent as Connellan and Carroll, had described, but perhaps it was not as innocent as the police described. 'You may feel that the real truth of the matter lies somewhere between the two versions,' he said. 'But did some unusual and dangerous aspect, such as it occurring just after a meal, take over and control the outcome to the extent that an unusual

The inquest

injury causing death was imposed on the victim? If you believe this, then manslaughter is the finding you should introduce,' Mr Pascoe said. 'Joint and concerted efforts in manslaughter is now part of our law, and if you feel the death occurred in the manner I have just described, the finding should be against both participants.'

Brian was preparing for the worst but hoping for the best. After hearing the summing up, he didn't think it was in their favour overall, but hoped that the jury would consider the vast difference between the stories of Connellan and Carroll and the lack of injuries to Collingburn.

The jury deliberated for 80 minutes. When they returned, not one of them looked at Brian or Stillman. *Not good,* Brian thought, leaning over to Stillman. 'We're gone,' he said. 'We're going for trial.'

And sure enough, the vote against them was 4 to 3 to commit for trial

Senior Sergeant George Morris was in charge of Brian's protection that day and was armed. When they left the court, there were half a dozen members of the Painters and Dockers outside. They took one look at Morris and didn't say a word.

Brian hurried home as quickly as he could because Margaret was home with the kids when the verdict hit the radio and he was scared the Painters and Dockers would stack on a turn at the house after they heard about it.

She was standing at the laundry when he got back. 'What's the next step?' she said, tearfully.

Brian was blunt. 'Well, if I'm found guilty, I'll go to jail.' She needed to know.

Plattfuss was optimistic. 'Mate, you're better off going to trial. You'll beat it. Everyone reckons you'll beat it.'

Brian snapped. 'Don't say that!' he said angrily. 'Everyone said we'd beat it at the inquest but that hasn't happened.'

'Don't question the inquest because you'll need to look at the whole bloody judicial system.' Plattfuss snapped back.

He was right. A Coroners Court could hear any sort of evidence whereas the Country Court where Brian and Stillman were headed, had much stricter rules of evidence.

There was the issue of cost. A trial didn't come cheap. Brian and Stillman went before a panel at the legal aid office. When they asked Brian why he should get legal aid, his response was immediate.

'I've spent the last 17 years looking after the people of Victoria without fear or favour. These allegations are without foundation and I think that I deserve to be funded.'

'You've got no argument with me,' said the legal aid solicitor.

The wheels were set in motion. Ray Dunn organised barrister George Hampel for Brian while Stillman had John Phillips. Both men would go on to become judges.

Brian was impressed with George Hampel from the start. He was very affable. Ray Dunn passed on all his notes about inconsistencies and downright lies to the barristers, who set about building a case.

One Monday morning, not long after the inquest, Brian got a phone call from a friend who said that he had some news that would be a bit of a shock.

'Mate,' Brian laughed, 'after what I've been through, nothing could shock me!'

'Ray Dunn dropped dead of a heart attack last Thursday.'

Brian was wrong; things could still shock him.

28

ON TRIAL

It was only two years since the Abortion Inquiry of 1970 had resulted in the charging of Inspector Jack Ford, Superintendent Jack Matthews, former detective constable Martin Jacobson, and former station officer Frederick Adam, for running an abortion racket. The police officers had taken money from medical professionals and in return, had turned a blind eye to them performing abortions, which were illegal at the time. Their trial made headlines in February 1971. Witnesses told the court that the police officers charged were prepared to cover up deaths if need be in order to protect the doctors. It was alleged that Superintendent Jack Mathews had been paid $600 a month by the abortionists.

Jack Mathews had come a long way since Brian's mother Maggie had chased him off her porch with a broom when he'd come calling after Brian's car had been torched all those years ago.

Conservative Liberal Premier, Henry Bolte, who had withstood a huge public campaign to commute Ronald Ryan's death sentence, was keen to restore public faith in the police force. All of this formed the backdrop in which Brian and Stillman faced trial. Confidence in the Victoria Police had taken a battering by the time their case went to trial in February, 1972.

As the date of the trial loomed nearer, Margaret had faith that Brian would be okay—literal faith. The Murphys were so well known in the Catholic community that not only were the locals saying prayers on their behalf, a friend who'd been in Perth told Brian and Margaret that his name was mentioned in a Mass over there. They were also praying for Brian in his brother's parish in Orbost. A mate's wife even got them to say prayers in the Church of England. Brian figured he'd take them where he could get them.

Margaret believed that heaven was stormed with prayers for her husband.

Brian was humbled by the army of people looking out for him in small ways. There were a couple of kind parishioners who would arrive early at their church each Sunday, and wash off chalked slogans and peel off posters from the door—the general message being that Brian Murphy was a killer.

The priests were unbelievably supportive. So were the nuns. On the day the inquest started, the nuns had held a special Mass at the convent, followed by a breakfast.

In preparation for the trial, Brian visited George Hampel in his chambers. The barrister had read the transcripts from the inquest and had a lot of questions. His questions were astute and often when he asked a question, Brian thought: *that's the question I'd ask*. Brian told Hampel what had happened with McLeod and how his colleagues had followed him home, drunk, and left him lying in his driveway.

Hampel replied, 'It won't serve you to get into the witness box and attack other police. We will hold it in case we need it, but I don't think we will.'

Not only was Hampel astute, but he had a pleasant attitude. He didn't look down on Brian, but rather, he seemed to trust that the experienced police officer would be fine in the witness box.

At the trial, Judge Leckie was presiding and Paul Mullaly was the Crown Prosecutor. Mullaly had insisted on prosecuting the case, even though another prosecutor, Geoff Byrne had wanted to do it. Brian liked Geoff Byrne; he was a good bloke and would have given them a fair go. As far as Mullaly went, there was no love lost between the cop and the prosecutor.

There was a false start to the trial after the jury was chosen. Brian and Stillman checked the jury list and found one of the jurors knew Carl Stillman's mother—they both worked at the same shop—which meant they needed a whole new jury.

It took another day to get a new jury which was made up of four women and eight men. They looked like average decent citizens. The jury were to be sequestered during the trial which meant they wouldn't be influenced by the media since the trial was sure to be front-page news

Paul Mullaly asked that the jury visit the Russell Street Crime Car office where it had all happened. Brian welcomed the visit because it would help everyone see how small the muster room was and how impossible some of the parts of Connellan's and Carroll's statements were. The visit would also prove important in an unexpected way that hadn't occurred to any of them at the start of the trial. The devil would prove to be in the detail … or in this case, the toilet.

The medical evidence was heard first. The pathologist was followed by the doctors at the hospital. As Brian listened to the doctors, he believed that what they were saying was not favourable to his case. On cross-examination, the defence barristers did well to leave the jury in no doubt that there was a conflict of interest. Collingburn might have sustained his torn duodenum in the Crime Car office, but once he was their patient, he had been pushed aside and left untreated until it was too late. One doctor from the Alfred Hospital said that the injuries Collingburn suffered were consistent with a car accident. The only problem was that he'd never seen Collingburn so his evidence was swiftly rebutted by defence barristers.

The trial went for about three weeks. For Brian, the best part was the destruction of Connellan and Carroll. At the inquest, the police prosecutor had encouraged them to gild the lily as much as they liked because then the defence would know their full story. Most trials are won by the questions asked at committal which then tie witnesses to certain facts that they can't change later. In this case, the inquest served the same purpose.

As galling as it was to hear Connellan and Carroll lying about him at the inquest, Brian was happy because most of the things they said were blatantly untrue and could be disproven. He was also glad they weren't smart enough to realise this.

Ian Revell Carroll looked like a regular knock-about bloke and the jury would have taken him for such. He wore jeans, a shirt and jacket to the trial. At the inquest, Carroll had been questioned about the knife found in the waste bin in the men's toilets. Carroll had admitted standing at a urinal, but denied dropping the knife.

One night during the course of the trial, Brian lay in bed pondering this. He suddenly remembered that at some time the men's toilets had been switched with the women's toilets at Russell Street, so there was no urinal in the men's toilets. Carroll must have used a cubicle, which put a lie to his story that he stood in front of a urinal. Brian rang George Hampel in the early hours the next morning and also contacted Phillips and Stillman. At 7 a.m., they all met at Russell Street to plan that day's court strategies.

In cross-examination during the morning, Phillips and Hampel destroyed Carroll on this point.

'So what?' said Carroll, when he was proven to be a liar. He did not understand that a man who lied about a small thing might be seen by a jury as a man who might lie about other things, too.

When they questioned him about the knife, Carroll tried to demonstrate how he couldn't have had the knife because he was wearing tight jeans.

It's one thing to rehearse the questions you think the opposite side are going to ask, and quite another to counter something out of left field. In the blink of an eye, Carroll changed from being a trained witness to the cocky petty criminal that he was. Brian watched the jury looking at him, taking his measure. It wasn't hard. The men on the jury who had been sitting forward earlier, listening intently, sat back as Carroll fired up angrily. Brian read their body language and guessed scepticism. The women jurors looked at one another as if to say: *Get a load of this bloke*!

On trial

By contrast, Connellan had a insolent attitude when answering questions. He would say, 'nah,' instead of 'no', and was unimpressive from the moment he took the stand, coming unstuck soon after. He repeated his story from his original statement that police officers stomped and jumped on Collingburn. When the Crown produced the post-mortem photographs for Connellan to point out the injuries—which weren't there—he shrugged and responded along the lines of: 'I dunno. But he did it.'

Brian watched the jury and sensed they didn't believe him. There was even a bit of head-shaking as Connellan stuck belligerently to his story. And that was his undoing. If Collingburn had indeed been rammed head-first into the edge of a steel filing cabinet, and been jumped on from a height, where was the proof? When he talked about Brian jumping off a table, the jury all looked over at Brian who made eye contact with them, one at a time. He hoped this frank exchange would ask them to decide between who was telling the lies and who wasn't.

The jury looked at pictures of the post-mortem with interest.

On Friday 25 February, the surgeon, Graham Collopy, explained what he had found when he operated on Neil Collingburn, telling the court that there was a small tear in the duodenum which had caused peritonitis when semi-digested food leaked into the abdominal cavity. He stated that Collingburn was in the one percent of the population of people who carried a normally dormant organism which multiplied in damaged tissue. This produced a toxin which destroyed the blood. This, he concluded was the cause of death. Collopy said that the injury was consistent with a knee to the stomach or possibly an upward kick. Asked if the injury could be caused by being jumped on or punched, the surgeon said, 'Possible but not probable.'

After hearing the full story from Kevin Carton, Brian watched with great interest as Collopy gave evidence. Interviewing the hospital staff, Carton had discovered that Collingburn had been abusive to the nuns on arrival, so they had promptly shunted him to the furthest part of the casualty ward, reserved for rowdy patients. He was thereafter ignored until Collopy spoke to him the following morning. Brian heard that Collopy had said to the head nun: 'We have a patient down the back there who is in a very serious condition. Unless we operate on him, we might lose him.' The nun is alleged to have replied: 'We have *paying* patients before him.' To which Collopy said: 'You make your own mind up, but he is in need of urgent attention.'

By the time Collingburn was operated on, it was too late. Blind Freddy could see that the hospital had been negligent. Brian knew this was arse-covering. Kevin Carton had seen Collingburn's chart where someone had scrawled 'allergic to penicillin' on it. That was one of the treatments that could have saved him. Brian didn't know if Collingburn was allergic or not, but Carton told him he'd seen it written on the chart. Brian wondered if it could have been written later in an attempt for the hospital to cover up the fact that they hadn't administered it.

The doctors from St Vincent's had offered shallow excuses for the reason that Collingburn died—considering that he hadn't been given proper medical attention when he was admitted.

The Defence got their star witness through serendipity. Professor Hughes from the Royal Melbourne Hospital was one of the leading surgeons of the day. Someone from Brian's parish knew his PA. Professor Hughes had overheard her talking about the case and declared that it shouldn't have made it into court. 'He died because of what happened at the hospital.'

When Brian found this out, the Defence subpoenaed him to give evidence.

Professor Hughes was an impressive man. When he took the oath and gave his name and qualifications, the judge asked him to assess himself as to his standing in his field.

'I am the best,' said Hughes, matter-of-factly. And the way he said it, left no doubt in anybody's mind that he was.

The jury was hooked.

Hughes said that Collingburn didn't die as a result of the injuries he sustained, but rather, he died of neglect. Had Collingburn been operated on straight away, Hughes told the jury, the contents of the duodenum being released into the body could have been arrested. Twenty-four hours later, this was impossible. Professor Hughes also reaffirmed the fact that there were no corresponding injuries to the assault described by Connellan and Carroll.

Any questions that Mullaly asked, Professor Hughes reiterated his view that Collingburn did not die as the result of what the police did.

By the end of his evidence, Brian felt a bit less worried. Looking over at his co-accused, he sensed Stillman felt a bit better, too.

Next, Gosney gave evidence. He was genuine and honest, and remained as solid as a rock on cross-examination. He described the yelling and screaming and then the fact that he and Brian had both come in and helped bring things to order.

Several witnesses for the Defence, followed in the witness box and confirmed the defendants' stories. One cop said that when he had grabbed Collingburn's shirt, he noticed a spot of blood the size of a coin. *The Herald* later reported it as 'blood-soaked' clothing.

The trial hit the presses as far away as London where Mick Miller, then an Assistant Commissioner, was on a Churchill Scholarship. He sent a message through a superior officer to Brian which read: *One way or another, I am ready to give evidence for you.* To know that a colleague of Mick Miller's calibre and seniority still thought enough of Brian to go to court on his behalf was a big morale booster. Ironically, the Chief Commissioner, Reg 'Judas' Jackson, made no attempt to contact Brian. They both knew each other, but when Brian bumped into him and greeted him, the Chief Commissioner acted as if Brian was a complete stranger.

The night before Brian was to give evidence, he spoke to George Hampel. 'Any advice?' he asked him.

'No,' Hampel said. 'You've given evidence hundreds of times before and no doubt, your evidence for yourself will be just as strong.'

Some barristers advise their clients not to give evidence, but as a police officer, Brian knew that if he didn't, it would look as if he had something to hide.

When the time finally came to step into the witness box, George Hampel started the questioning by asking what happened on that March day in 1971. Brian told the court that when he'd heard mention of Collingburn, Carroll and Connellan over the radio, he had warned Gosney and Stillman to be careful of them. Later, he had seen Gosney in the squad's reception area and went in to ask how the arrest had gone. When the ruckus happened in the main office, he went in and restrained the other two. Hampel asked if Brian had jumped off a desk and rammed Collingburn's head into a filing cabinet.

'Those things never took place,' he answered, looking straight at the jury.

When it came time for the cross-examination, Brian was confident that Paul Mullaly couldn't knock a chip off him.

Mullaly came in hard right from the start.

But two could play at that game. Just as barristers try to knock witnesses off their game, Brian did the same to Mullaly. When the prosecutor lowered his voice and asked a question, Brian took his glasses from his pocket, cleaned them with a hanky, and then looked up.

'Can you repeat the question?' he asked, innocently.

'For you, Mr Brian Francis Murphy, I'll ask the question again,' Mullaly said in a voice dripping with condescension, intended to put Brian down.

At that moment, the judge said, 'Mr Mullaly, it won't be for Mr Murphy's benefit, it will be for the benefit of the jury who most probably didn't hear it since I didn't hear it, either.'

Mullaly reddened.

On trial

Brian was chuffed to see his tactic had thrown Mullaly because the question he repeated was not the same one as he first asked. When Brian answered, he didn't look at Mullaly, but instead, made sure he had the eyes of the jury members, and ended with most of them nodding in agreement with what he was saying.

Brian spent the morning in the witness box. Because his evidence was of such a minor nature, it was over pretty quickly. When he finished, he thought the jury members were on his side. He had seen their faces when Carroll and Connellan gave evidence and he thought they looked like they found Brian more plausible and honest.

Because Mullaly didn't knock any chips off Brian's story, George Hampel didn't bother with a cross-examination.

When Brian finished giving evidence, he asked Hampel how he thought it went.

'I know people at 20th Century Fox. I could get you a job there any time,' he said, smiling.

Because evidence is given in alphabetical order where two or more are charged, Brian had gone first. Stillman was next. His evidence was clear and forthright. On cross examination, Mullaly didn't put a dent in his story either.

It was even clearer that there was no crime here. Collingburn had attacked Stillman and they had both restrained him. End of story.

While the trial dragged on, Brian tried to go about his usual business when he was not in court. He found going to Mass on a Sunday a great comfort. Not only could he pray for a good outcome, but the parishioners were a wonderful support.

There was the odd faux pas, though. One Sunday at Mass, Margaret's bag slipped off the seat and Brian's gun fell out and slid nosily across the floor. He tried to be as unobtrusive as possible in retrieving the weapon and returning it to its hiding place. He thinks only half the church saw what happened.

At the end of Mass, a woman approached Brian. He had become

accustomed to people approaching him after Mass. Thankfully most offered their support and well wishes. This woman offered him $500—a small fortune at the time. Brian thanked her but told her he couldn't take her money. She burst into tears and Brian followed her back into church so she could compose herself.

'You don't remember me,' she said through her tears.

'No I don't.' Brian searched her face for signs he knew her.

'The corner of Canterbury Road and Westbeach Road … the little dog over the fence …'

Then it came to him. He did remember. She was the wife of a Painter and Docker who had turned to prostitution to feed her kids. She had used the little dog to signal her customers of her availability.

'How are things going?' Brian asked kindly.

She told him that all of her kids had done well. There was pride in her voice.

'What about that husband of yours?' Brian remembered talking to her about him. There was no love lost.

'He died about 15 years ago.'

Brian couldn't help himself. 'Lucky you!'

The woman laughed.

They chatted for a while longer. Brian had never seen her at his church before and supposed she had come to offer him the money because she'd read about his trial in the newspapers. Maybe she wanted to pay back the kindness he had shown her all those years ago.

Brian was humbled by each small act of kindness. He had served the community for many years, and when he most needed it, the community was right behind him.

On Friday 3 March, John Phillips gave the closing address on behalf of Carl Stillman. He made much of the fact that Carroll and Connellan changed their stories to fit the medical evidence.

On Monday 6 March, George Hampel summed up Brian's case for the defence. He told the court that if Stillman and Murphy were

On trial

convicted, it would be the greatest miscarriage of justice.

At the end of his address, it was the judge's turn.

In his summing up to the jury, Judge Leckie described the two versions of the case—the one given by Connellan and Carroll saying that Collingburn had been punched, jumped on, stamped in the face, kneed in the groin and slammed head-first into a locker. The other version, given by police witnesses that said Collingburn attacked Stillman and that the police officer defended himself while Brian Murphy helped by getting Collingburn back to his chair.

Brian thought the summing up was fair. He said that Brian had in no way contributed to Collingburn's death, but because he was the senior member in the room at the time, the Crown had alleged that Murphy should have controlled the situation better than he did. With that, Brian breathed a sigh of relief.

The judge gave Stillman a good rap too. Collingburn had been the aggressor and Stillman was defending himself.

As the jury retired, Brian thought about the conversation he'd had with his two oldest children that morning. The thought brought tears to the tough detective's eyes. It was a conversation no dad should ever have to have with his kids. But the words had to be spoken in case the jury went the other way, and Brian didn't come home. He had taken Bernadine and Reg into the shed and told them that they should be good to their mother and help her if he didn't come home.

With tears the size of stones, his children stood before him, and realised that something terrible could happen. Brian tried to reassure them, but he could only reassure them so far. He told Reg that a couple of policemen he trusted would help him. There were also lots of aunts and uncles to help.

'I'll look after Mum, I promise, Dad,' said Reg.

'And I'll look after the brothers and sisters,' promised Bernadine.

They had finished the conversation with a big hug and then Brian ushered them back into the house. His sister-in-law who lived with the Murphys and earned a good wage promised that if he went to jail, she would look after the mortgage and the financial side of things. Brian's brother promised the same thing.

And that was all he and Margaret discussed. She was doing a great job with the kids and there was nothing more to say.

When the jury went out at lunch time, Brian and Stillman were put in cells beneath the County Court. While he waited, Brian read the cell graffiti about himself with great interest—his heritage, parentage and masculinity had been questioned several times. He was able to see the irony and the humour. He joked with the warder until he told Brian that instead of joking, he should be worried.

'Just trying to get you onside early,' Brian said to him.

While he felt confident, he could not relax until the verdict was in. He believed that fair-thinking people couldn't return any other verdict than 'not guilty'. The jury came back quickly, so Brian and Stillman didn't have long to wait before being escorted back into court.

On the way up the stairs from the holding cells located in the bowels of the courts complex, Stillman turned to Brian and said, 'If we come out of this, thanks for your help. If we go down, I'm sorry you were involved in this with me.'

'No worries,' Brian said. He had always believed that if he hadn't gone into the room that day, there would have been a serious situation for Carl Stillman. He believed that Collingburn and his two tough mates might have severely beaten the police officer who had arrested them. Even considering the repercussions, Brian would not have done anything differently if he had his time over.

Arriving back in the courtroom, he was feeling pretty good until he walked past Margaret in the first row of the courtroom, sitting with a priest and two of her sisters. Brian's mother Maggie was too crook to attend. She was home doing the hating from a distance. Seeing them there, the thought hit him in the guts: *What if I go down? What will this do to Margaret?*

On trial

A conviction could mean six to eight years, even ten—and that was only if he survived jail. Rumour had it that if they were convicted, their prison welcoming committee would be made up of Painters and Dockers. It was a sombre trip to the court that day. Seeing Margaret clutching her Rosary beads, looking terrified, brought home what was at stake.

When the jury returned, one of the female jurors looked at Brian, smiled and winked. He turned to Stillman and said, 'I think we're home and hosed.'

The jury found Carl Stillman not guilty first. And then it was Brian's turn. He heard the sweetest two words in the English language: 'Not guilty!'

The court erupted into cheering and clapping. The warder grinned, opened the door to the dock and said, 'Go for your lives!'

The judge banged his gavel on the bench and roared, 'Put those prisoners back in the dock! I haven't finished yet!'

Brian wanted to head straight to Margaret, but he sat back down beside Stillman while the judge thanked the jury and dismissed them. Brian rushed out of the dock into the arms of his wife. All he wanted was to be with his family. The verdict was announced on the radio and Brian's brother raced out to ring the kids at home to let them know. Margaret's sister took the kids straight away to the milkbar to buy half a dozen bottles of red lemonade—Brian's favourite drink.

On the steps of the court, Brian faced the press.

'Are you happy with the verdict?' they yelled.

Brian needed to tread carefully. A victory for him was no consolation to Collingburn's family. 'Yes I am,' he told the press, 'but remember, there are still parents without a son, and a woman without a husband, and a child without her father. But it had nothing to do with me.' He hadn't prepared a speech, but he knew that he had to acknowledge that at the heart of all of this was a loss of a life.

'Very wise move, Brian,' said George Hampel, standing by his side on the steps of the court.

Brian and Margaret were quickly surrounded by a couple of hundred people spilling out onto the road. He had wanted to head straight home to the kids, but the police force had organised something else. They all had to push their way through the crowd to get to the waiting police cars which took them to Russell Street. The media were there in droves; the mood was buoyant. They had heard all the evidence and, while they had sometimes written it up adversely, it seemed they thought justice had been done.

At Russell Street, Brian and Stillman stood before Assistant Commissioner Carmichael. He was arrogant. 'You have been found not guilty of manslaughter today; that doesn't mean to say you are innocent.'

'Bullshit!' Brian said. As he got up and went to walk out, Mick Patterson, the commander of the CIB told him to put his arse back in the chair. Brian sat back down, mouth clamped shut. He had been so engulfed by the trial, that he hadn't given much thought about coming back to work, but had assumed his superiors would accept a not guilty verdict and things would return to normal. Clearly this might not be the case.

'Consider yourselves reinstated,' said Assistant Commissioner Carmichael, before dismissing them from his office.

Brian signed a paper, collected a gun, and walked out of Russell Street a working police officer, again.

Back at home, there were lots of hugs and visitors and red lemonade. Every visitor said the same thing to the kids, 'Do you realise how lucky you are to have your dad at home!'

They did.

Twenty-four hours after the acquittal, Brian finally slept. The best feeling was waking up and knowing the acquittal wasn't a dream. The best morning ever.

Letters began arriving at Russell Street the following day.

Have you ever been dead like Collingburn
You'll be Still Men

On trial

> *How's your conscience??????*
> *Dear Sir,*
> *The other day I noticed that the tie you are obliged to wear around your neck was not tight enough.*
> *Yours truly,*
> *Bob*
> *A Liberal Voice*

The thing his detractors seemed to have in common was bad spelling.

> *Sen Det Brian Francis Murphy*
> *You are a filty doog*
> *And you will pay*
> *Just remember you children*
> *This will be for ever*
> *Because you are guilty*
> *M*

On the flipside, the nuns were happy to welcome a *filty doog* to the convent for a celebratory breakfast. Several Christian Brothers wrote Brian letters of congratulations and thanked him for the work he'd done to enhance the welfare of people in the neighbourhood. Even the American Consul General added his voice to the many supporters.

> *Dear Brian,*
> *The power of Prayer is indeed great.*
> *May I say how happy I am for you and your family.*
> *Sincerely,*
> *Bill Hume*
> *American Consulate*

All up, there were hundreds of congratulatory and supportive letters and cards which far outweighed the few negative ones—one of the latter being addressed to Stinker Murphy. Telegrams came by the dozens. In those days, people paid by the word and it was an expensive form of communication so all of the messages were short and succinct. One from the boys from South Melbourne police said: *Congratulations on an inevitable verdict.*

There were so many cards from people Brian didn't even know, offering their heartfelt congratulations. It made him appreciate just how many people out there were on his side. It was especially gratifying to hear from people he'd helped in the past; they remembered and appreciated what Brian had done for them and, in his hour of need, were there in return.

Brian was humbled.

The support for him among the rank and file of the Victoria Police had always been absolute, so Brian imagined there were a lot of cops around the state celebrating the acquittal. It was one of the first cases in Victoria where police had been charged like this. There had been a collection taken up when he and Stillman were first arrested which had raised the princely sum of $2,000 which the two shared evenly. The support had continued throughout the year that Brian was suspended and waiting for the trial; not a day went past when the Murphys didn't get calls from people all over the country offering their support, and police officers from interstate whom they had never met, would ring to wish them luck.

Among the bosses who offered their support were Keith Plattfuss, Mick Miller and Kevin Carton. Afterwards, people who hadn't been around for Brian during the trial, came back with open arms. One of his old bosses had ignored Brian completely when he was arrested. Within a couple of days of the acquittal, Brian ran into him. His superior walked up and offered to shake his hand. 'Welcome back to the police force,' he said.

'You've got to be joking,' Brian replied. 'You didn't want to talk to me three months ago and now you want to be my best friend.' Brian turned away and never spoke to him again.

Some ethnics in the community believed that Brian had killed Collingburn and that he had done the right thing. The more he

On trial

tried to explain, the more they believed he did it. 'We're your friends,' they said conspiratorially, 'you can tell us.'

Brian would shrug it off. People would believe what they wanted to believe.

He appreciated John Link for giving him a job and sticking with him. People would give Margaret eggs in church. One woman from church asked Margaret to make her a fruit cake. Margaret did and the woman pushed $20 into Margaret's hand—a small fortune then. Margaret was heartened that no one ever said a bad word to her about Brian. The Christian brothers at the Catholic school told them that parents had agreed to keep the newspapers out of sight of their kids and turn off televisions when his story came on. That meant the kids at school didn't talk to the Murphy kids about the case.

The community support often came from least expected corners. 'Howya going, mate? Do you need anything?' became the sweetest words—after 'not guilty' of course.

The Herald marked the acquittal with an article on page 3. The heading read: **'Guard to Stay on 2 Police'**. Armed guards were placed on Brian and Stillman for fear of reprisals. The article said that the two police officers would both be back on duty the following day and that they had both benefitted from a change in the ranking system during their absence. Stillman went from being a First Constable to a Senior Constable, while Brian moved to Detective Sergeant. With the new ranks came what the paper termed 'substantial' pay rises.

Brian could only imagine how that sounded to the Painters and Dockers.

While he was mostly left alone after the trail, on a couple of occasions, Brian came face to face with mates of Neil Collingburn's. Once, he was taking Margaret and the kids to lunch at a hotel. He saw two Painters and Dockers outside, glaring at him.

Brian hustled Margaret and the kids into the pub and told her to order. 'I need to pop out and talk to a bloke,' he told her.

As soon as his family was safely inside, Brian took a gun from his holster and pointed it in the faces of the two men.

'We didn't know you were here!' they both protested.

Brian searched them both and sure enough, they were both armed. He took their guns, walked to the gutter, and flung them down a drain.

'I see you again, I'll kill you,' Brian said, letting the cold glint in his eyes and the barrel of his pistol leave them in no doubt that he meant what he said.

29

BILLY AND PAT

The Painters and Dockers had a long history of violence, both within and outside its ranks. Over 15 murders were attributed to the legendary power struggles and that's not counting the men who disappeared off the face of the earth.

One day a small furniture van pulled up around the corner from Billy Longley's house. One of Billy's neighbours was a friend of Brian's and she rang him with an odd story. Two men opened the back of the truck, pulled down a ramp and minutes later, rode down it on small motorbikes. Brian rang Billy straight away and told him about the two motorbikes headed his way.

'They'll get a hell of a shock if they come to my place!' he said.

Brian could only imagine the kind of firepower that Billy might keep at his disposal. After warning Billy, Brian rang the police at Port Melbourne who sent a van with lights and sirens. The motorbike riders hearing the sirens, high-tailed it back to their furniture van. Afterwards, Billy said he knew who the men were but refused to name them.

It was around closing time in mid-October 1973 when Painters and Dockers boss Pat Shannon was gunned down at the Druids Hotel in South Melbourne. Adhering to the crims' code of silence, no one saw a thing, but everyone knew what had happened. Billy Longley's name was bandied around.

Days after Pat Shannon met his end, a criminal called Gary Harding received a threat. The Painters and Dockers were after his son, and a threat like that never ended well. Word on the street was that Harding was ready to talk. A detective named Murray Burgess, asked Brian to find Gary Harding.

'What for?' asked Brian.

'Harding's a witness. Tell him he's got immunity if he comes in. We need him,' said Burgess.

Brian spoke to a mate of Harding's and repeated Burgess's guarantee that Harding wouldn't be charged. As a consequence, Harding agreed to come in.

It turned out that Harding had disposed of the gun used to shoot Pat Shannon. He was promised immunity from prosecution, but a verbal promise isn't worth the paper it's written on. Harding admitted to pointing out Pat Shannon to the shooter, a man called Kevin Taylor. He even led police to the murder weapon—a gun he'd dumped off a wharf. Harding gave police enough to charge Taylor and involve Longley who the gun belonged to. As soon as the interview was over, Harding asked if he could leave. He was told that he was going straight to the cells after being charged with murder.

When Brian found out, he was furious. The next time he bumped into Burgess he shirt-fronted his colleague. 'Gees, you're a nice bastard,' he said, getting right in Burgess's face.

Burgess held his ground. 'Harding is just a shit-box criminal. Get over it!'

'You should have told me the truth,' said Brian. 'I broke my word to him that he wouldn't be charged.'

Burgess shrugged. But Brian was incensed. His word was his bond—this is how he kept his reputation with the criminal world—pure gold when it came to getting information he needed to find the baddies. And Burgess had forced him to break it.

When Taylor was brought in and confronted with the still-wet gun, he caved. His story was that Billy Longley was an old prison mate from Ararat and that Billy had told him that someone was harassing his wife and needed taking care of. Billy drove him to the pub and told him to shoot the man Gary pointed out. He would be paid $6000 for his trouble.

On the day of Pat Shannon's funeral, as Brian left for work, Homicide detective, Murray Burgess and another detective turned into his street. Brian saw them and wondered where they were going. When he got to work, he rang Margaret to check.

'Oh, I'm glad you rang,' she said. 'Murray Burgess has been here and searched the house. He said there was a bomb here.'

'Was he nice to you?' Brian asked, imagining the things he would do to Burgess when he next saw him.

'Yes,' said Margaret, sounding fine.

Brian stepped out into the corridor at work to cool off.

One of his colleagues followed him out. 'Mate, I had nothing to do with the police searching your house for Longley.' That sealed it. What infuriated Brian most was that Burgess had not asked *him* to find Billy. If he had, Brian would have brought him in.

Gary Harding stood alongside Kevin Taylor in the dock, charged with murder. In his absence, they both pointed the finger squarely at Billy. The Texan made a good target. Witnesses swore they were terrified of Longley, and the defendants made out that they couldn't refuse him.

Gary Harding was horrified to receive a death sentence, swearing his displeasure at the judge and jury, and wrestling with the court security. While his sentence was commuted, Harding died soon after anyway; he was stabbed to death in his cell. Those who saw the body later described a look of stark terror frozen on the dead man's face.

The echoes of the shots that killed Pat Shannon had barely faded when Billy went into hiding. He began ringing Brian a couple of times a week in the small hours of the morning. He told Brian he was up in Monegeetta, resigned to the fact that all of his mates had deserted him. 'You've gotta have your guard up all the time,' he told Brian in one late-night conversation.'

Brian knew Billy was using him as a sounding board. Ironically, when the shit hit the fan, a policeman was the only one Billy could trust. It was the Painters and Dockers he feared above all. For Brian, Billy was someone who could paint a clear picture of what was going on in the Painters and Dockers. But, at the end of the day, if the Homicide Squad asked Brian to set Billy up, he would have.

But it wasn't simple. Billy had protected Brian's family after Collingburn's death; Billy had stepped outside the parameters for Brian, and Brian would return the favour—but drew the line at murder.

During one phone call, Billy told Brian that a Painter and Docker called Charlie Wootton and several others were going to meet down at the union rooms and they would all be tooled up—armed—so Brian had to be very careful of them; Billy reasoned that if they couldn't find *him*, they might have a whack at Brian.

Brian rang a policeman he knew at the South Melbourne CIB and, as a result, detectives pulled up two carloads of Painters and Dockers in South Melbourne. The men were taken to the South Melbourne CIB and their guns were confiscated. Oddly, the copper in charge on the day who questioned all the men, refused to charge them. It was hard not to wonder if some nefarious business had been done.

Brian knew from this who he could trust and who he couldn't in that police station—colleagues who had picked up the Painters and Dockers proved themselves. The boss, however, had failed the integrity test.

So Brian was faced with a choice: he could drop Billy like a hot potato because some of his colleagues didn't like it, or he could keep being Billy's sounding board and hopefully pick up handy bits of information like when people were trying to kill him. Brian would've returned the favour, too, and warn Billy if he found out someone was after him just like he'd do for anyone.

Over the intervening months, Brian would get the occasional call from Billy. First and foremost, Billy wanted to know if he was 'tropical', meaning was the heat still on him.

Billy and Pat

'There's no warrant for your arrest,' Brian told him. 'but if you're innocent, go in and talk to the boys in Homicide and clear it all up.'

One night, Billy said that he'd been reading a book about a priest in New York. Someone had confessed a murder to him. The police found out and interviewed the priest who wondered how he could get out of giving evidence since he couldn't break the seal of Confession. The priest was told by a colleague that God would find some way of getting him out of giving evidence. The night before the trial, the killer was murdered in prison. God worked in mysterious ways—brutal, but mysterious. Billy was fascinated by the story.

In other long late-night conversations, Brian and Billy discussed crime figures like Twist and Harrison. He couldn't understand why Billy idolised them.

'This is the side I'm on,' Billy said, 'and that is the side you're on.'

One night, Billy tried to explain why he had ended up a criminal. 'The cops treated me bad when I was a kid,' he told Brian.

Brian snorted. Every red-blooded boy in his neighbourhood got an occasional boot up the arse from the coppers. 'The cops treated everyone badly,' he replied.

With long negotiations that had reached as high as the chief commissioner, Billy finally agreed to be interviewed. He wanted to avoid the bashing he had been given when he turned himself in over the death of his wife back in 1961. Billy Longley arrived at Russell Street with a barrister and a solicitor. The media was pre-warned. Homicide detective, Jim Fry, interviewed him. Billy followed the advice of his lawyers and refused to answer any questions—not even when asked if he wanted a cup of coffee.

Gary Harding was two months in his grave by the time Billy's trial began. Evidence was confused. Taylor changed his story as often as he changed his undies. At one point he even said that Gary Harding had received $6000 from a man called Putty Nose to kill Pat Shannon. It made a great story since Putty Nose Nicholls took over the Painters and Dockers just weeks after Pat Shannon's murder. And since Gary was dead, he couldn't refute it.

When Billy's trial finally commenced, Brian was stationed out at Heidelberg. He got a phone call one Friday afternoon at 4.30 p.m. from Detective Jim Fry who said that he needed Brian in court to back him up. While Brian knew Jimmy Fry, he had never worked a case with him.

'What are you talking about?' Brian asked.

'Mate, I'm giving evidence against Billy Longley and they asked me where I got certain information from. The only one I could think of was you. I told them it was you.'

'Get stuffed,' Brian said, imagining it was a set-up. 'I'm not going to court for you!'

Brian told his boss, Plattfuss what Fry had asked him to do.

'You're not going to court on Monday,' declared Plattfuss. 'And if anyone says anything, refer them to me.'

With the Puss on his side, Brian spent the weekend feeling smug. Fry's bosses could take on Plattfuss and Brian would sail under the radar.

It didn't work out that way, though. Just before midnight on the Sunday night, Plattfuss rang Brian and said he had to go to court the next morning, no fucken questions.

Someone further up the tree had made the decision.

On Monday 17 November 1975, Brian drove out to the Heidelberg police station to see the Puss. 'What's going on?' he asked, careful not to antagonise his volatile boss.

But Plattfuss wasn't elaborating. 'Get your arse into that car and get yourself into the Supreme Court.' He ordered two of the young detectives to drive Brian straight in.

The lack of information from the Puss spoke volumes. He looked visibly embarrassed, and for this big fearsome bloke, that was a rarity. Brian deduced that wherever the orders had come from—he suspected a Sunday night meeting—they had put the wind up the Puss. If Brian pushed things, it would embarrass his boss in front of the troops. A small consolation was that the Puss's orders clearly went against his grain.

Brian suggested the two young detectives accompany him into the Supreme Court police witnesses' room. 'There's going to be a shit-fight,' he assured them.

The first thing Brian saw when he walked into the witness room, was Jimmy Fry, sitting at the ornate cedar table covered in deep green leather with gold embossed curlicues around the edges. He was lounging back, smoking a cigarette in a poncy cigarette holder.

'Brian Francis Murphy,' he began in his pompous voice, 'Today is the day you decide which side you're on: law and order or the side of the crims.'

It took about half a second for Brian's blood to boil. He dived across the table, grabbing for Fry's throat, knocking his pompous cigarette out of his pompous hand.

Homicide Squad detectives grabbed at Brian, but got his coat instead. They dragged the coat down so that Brian's arms were trapped, and pulled him off his quarry.

Fry screamed: 'Get 'im off me!' over and over again.

At that moment, the prosecutor and the defence lawyers arrived at the door to speak to the detectives. When they saw the fracas, they thought better of interrupting.

At that moment, the tipstaff's voice echoed off the bluestone floors that dipped in the middle, worn away by a hundred years of crooks and witnesses. 'Brian Francis Murphy!'

The Homicide Squad detectives let go of Brian who struggled to untangle his arms in the twisted jacket, turning it inside out in the process of removing it. He headed straight to the courtroom and was still trying to pull his jacket back to rights when he entered.

'Are you Brian Francis Murphy?' The judge's voice dripped with distain.

Brian was in no mood. 'Yes, Your Honour.' His voice was

grumpy.

'When you finish dressing, Mr Murphy,' he said, 'you can go straight into the witness box.'

Brian didn't answer. He was still trying to compose himself—it was a hard shift mentally from sliding across a table to attack Jim Fry, to stepping up into the witness box. After solemnly taking the oath, he readied himself to begin, still unsure of why he was there.

'Did you know that Billy Longley was wanted?' asked the prosecutor.

'Yes,' Brian said.

'Did Longley know that he was wanted over this murder?'

'Yes, but only by the Painters and Dockers,' Brian answered.

'So it was common knowledge that Longley was wanted by the Painters and Dockers who were seeking retribution for the killing of Pat Shannon?'

'Yes.'

'Did you ever tell him he was wanted by the police?'

'No.'

The Crown Prosecutor sat down and the Defence had no questions for Brian.

Brian looked at Billy who gave a little shrug as if to say: *you couldn't help it, Chief*. Brian suspected both barristers trod lightly because there could be trouble over this. He didn't speak to Fry again for years and never found out what he said in court.

Billy knew that he wasn't wanted by police because Galbally was making discrete enquiries with the Homicide Squad. As soon as Billy was wanted, the lawyer arranged to take his client in.

Billy Longley was found guilty of conspiracy to murder Pat Shannon and began a thirteen-year stretch in prison. On a couple of occasions, Billy sent messages to Brian to warn him about crimes that were about to happen. Brian visited Billy twice in jail at the prisoner's behest because Billy wanted to pass on information.

30

BRIAN KANE

In the mid-1970s, Brian bumped into the notorious crime figure, Brian Kane, in a coffee shop in Carlton. They had both ordered coffee and when the barista called coffee for Brian, they both stepped forward. To avoid a gunfight over a coffee, the wily proprietor came around the counter with a second coffee.

'Sit, sit,' he implored.

The cop and the crim sat opposite each other. Brian Kane opened with, 'I was going to kill you, Murphy.'

'What's stopping you?' Brian asked. It was late and the place was nearly empty. Under the table, he readied his gun, pointing it at Kane's important bits.

There was a bit of a Mexican stand-off so Brian asked the café owner to slide away the small table separating them.

'You bastard,' Kane roared when he saw the gun. 'Put that away!'

Brian put it away; it was enough to prove to Kane he was willing to shoot him. And for some strange reason, Kane seemed chuffed that Brian had got one over him. The man laughed and raised his coffee in a toast. 'You're all right for a copper.' He stood up then, leaned over and grabbed Brian's head and kissed his forehead. 'That's the way coppers should be. You gotta be fucken prepared. These coppers come in here and drink with their guns holstered. They couldn't knock a kid off a pisspot.'

The two Brians chatted for hours and matched each other coffee for coffee like seasoned drinkers at a pub.

'I'm glad I didn't shoot you,' Kane said after a while. 'I was offered money years ago to shoot you. But I saw you walking down the beach with your family and I thought, *he's never done anything to me*. Now, I'm glad I didn't shoot you.'

'Me too,' Brian said, raising his coffee cup. 'Very civilised of you.'

Over fourteen espressos, the cop and the crim talked the night away. Kane told Brian about his childhood and said that whenever he asked his father for school books, he was told to go out and fucken steal them.

'If I had an education, I'd have been a copper,' Kane said wistfully. 'But my old man wouldn't even buy my fucken school books.'

A lot of crims tell a similar story, but Brian felt there was a truth to what he was saying. The fact that he'd been offered money to shoot Brian and didn't, said something about the man he was. The kind of family life people like Kane had been brought up in, completely buggered their future.

'I couldn't believe it,' said another detective afterwards. 'You pulled a gun out on him in front of everyone. Would you have shot him?'

'Too right,' Brian said. 'If *he* had a gun, I would have shot him right in the guts. But after our chat, maybe I would've hesitated.'

Brian's list of unlikely allies grew longer each year. One of the most unlikely ones came in the form of Norm Gallagher in the heyday of the Builders Labourers Federation. They met at a BLF rally when Norm Gallagher greeted Brian with: 'Get fucked ya fucken dog!'

'Norm,' Brian said. 'No need for that. We're treating you nice.'

But Gallagher was not to be appeased. 'Fucken coppers! You never listen to me. I give coppers names when people knock off tools from building sites. What do the coppers ever do? Nuthin!'

'Norm,' Brian said, looking him straight in the eye, 'if you ever give me a name, I will look into it. I promise.'

Gallagher's eyes narrowed and something shifted in his thinking. He asked if Brian ever visited a certain inner city hardware shop. Brian nodded; he was a keen handyman and went there often.

Gallagher issued a challenge. 'Next time you're in there, I'll give you a name and we'll see what you fucken do about it.'

From that day on, every time Brian visited the hardware shop and Norm Gallagher was there, they played out the same scene. Norm would be up the front, leaning on the counter. He'd see Brian, lift his head up and sniff disdainfully. 'I smell a bloody rat,' he'd drawl.

Then it was Brian's turn. He'd look down at his shoe, sniff, and reply: 'Oh look, I've got a bit of Norm Gallagher on my shoe.'

Norm would slap his hand on the counter and declare that he was off to get some fresh air, then he'd storm out.

On the counter would be a slip of paper with a name and address on it. When Brian followed it up, it would always be the name of someone who was pinching tools worth tens of thousands of dollars from job sites.

Later, Norm Gallagher would be accused and convicted of all sorts of things, but the brief interludes Brian shared with him suggested that at heart, Norm wanted to do the right thing by his men. If a young bloke had his tools stolen from a building site, he would have no option than to blow his wages to replace them. Norm wanted to stop that and lowered himself to meet with a copper to do it.

And Brian knew more than most that a man's public persona can be very different from what's in his heart.

31

THE VALOUR AWARD

It was a summer's evening in the week before Christmas in 1975 when Heidelberg police received a call from residents in a quiet suburban court in Greensborough. Neighbours heard the sound of gunshots coming from a house where Corporal James Gardiner lived with his wife and two children. One of the calls was from Mrs Gardiner herself. She was babysitting for a neighbour and she, too, had heard the shots. Her husband, she told police, was a Vietnam veteran and had been agitated earlier in the day. He had his rifle out, claiming there was an intruder near their house.

When Brian got to work that night, he got a full briefing about the siege. He thought of the hollow-eyed men he'd seen as a boy, returning with shell shock from the Second World War. He'd dealt with these men all his career—men 'going troppo' and doing strange things. Brian wondered if Corporal James Gardiner had gone troppo too.

By the time Brian arrived at the scene at 9.30 p.m., there were a dozen police cars in the small suburban court and twenty coppers dotted around the place. They were crouched, taking cover, as intermittent shots rang out from the Gardiner house. Bullets shattered windows and roof tiles of neighbouring homes. They smashed with deadly accuracy into the headlights of police cars.

As the senior officer at the scene, Brian immediately took charge. The lights made them all easy targets. He sent a colleague to tell all the neighbours to turn off their lights and keep away from windows. The newly-darkened street gave police a better view into

The Valour Award

the house. It was a cream-brick home with stairs leading up to a small porch and a front door—a common spec house springing up in suburbs around the outer edges of Melbourne in the 1960s and 70s. Brian could see Gardiner sitting on the ledge of his front window; given the raised property, he was about ten feet off the ground. He wore a T-shirt and some old trousers and was barefoot. His jaw was clenched which made it hard to tell if he was drunk or agitated—or both.

Brian had dealt with a lot of aggressive individuals in his career, and his first priority was always to quieten things down. He discussed this with one of his colleagues, Griff Morris.

'I'm going in,' said Brian. 'If I can get him talking, it might help.'

Morris shrugged. Nothing else had worked and there seemed to be no end in sight.

Moving towards the front gate, hands in the air, Brian called to Gardiner. 'Hey, mate!'

As soon as Gardiner heard Brian's voice, he pointed the gun at him.

It wasn't the first time Brian had a gun pointed at him, and probably wouldn't be the last. He walked slowly forward. 'My name is Brian Murphy. I'm a detective and I just want to come up and talk to you.'

Gardiner was nervous and jumpy. He called back: 'If you've got a gun or handcuffs, I'm going to kill you.'

'I hope you don't,' Brian said. 'I'm taking my kids fishing tomorrow and they'll be disappointed.' His heart was pumping like a two-stroke engine. He handed his gun and handcuffs to Griff Morris.

'Want me to come with you?' Morris asked in a low voice.

Brian shook his head. 'Two coppers might spook him.'

'I'm coming!' Brian called. 'I've got no gun and no handcuffs.'

'Well, you fucken make sure you haven't,' called Gardiner.

'Hey,' Brian said, arms raised, coming closer, 'I just want to talk to you.'

Gardiner sat on the window ledge; Brian moved slowly up the front steps and stopped on the porch, about ten feet from him. The agitated man rolled a cigarette, resting the gun across his knees.

'I forgot my smokes,' Brian said. 'Can I have one?'

'You mean bastard. You probably wouldn't even know how to roll a smoke.'

'Give me the fixings for one,' Brian said, keeping his voice even. Every minute the man wasn't talking about shooting him or firing the gun on the coppers in the street, was a good one.

'Don't you lean over here!' Gardiner said, eyes narrowing. 'I'll throw you the packet.' He tossed the packet of tobacco.

Brian rolled a cigarette.

'I didn't think you could do it,' Gardiner said begrudgingly.

'I've been around a long time.'

They both smoked in silence for a moment.

'Why don't we talk inside, not in front of all these blokes.' Brian nodded towards the police circus surrounding the house.

'All right,' Gardiner said finally. 'I'll come to the front door, but I'll search you.'

Brian took off his work jacket and hung it on the porch post. No sense making the man with the gun wonder what was in his pockets. He stood at the front door which opened almost immediately. Gardiner pointed the rifle at him.

'Get your hands in the air. I'm going to search you. Open your mouth.'

In disbelief, Brian stood like a stunned mullet while Gardiner put the end of the gun in his mouth and held it with one hand while he patted Brian down with the other. It felt as big as a cannon. Residue on the recently-fired muzzle reminded Brian of when he was young and used to burn matches, blow them out, and then stick them on his tongue.

Standing there, the gun jammed in his mouth, all he could do was pray.

The Valour Award

He imagined that all the millions of prayers he'd said in his life could join together and protect him like a shield. It was all in God's hands now.

In the light of the doorway Brian knew his colleagues would be able to see what was happening. He could only imagine what was going through their minds. There was no clear shot of Gardiner so they were as stuck as Brian was. The gun-in-the-mouth pat-down lasted about twenty seconds but it seemed like forever. Once Gardiner was finished, he took the gun barrel from Brian's mouth.

'Come inside and no fucken smart moves.' Gardiner led the way inside. Brian followed him into a kitchen in the middle of the house where there was no view of the street or the backyard. Gardiner pointed to a chair. Brian sat while Gardiner leaned into an alcove.

Brian wondered where to start. 'You're a Vietnam vet?' He realised it was the wrong thing to say, when Gardiner flew into a rage.

'You fucken wouldn't know what happened in Vietnam?' Gardiner yelled, agitated and sweating.

'I'm glad of that,' said Brian quickly. Talking to this man was like walking through a minefield.

'You fucken wouldn't know!' Gardiner shouted.

'Do you want a cup of tea?' Brian said, making a mental note not to talk about the war.

Gardiner raised the rifle. 'Don't you fucken make yourself a cup of tea!'

'No.' Brian's voice was firm. 'I asked if *you* wanted a cup of tea.'

Gardiner glared at Brian. 'All right,' he said finally, 'make two cups of tea.'

While Brian didn't drink tea as a rule and regarded himself as a coffee man, he felt it would be the wrong time to point this out. He made two cups of tea.

'There's some chocolate ripple cake in the fridge,' Gardiner said. 'My wife made it. Have some.'

Like every Australian at the time, Brian was a fan of chocolate ripple cake, but the last thing he wanted to do was to eat anything. Nevertheless, he took a slice; Adrenaline pumped through his blood. He might not have been to Vietnam, but sitting in this kitchen drinking tea and eating chocolate ripple cake was like being on the front line. The cake sat like a ball of dough in his mouth until he forced himself to swallow.

'That's great cake,' Brian said. 'Your wife's a good cook.'

With that, Gardiner burst into tears. He wailed that he didn't deserve her and, like a floodgate opening, the distraught veteran spilled a lifetime of woes. Recently, he said, he had tried to kill himself and drove off into the hills at the back of Healesville to do the job. On the way, he had a flat tyre and stopped by the side of the road. Just as he decided to shoot himself then and there, two men had pulled over and offered to fix his tyre. He stood by and watched them. Then they offered him a beer and by the time they waved him goodbye, the impulse to die had deserted him. It was only a temporary reprieve though. Tonight, he had snapped again.

Brian felt so bad for the poor bloke. He listened and tried to forget that he was a cop and Gardiner was a gun-wielding vet and soon, in the small suburban kitchen, they became just two blokes—one upset and the other one trying to make him feel a bit better.

After a long while, Gardiner put the gun down, resting it safely on the floor. Brian did not reach for it. They weren't finished yet. Gardiner was wretched, nose running, dribbling, wailing. Brian didn't want to see him dragged away in that state.

'What's going to happen to me, mate?' he asked finally.

'We're going to take you away. There are too many bad vibes for you here.'

Gardiner looked haunted and scared and in need of reassurance.

'You're not going to be hurt by me or by anyone else.' By this time, Brian had tears in his eyes. He felt for him so much. Gardiner looked up and saw Brian's reaction and seemed to slump. Brian moved over to him and put his arm around him. 'Don't worry

The Valour Award

mate,' he said in a soft voice. 'You haven't hurt anybody. We'll sort it out.'

Brian picked up the gun, removed the magazine, and took the bullet from the breach. Carrying the gun in one hand, he led Gardiner to the front door with the other. As soon as they appeared, an inspector hurried up the stairs and took the gun.

'That's the longest forty minutes of my life,' Brian told Griff Morris when he was safely back out in the street.

'Mate, you were in there for over two hours,' Griff replied.

Brian didn't want to leave Gardiner now that they had a rapport, and travelled with him to hospital. Brian grew agitated when the doctor in charge refused to treat Gardiner because he had mental problems.

'If he had a broken arm, would you treat him?'

'Yes,' said the doctor.

'But if he has a broken mind, you can't.'

The doctor shrugged. In the end, he gave Gardiner a small sedative which calmed both he and Brian down. When Gardiner was finally asleep, Brian left him to his police guard; he wanted to find out what had sparked the siege.

Overnight, Brian made some enquiries. It turned out that Gardiner had taken some money from the RSL where he worked because he wanted to buy his kids presents for Christmas. Brian called his brother who was a barrister and explained the situation to him. His brother knew a bank manager and phoned him in the middle of the night. By morning, they had arranged a loan of $2,000 to tide the family over. Brian and his brother and his brother's mate guaranteed the loan. If Gardiner didn't make good, they would split it three ways.

By morning, Brian was back at the hospital. Sitting by Gardiner's bedside, he told him that he knew about the stolen money from the RSL, but that he had arranged a loan to pay it back.

'But they'll know I'm a thief.' Gardiner's protests were feeble.

'We'll tell them you can return it straight away,' Brian said.

Gardiner hung his head in shame.

Even though the police had to charge Gardiner with offences regarding firing shots in his neighbourhood, they made sure he was bailed immediately. Brian took him to the repatriation hospital who agreed to treat him on a daily basis.

By the time Brian got home, he was exhausted and drained. He told Margaret what had happened, and the kids heard the story too. Gardiner's behaviour that night was a cry for help and Brian felt honoured to be there for him.

Margaret was as moved by Gardiner's story as her husband was. The following week, they both took presents and a Christmas cake to the family. The feeling of the house was so different now with Gardiner and his lovely wife and children, that Brian didn't give a thought to the peril of the week before in the same house. He looked over at Gardiner then to his own wonderful Margaret, and thought: *how lucky are we*.

Brian spoke up for Gardiner in court. The judge commented at the end of the trial that because the police had spoken up for Gardiner, there was some hope for him. The judge let him off with a bond. It was a good result.

When Brian arrived back at Russell Street, his boss called him into his office and told him that he would get a Valour Award out of the incident. Before Brian knew it, he was being photographed for the occasion. There he was grinning, wearing a patterned shirt and a patterned tie, with more hair then than he would ever have again. The photo was released to the press. Soon after, Brian found himself at a ceremony out at the Police Academy.

Every family member he ever had was seated in the academy parade ground, looking proud. Brian stepped up to receive the badge from Deputy Commissioner Salisbury.

'Howya going, Murph?' he said.

'Good,' Brian said, grinning.

Salisbury leaned forward to pin the badge on Brian's lapel. 'Murph,' he said, 'one minute we're trying to convict you for

The Valour Award

murder and the next, we're giving you a Valour Award.'

Brian laughed. 'That's how it goes.'

Three years later, Brian got a phone call from a bank manager who was a friend of James Gardiner's father, informing him with a sad voice, that Gardiner had killed himself the day before. The news shocked and saddened Brian deeply, but in the wash-up, he figured that Gardiner had an extra three years with his wife and his kids that he might not have had otherwise. He'd seen that sometimes distress and trauma becomes so bad, people can't see the forest for the trees. The hopeless sensation of impending doom never leaves them and death seems like the only release.

Brian thinks of Gardiner quite often.

32

THE SKULL

Brian got the call minutes after it started. An aggressive young man launched an attack on a man and a woman just 100 metres from the Heidelberg police station. Brian and a fellow detective flew out the door and ran towards the fray. The victims were huddled against each other, trying to ward off the blows, and anyone brave enough to try and help was bashed for their trouble.

The arrival of a couple of detectives didn't make any difference to the assailant; he continued yelling and screaming and carrying on a treat. Brian's police colleague biffed him on the chin which sent him reeling backwards. Brian jumped on him and wrestled him into handcuffs, trying not to trip over his own brown flared trousers, in the process. The fashion of 1976 was not necessarily conducive to arresting struggling mad blokes.

As soon as everyone was upright, it was time for a chat around the corner. They dragged the fellow away from his victims.

Brian got up close and personal, and used his baby blues to good effect with a cop stare. 'Mate, you've already had one clout in the jaw. If you keep playing up, you're going to end up with a shirtful of broken ribs and a broken nose. It's up to you how you want this to go. Make up your mind.' The tone of his voice left the man in no doubt that his choices were hospital or the police station.

'I know I'm going to get a biffing,' sniffed the attacker, shrugging.

Brian fixed him with a cold stare. 'You've never had a biffing from me.' He let that thought hang in the air.

The Skull

The man's eyes widened. He got the message.

They radioed the divvy van to come and collect him. While the van crew carted the scruffy lout to the lockup, Brian and his partner took the shaken victims and witnesses to the police station to take their statements.

When it came time for the offender to be put through the interview register, he was asked by a senior officer if he had any complaints about his treatment.

'Yeah, I got a complaint,' he said. 'I was belted by a cop with a head like a skull.'

Brian had to admit that by this stage, he was pretty bald, but luckily, there was another copper called Ian Dunn who was balder than him.

'Must be Ian Dunn he's talking about,' shrugged Brian when the boss asked him about the alleged assault. Brian pointed to Dunny over at his desk.

Dunn who had been in the police station all afternoon, denied it. 'Sounds more like you, Murphy,' he said, without missing a beat. He looked at Brian critically: 'You look more like a skull than me,' he said. And then he winked.

The boss asked the two of them to take part in a line-up which Brian insisted they populate with seven other bald-headed blokes. Luckily, it was a court day at the Magistrates' Court next door and his colleagues quickly gathered a bevy of baldies. Brian stood innocently alongside Ian Dunn and the rest of his follicly-challenged compadres. The man who'd bashed innocent passers-by walked up and down the line, squinting at each bald guy. In the end, he couldn't pick anyone out.

As they walked away from the line-up, Ian Dunn called Brian 'Skull', and the name stuck.

Brian's boss gave him a talking to later that day and told him if he was going to get into trouble, he needed to start wearing a hat.

'You stand out like a nipple on a lemon,' he grumbled.

So that was where the nickname came from. And Brian's

propensity for wearing hats. The irony, of course, was that he hadn't laid a hand on the man—it was his partner who had biffed him—and this was supported in the statements of the victims.

In the end, the nickname worked for Brian; the name Skull made him more feared than the name Brian. 'Think about it,' he said, 'if you were a crook and you heard Skull Murphy had come around looking for you, you'd be more afraid than if you heard that Brian had paid a visit.'

33

THE GREAT BOOKIE ROBBERY

Paul Egan—aka The Tooth Fairy—was a dental technician who loved cutting safes. By 1976, he had been Brian's informer for five or six years. Informing wasn't his first inclination and he'd needed a bit of convincing. Egan had been arrested with Graham 'The Munster' Kinniburgh and Charlie Wootten in a hardware store at midnight cutting a safe in the early 1970s.

When the three were being questioned, Brian poked his head in each interview room and took a look at the surly arrestees, to gauge their mettle. None of them looked willing to talk, but there was something about Paul Egan ...

'Do you know who I am?' Brian asked him.

Egan nodded. 'Yeah, I know who you are,' he said, shoulders slumping.

As soon as Brian saw this, he knew Egan was the one who would talk. And he was right ... to a point. Egan begrudgingly told Brian where the three had parked their car, loaded with extra tanks of oxyacetylene, then he clammed up. Of course things were different in those days. Nowadays, there would be negotiations—cops would offer him something, then he'd give a bit of information. Back then, all Brian offered him was water.

Quite a lot of it in fact. Not to drink, to stand in.

Brian took Egan on a nice country drive to Gippsland and then gave him a couple of hours to literally cool his heels in Picnic Point Creek until the feeling in his feet was as far away as Melbourne. To Egan's credit, it took a while, but then the cold got the better of him and he started singing like a numb-footed canary. He told the detective about Joseph Patrick Monash—aka Joey Turner—who had absconded on bail after the MSS robbery in South Melbourne. He knew a couple of other safe-breakers.

It turned out that Egan was quite a nice bloke. Brian reckoned that for him, safe-breaking was more about the thrill of pitting himself against the coppers. The money that flowed thick and fast from his crimes was an additional bonus. But once the coppers caught up with him and he faced jail time, things didn't seem as exciting.

Paul Egan frequented the Hollyford Hotel in Carlton and knew the criminals who drank there—among them, Ray Chuck Bennett, Greedy Smith, and Normie Lee. One day, Egan got a whisper that there was a big job planned over the long Easter weekend.

'It's going to be humongous!' he told Brian. The problem was that he didn't know where the robbery was, but he knew who was going to do it. Ray Chuck Bennett and Greedy Smith.

While a lot of crooks exaggerate, Egan was usually pretty much on the money. At that time, Brian was a detective sergeant at the Heidelberg CIB and had nothing to do with armed robberies unless they were minor and on his turf. So after he passed on the information to the detective district inspector of the Armed Robbery Squad, he pretty much forgot about it—until Easter loomed closer. On the Thursday before the long Easter weekend, Brian rang the DDI to check whether he'd done anything with the information.

The inspector cursed. He'd forgotten. Slipped his mind.

At Brian's reminder, the DDI passed it on to a detective in the Armed Robbery Squad, but everything closed down over Easter, so there wasn't much they could do. While Brian was a little annoyed, none of the police had any inkling of the cost of ignoring Egan's information.

At midday on Wednesday 21 April, in the heart of Melbourne, an armoured van made a delivery to the Victoria Club in Queen Street. It was well known that the Victoria Club was the place

The great bookie robbery

where bookmakers settled up on the first day after a weekend's racing. The cash that went through the club was looked after by a couple of detectives who would moonlight on settling day and make sure all was well. With over a hundred bookies present after the long Easter weekend of races, there was a huge amount of money for the settling.

Unusually, the two detectives were absent.

Not long after the cash arrived, a group of six heavily-armed men burst into the second floor settling room. One wielded a sawn-off double-barrelled shotgun, and another robber held an Owen submachine gun.

'This is a hold up! Get down on the floor,' one of them yelled.

Startled men scrambled to lie down on the floor.

'That means you, Ambrose,' one of the masked men said to prize fighter, Ambrose Palmer. It would later be claimed that Palmer recognised the voice.

Calico bags filled with untraceable bills were loaded up, and eleven minutes later, the robbers were gone.

Brian was in bed in the afternoon that day getting a bit of shuteye before working a nightshift. It was around 3 p.m. when the phone rang.

On the other end of the line was a very excited Paul Egan. 'Mate, they got thirteen fucken million!'

'You're bullshitting me,' Brian said, suddenly awake.

Egan refused to say more.

Before long, the phone rang again. 'Commander Bennett, here,' said a voice.

Brian thought it was his mate, Paul Higgins, playing a joke. 'Don't bullshit me,' he said, and hung up.

Margaret picked up the phone when it rang again. She listened for a couple of seconds, then handed it over to her husband. 'Mr Bennett wants to talk to you and you're not to hang up.'

'Don't you ever fucken hang up on me again!' Fat Harry Bennett boomed into the phone. He demanded Brian's presence at work. 'You are now a member of the Consorting Squad and you're in charge of the bookie robbery.'

This was a convenient move because Brian already knew two of the key players on account of Egan. At the Consorters, Brian was allocated Peter Halloran and Alan Johnson to work with him. Their first job was to visit the Victoria Club and talk to the bookies. The robbers wore masks so none were immediately identified. Logic said that while Greedy Smith might have been a part of the planning, he wasn't present on the day; because of his size, he'd stand out like a sore toe. So if Chuck Bennett was one of the masked men, that left five others for police to name.

From the time Brian and his colleagues were asked to investigate the bookie robbery, there was a stench about it. Brian met with Commander Bennett, Frank Green and the District Inspector who he'd first reported Egan's suspicions to. The commander insisted on an air of secrecy to the investigation, not least because the last thing he wanted was the public to know that the two coppers hadn't turned up on the day. Bennett went even further and told Brian not to question the two detectives. 'Keep away from them,' he warned. Brian assumed that he must have had operatives from the Bureau of Criminal Intelligence—the BCI—taking a closer look at them. He was wrong.

'We need to talk to Paul Egan,' Brian told his superior.

'No,' said Bennett. 'We'll put them all under surveillance.'

Brian couldn't understand it. His natural inclination was to ignore the order, but this job was too big to let his ego get in the way.

Brian trusted Peter Halloran and Alan Johnson as investigators, and the three made a good team. Even though they knew two of the people involved in the robbery, quickly dubbed The Great Bookie Robbery, they weren't allowed to go anywhere near them. Bennett wanted the investigation run differently. Instead of Brian's crew going straight to people they suspected of involvement and dragging them in for some meaningful dialogue, they were told to keep away from all the suspects. Instead, Bennett instructed, Frank Green, who was in charge of the BCI, to use the Observation Squad to follow the suspects and organise the bugging of phones and houses. All this information would be fed to Frank Green who would then instruct Brian's crew when to move.

What this did was effectively distance the detectives from the investigation. A couple of times Brian would take Green aside and say, 'Mate! What's going on?'

'This is how Fat Harry wants it run,' Green told him. And that would be the end of that.

The best Halloran, Johnson and Brian could do was to get information where they could find it. Names were bandied about and everyone had a theory. Ian Carroll, who Brian knew well from the Collingburn incident, and Normie Lee, erstwhile dim sim maker and armed robber, and of course, Ray Chuck Bennett were all said to be part of the gang.

But without being able to interview or even approach any of the suspects, the three detectives made little progress and the commander called them to his office.

'You're not working fast enough,' he said.

'We're not allowed to!' Brian exploded. 'For Christ's sake! We're not allowed to go near Chuck or Normie Lee. How can we lock 'em up?'

'Don't worry about that,' declared the commander. 'I'm replacing you with a new crew. They'll make arrests soon.'

'Don't charge anyone until you've got more than what I think you've got,' Brian warned. 'If you charge one and he gets off, you won't be able to commit anyone else on the same evidence.'

Harry Bennett waved away Brian's protest.

It turned out, that's exactly what they did with Normie Lee.

Police are always on the lookout for criminals who suddenly live the high life and start throwing cash around. Ray Bennett was canny enough to stop his bookie robbery colleagues from doing it, and rumours later spread that the robbers had rented an office adjacent to the Victoria Club and the money stayed put for months. Until Normie Lee started splashing it around. He suddenly had $270,000 in cash; he delivered $50,000 to his accountant's office—a gambling win, he explained—then paid cash for work on his house and his dim sim factory.

Brian suspected a certain member of the police force was involved. Someone had sent the two Victoria Club detectives elsewhere on the day of the robbery, and someone was hobbling the investigation. He had a fair suspicion who it was and passed his name onto Frank Green.

Brian also wondered if he had been brought on board so the hierarchy could watch him fail. As new detectives took over the case and failed to get a conviction on Normie Lee, Brian stayed on at the Consorting Squad.

Brian's suspicions that there was police involvement in the Great Bookie Robbery gained momentum soon after he was taken off the case. A certain detective called Brian's mate, Paul Higgins, to find out which crews were working the afternoon shift at the Consorters because they might be needed to assist another squad. Higgins told the detective that both his crew and Brian's crew were working the afternoon shift. It turned out that they weren't needed, which was just as well because that shift, the Consorting Squad was one of the busiest Brian had ever experienced. The squad offices were suddenly filled with people, and there was even a crying baby somewhere in the office.

While Brian and his colleagues were trying to sort things out, another crew from the Consorting Squad—who weren't rostered on—was asked to pull over Greedy Smith's car. Cops privy to the listening devices planted on Greedy Smith had found out that he had $150,000 in the boot of his car. Brian would later find out from Greedy himself that the police who pulled him over that night had taken nearly all of it, leaving him with $5,000 to buy himself a ticket back to his bar in the Philippines. Rumour had it that two Consorters shared the money with the detective who had phoned

The great bookie robbery

Higgins.

When Brian spoke to Greedy Smith in a candid moment later, Smith said there was no hope of solving the Great Bookie Robbery.

'What do you mean?' Brian asked.

He smiled, a little smugly. 'Look around you,' he said.

It was as Brian suspected.

If the haul was 13 million dollars as suggested by Paul Egan, it did none of the robbers any good. Brian Kane and his brother, Les, tried to muscle in on the cash. Ray Chuck Bennett retaliated by killing Les in his own home while his family cowered in another room. When Bennett was arrested for the killing along with Vinnie Mikklesen and Laurie Prendergast, they were found not guilty—probably because Les Kane's body was never found. Bennett did not walk free, though; he faced other charges over a payroll job.

On Monday 12 November 1978, Ray Chuck Bennet was escorted into court by Consorting Squad detectives Phil Glare and Paul Strang. Another detective from the Armed Robbers was also allocated his protection. Strang went upstairs to check the courtroom. Up two flights of stairs, sat a bearded man in a suit who'd been waiting patiently outside the courtroom. He looked like a lawyer. The man stood up, pulled a snub-nose revolver from his jacket and shot Bennett three times—twice in the heart, once in the hand. In the ensuing chaos, the killer calmly walked down the stairs and out the back exit. He escaped through a gap in the fence into the RMIT car park behind the court.

Because of Brian's long-standing mutual loathing of Ray Chuck Bennett, he was one of the many suspects looked at closely after the brazen court shooting. He fit the general description. But stronger in the suspect stakes was another Brian. Brian Kane fled Melbourne straight after the murder and resurfaced three years later, only to be gunned down at the Quarry Hotel in Brunswick.

34

MURPHY'S MARAUDERS

In the late 1970s, Superintendent Stanfield called Brian to his office. He explained how Fat Harry Bennett was thinking of starting up a Metropolitan Regional Crime Squad and wanted Brian to lead the new squad, beginning with investigating a spate of recent fires in massage parlours.

Brian was immediately suspicious. Either Fat Harry had finally recognised his ability as a detective at the same time some pigs had flown backwards past his office window, or the more likely option: he wanted Brian to stuff up so he could get rid of him once and for all. Either way, if he accepted the post, Brian knew he would have to be very careful.

Taking charge of the new squad, Brian had a prevailing philosophy—he wanted to be the kind of boss who people would work best under—someone like Mick Miller who was a strategist and clear thinker. Or Keith Plattfuss who was brave and fearless. Honesty and integrity were what both leaders had in common. Brian tried to take their best qualities and amalgamate them into his own style. From Mick Miller, he tried to take his skill of methodical planning and letting his men know the reasons for what he wanted and why it was the right way. From the Puss, he took his heart—if someone committed a crime, it was a personal affront to him; he could *feel* it. The Puss felt that the public of Victoria didn't deserve to have their houses broken into, and it was the job of the police to stop it.

Brian's squad quickly became a dumping ground for misfit

coppers; he suspected that half a dozen senior sergeants around Melbourne who were asked to volunteer an officer rubbed their hands in glee, looked down their long noses at their troops, and chose their biggest moll chasers, drunks, thieves, and malcontents. Transfers were signed with a flourish.

When the six men stood face to face with the notorious Skull Murphy, Brian would open with: 'I'll forget what I've heard about you if you forget what you've heard about me. Understood?' It was his way of giving them a fresh start and a free rein. To everybody's surprise, the men rose to the occasion. It's human nature to be a better person when there's a boss and a team supporting you. They were all underdogs with something to prove.

Brian encouraged them to come to him with ideas, and he would support them.

One of the detectives had an informer who drank at a pub with a lot of men who drove delivery vans for a living. According to the informer, some of the van drivers had a scheme: they would buy vans at auction and park them in Flinders Lane where the rag trade operated. During the day, trucks would pull up with thousands of dresses to be delivered. As the truck drivers unloaded racks of dresses, instead of padlocking the delivery trucks, many simply hooked the padlocks over the lock while they took the dresses inside. As soon as they were gone, the van drivers would jump into the back of the trucks and do some unloading of their own. The legitimate drivers would return to find their stock gone.

The informer offered the name of the pub so police could set up surveillance to get the registration numbers of the vans. They could then follow the drivers home to where they lived. The squad locked up about six of them in the first couple of months of doing this. When they seized a couple of vans used in the theft, they used them to follow people covertly.

The squad that became known as 'Murphy's Marauders' ended up with some really good officers – men who learnt the ropes with Brian and copied his dash and daring. They learnt to stretch rules to the breaking point, but most of all, learnt that some problems required unorthodox solutions. Brian always had their backs. And before long, they always had his.

At the beginning of each new job, Brian delivered the same speech: 'I'll tell you what I am going to do and if you have a problem, tell me immediately. Some of the things may not be kosher according to the law, but if you're against it and you tell me, I'll admire you forever. But if you say you're for it and you give evidence against me in the Supreme Court, it might be the sorriest day of your life.' The speech also served as a motivational one because nothing quite stirs an honest policeman's blood like sailing close to the wind to catch the bad guys.

One morning, in the early hours, a couple of Murphy's Marauders were called to the Maidstone police station. Shots had been fired into a flat in a suburban street, and someone in the flat had returned fire. Maidstone coppers had the tenant of the flat in custody, but she wouldn't speak to them. Nightshift CIB had given up but wondered if there was anything Brian's team could do.

The woman was in the interview room, beautiful, feet up on a chair, smoking, and laughing with the young constables. She had clearly charmed them all and that was not going to make her talk—not if she thought she had them all wrapped around her little finger.

'Get your feet off the chair,' Brian commanded as soon as he walked into the interview room.

'Who do you think you're talking to?' she said, unruffled and a little amused.

'You! Get your feet off the chair and put out that cigarette! Anyone on the street could have been shot tonight and you're sitting up there like the Queen of Sheba.'

'What gives you the authority to come in here speaking like that?' she yelled back.

Since words weren't working, Brian picked up one of the hardwood chairs and smashed it against the table. The woman's haughty attitude dissolved as quickly as her arrogant expression. She screamed, and the odour that filled the room suggested she might have lost control of her bladder. But that was a necessary evil. If there was a gunman on the loose and this woman knew who he was then they needed to get her to talk.

Brian's voice softened. 'If you want to go to the toilet, I'll get a policewoman over here.'

'No. I'm fine.' But her voice was quiet. She was ready to talk. Her tale included a very dangerous man—Alex Tsakmakis—made even more dangerous by the fact he was her ex-boyfriend. Brian had heard of the mad man but had never met him. There were mug shots of him in police folders of red-hot crims. The guy was a killer. In 1978, Tsakmakis was wanted for the murder of Bruce Lindsay Walker—who, ironically was a professional runner—over a dispute involving a vintage car. The two had gone out on a fishing boat, but only Tsakmakis returned. Walker's body washed up at Point Lonsdale soon after with his hands and feet bound with chicken wire. The woman said quietly that she had started seeing another man and Tsakmakis had come looking for them both.

'Who is the other bloke?' Brian asked.

She was suddenly stubborn again. 'I'm not going to tell you.'

Brian fixed her with his baby blues. 'You have a fair idea of my bad manners ...'

Her voice became pleading. 'The person I'm seeing will get the sack if this comes out.'

'He's a copper?' *Bloody hell!* It explained why he had been armed to fire back when Tsakmakis fired into the flat.

She nodded.

'I can protect him,' Brian said to her, but she still refused to name him.

Brian left her to stew for a while and went and had a cuppa with the Maidstone coppers. It wasn't long before he heard that she wanted to speak again. Her new beau was a detective from the Vice Squad.

Proving that the beautiful woman had the most appalling taste in men, when Brian rang the detective and invited him in for a chat, his answer was nothing if not concise.

'Fuck off,' he said. 'I'm on a day off.'

Brian was in no mood for games. 'You've got half an hour to come and see me, otherwise I'm going to the bosses.'

He finally agreed to come into the office. In his first breath, he asked for her. 'Is she there? I wanna see her.'

Didn't he realise the hot water he was in for shooting his weapon into a suburban street? Apparently not.

'Surely she told you her ex is wanted for murder!' said Brian.

The detective shrugged.

It was time to locate an associate of Tsakmakis—a man called Terry who knew about the murder of Walker the Runner. If he squealed, Tsakmakis might just go down for it after all.

Terry was cocky—until Brian's squad took him on a little drive to the backblocks of Sunshine in the dead of night, got him out of the car, and made a circle around him.

'Pull your guns out,' Brian told his six squad colleagues. And then to Terry: 'We're going to shoot you.'

The man was sharp as a tack. He looked from one to the next. Finally, he spoke to Brian. 'Can I talk to ya?'

'I'm right here.' The two stepped away from the circle.

'You're not going to shoot me,' he said. 'There's a bloke over there who's got a twitch. He'll give you all up.' He nodded to one of the detectives.

'You're wrong,' Brian said, coolly. 'He's the worst of the lot of them.'

Terry's shoulders slumped in defeat. 'All right, I'll talk.'

Back at the office, Brian rang the Homicide Squad. A detective said he would deal with it in the morning, but time was of the essence and this couldn't wait. With hours to think about it, Terry could turn from hot to stone cold. So Brian lied and said he'd just spoken to Mick Miller who was then the Commissioner in charge of organised crime who wanted a crew to interview Terry right now.

Homicide took a statement over three hours and got all the details about the murder of Walker the Runner. Without Terry's middle-of-the-night statement, Tsakmakis could have escaped scot-free.

In an interesting historical footnote, after Tsakmakis was convicted over the killing of Walker the Runner, he committed a brutal killing in jail. Convicted murderer, Barry Quinn, made the mistake of taunting Tsakmakis about an incident in which a girlfriend of Tsakmakis had been raped. Tsakmakis did not respond immediately, but rather waited until the two were alone in the prison carpentry shop, then Tsakmakis poured glue over Quinn and flicked matches at him till he caught alight. Quinn received burns to 85 per cent of his body and died soon after. Tsakmakis himself was later murdered in prison by Russell Street bomber Craig Minogue. Minogue's weapon of choice was a little kinder than death by fire. He put a bunch of weights in a pillowcase and donged Tsakmakis over the head. Death was pretty instantaneous. Tsakmakis left a trail of bodies behind him, including being a strong suspect for the Manchester Unity building triple murder in the jeweller's office on St Patrick's Day, 1978.

Luckily, Brian told that little white lie and got Homicide to interview Terry that night, which put Tsakmakis squarely in the frame. Like the Lord, justice works in mysterious ways. Sometimes it's poetic, and sometimes it's a pillowcase full of weights.

35

THE PARLOURS

In the 1970s, massage parlours sprang up everywhere. There was good money to be made. Girls could earn up to fifteen hundred dollars a shift—much more than an honest copper earnt. And, of course, the parlours attracted standover men like bees to honey, so it wasn't long before things turned nasty. Police were caught on the hop a bit. The Consorting Squad did raids on parlours to see who was in there, and some of the girls would mention names of criminals who had been in to try and stand over them.

It fell to the police to control them. Not long afterwards, the turf war fires started.

Murphy's Marauders were tasked with stopping the fires. Working from offices in an old decommissioned police station in Best Street, Fitzroy, the squad raided every parlour they could find, and checked out the sex workers and their clients. In the process, a lot of people were charged. Some were wanted on warrant for drug offences, some on violence charges. Some were thieves. Paul Higgins was still at the Consorting Squad at the time, and he backed Murphy's Marauders up on numerous jobs. Higgins' knowledge of the people in this world was better than most of his colleagues.

One girl the squad charged in a house in South Melbourne admitted to setting fire to a number of parlours with her boyfriend. When they arrested her, she told them she'd had a fight with some of the parlour owners. The boyfriend was an ex-con and was locked up when police found a gun in his possession. After he was released on bail, he committed suicide, and left a note saying that

The parlours

he killed himself because he'd been charged with possession of a gun he didn't have.

While Brian realised the accusation of his squad planting the gun on the man needed to be investigated, the raid on the squad offices the next morning to seize all their briefs was overkill. The brief in relation to the young man had been completed and had been filed to go to court. All the statements were vetted and members of the squad were interviewed and so was the girl. The investigation found the squad had done nothing wrong. The girl admitted that her boyfriend had a gun when they were arrested.

Brian was called to appear at the inquest. Fat Harry Bennett was there too, no doubt hoping Brian would get into strife. Brian arrived all dressed up and mingled with the crowd outside. He overheard four blokes—brothers of the dead man—talking about him, so naturally, he approached.

'I wish I had a fucken photograph of him,' said one brother, 'because we don't know what he looks like.'

'Are you blokes here to see what happens to Murphy, today?' Brian asked them conspiratorially.

One brother said, 'Yeah, we're going to give it to him when he leaves court.'

'He might not be as bad as you think,' Brian said.

'Nah, he's a dog,' spat the man.

Brian nodded. 'They reckon he can fight,' he said. 'And he always carries a gun.'

The men's eyes widened and their bravado diminished.

Once inside the court, the Coroner called Detective Sergeant Brian Murphy, and Brian walked up to the stand. The four brothers looked dumfounded when they saw who he was. At the end of the evidence, the Coroner found that the young man had died by his own hand.

There were no winners in a case like this. Brian felt sorry for the young wannabe gangster. His priors were only for housebreaking and he probably saw the girl as a ticket to a bigger life than just petty thievery. He was just out of jail and no doubt didn't want to go back.

Commander Fat Harry Bennett, who at the time headed up all of the Crime Squads, called Paul Higgins to a meeting at the Police Club at the back of Russell Street.

At the Police Club, Bennett asked Higgins what he wanted to drink.

'I'm on duty,' said Higgins, frowning.

His superior laughed and gestured to another cop at the table who got up and walked over to the bar to order a lemon squash. He delivered it to the table and then returned to the bar.

Bennett made small talk while Higgins sipped on his drink suspiciously, waiting to see what his commander wanted.

'Listen, there's a job we want you to do for us. Arrangements have been made to collect money from the parlours once a month. There's no one who knows the parlours like you. We want you to do it.' Fat Harry drew on a cigar and blew out a cloud of blue smoke.

Higgins couldn't believe what he had heard. It took a moment to process the fact that his boss had just asked him to collect protection money from the parlours. His first suspicion was that Fat Harry was setting him up. For a long while he stared at his boss.

'And what happens if something goes wrong?' Higgins asked, trying to buy time.

'I'll give you another diary,' he said.

'What do you mean?' Higgins had heard about other diaries.

'You can keep it six weeks behind and if something happens, you can bring it up to date to cover yourself and your crew.' Bennett grinned and raised his eyebrows.

'I can't do this,' Higgins said.

'No worries,' replied his boss.

Higgins stood up and left the table, never realising the far-reaching repercussions. On the walk back to Russell Street, Higgins

The parlours

was outraged. Was Bennett trying to set him up? If his boss was indeed collecting money from the parlours, that would put him in the same category as the hoons and bludgers who profited from the sex trade. Men who profited from women were the lowest of the low. After months of going into the parlours, interacting with the women, Higgins had developed a soft spot for a lot of them. Some were single women trying to support a family. There were certain quiet spots in the long nights where the women would open their hearts and tell a sympathetic copper their life story.

Most galling was the fact that Higgins had no one to tell. He'd had a couple of run-ins with the bosses, but he had worked hard to redeem himself.

And now, this.

It took a couple of days before Higgins broached the subject with Brian, and even then, he edged around it.

'Mate, I reckon these parlours are out of control,' he began. 'I reckon we should be harder on them than what we are.'

Brian looked at him closely. Higgins wasn't his normal self. Something had upset him. 'What's up with you?' he asked him.

Even though Paul Higgins assured him there was nothing wrong, Brian had a feeling in his gut. He didn't press it, figuring he'd find out in due course.

Around a week later, Bennett's sergeant came to Higgins and asked for two blokes from the Consorting Squad—Paul Strang and Phil Glare—to do an early morning raid with another crew from the Consorting Squad. Higgins agreed.

When Higgins arrived at 6 p.m. on the Friday for his afternoon shift, he was summoned to the Police Club where Fat Harry wanted to talk to him. Strang and Glare were there too.

'How was the raid?' Higgins asked Strang and Glare.

Oddly, the two were tight-lipped, and Higgins couldn't get a straight answer out of them. They kept moving away and returning to the bar when he wanted to speak to them.

Higgins felt that something wasn't right.

After they left, Higgins armed himself with a two-way radio to start his 6 p.m. to 2 a.m. shift on his own, without Strang and Glare, since they'd swapped their shift to work with Bennett. The radio was a bit of a brick and was awkward to carry. In those days, there was no belt to clip it to. Higgins headed in his police car and drove down to the Esplanade in St Kilda to inspect the clubs there, always ready to be diverted from his rounds if D24 called.

Higgins and Brian bumped into each other twice that night. Once at the Whiskey A Go Go night club and the second time at Mickey's Disco. They exchanged intel on who was out and about.

Around midnight, there was a stabbing at the newly built Warwick Apartment House on Beaconsfield Parade. The local CIB and uniform attended as did an ambulance. The victim had been taken to a local hospital. D24 called Higgins on several occasions over the radio but couldn't contact him. It happened frequently because the radios weren't that reliable. Several times that night, Higgins had checked in as he always did to report that he was back on air, but he hadn't been required. At 2 a.m., Higgins knocked off work and drove the police car back to his house.

The following Monday, his boss, Inspector Taylor, was furious.

'Where were you Friday night when the bloke got stabbed at the Warwick?'

'I was on all night,' said Higgins. 'I checked in all through the shift. No one told me anything about a stabbing.'

'Mate, they were calling you and calling you and you didn't answer the radio. Fat Harry has launched an inquiry to find out where you were. You could be charged with being absent from duty.'

'This is a lot of fucken bullshit!' Higgins told Taylor. 'You know what I'm like! I'd bite the arse out of a crim if I thought I'd get a good arrest.'

'Nonetheless, you will have to answer the questions,' said Taylor.

By the end of the meeting, Higgins was demoted back to

The parlours

uniform. Before long, he was being investigated with nuisance things like not having his diary up to date, and not signing the duty book—sins that every detective in Melbourne was guilty of. Higgins had no doubt it all emanated from saying 'no' to Commander 'Fat Harry' Bennett. While that rankled, it was part of Higgins' nature to stay loyal and never turn on his colleagues. Sometimes, all a man had left was to stay true to himself.

One of the bosses told Higgins that if he transferred back to uniform as a beat copper, there would be no charges.

Higgins refused.

'You *are* going to be charged. No doubt about it,' said Brian.

'Bullshit,' said Higgins and walked off.

A couple of months later, Higgins arrived on Brian's doorstep with a summons. Victoria Police had charged him with failing to sign off and failing to answer the radio and other disciplinary matters.

Higgins complained that they were all a pack of low bludgers; and he and Brian had a long conversation, grumbling about the system.

'It's more than the system,' Higgins said, but didn't elaborate.

Brian advised him to go straight to the Police Association.

Without telling Higgins, Brian did a bit of snooping. He wasn't above a dirty fight when those in power played dirty. One of the detectives spearheading the investigation on Higgins told his wife that he was going to Sydney for a fortnight for a trial. The word was that it wasn't a trial he was going away for. When Brian was ready to set the wheels in motion, he spoke to Higgins.

'I got a mate who's a private investigator. I'll get him to follow this guy and his girlfriend away for a fortnight while his wife thinks he's in Sydney. I'll have him photographed every place they stay at and everywhere they go—car, motels, the works. I'll make a big book of the photographs and nominate where all the pictures were taken.'

Higgins eyes stuck out like organ stops.

'On the day of the court case,' said Brian, 'walk up to him and say, "Boss, this is your life!" He'll never give evidence against you because he'll either have a friggin' heart attack or run away and never be found.'

Higgins shook his head. 'Thanks anyway, but I couldn't do that to another copper.'

Begrudgingly, Brian respected Higgins' form of honour, but warned: 'You get convicted of this, and they'll never get off your back again. You'll be the soft target.'

Brian was very worried. He'd asked around and the consensus was that Higgins had upset a few people and these charges would bring him back to earth.

The Police Services Board convicted Paul Higgins of the spurious charges, and his punishment was being sent back to uniform. The joke around the CIBs became: 'Get your diaries done, otherwise they'll do a Higgins on you.' But no one really took it seriously because the common understanding among his colleagues was that Higgins was the target, not the diaries.

Higgins took his conviction without complaint and went back to clerical duties. He appealed a short time afterwards, and was reinstated back into the CIB.

About six months later, Bennett came to Brian and made an astonishing announcement, 'There's an enquiry going on into the four of you—Strang, Glare, you and Higgins, but we only want Higgins. You'll be all right. Don't say anything to him. If he asks, tell him not to worry.'

'Fair enough,' Brian said. 'This is a funny way to do an enquiry.'

'Don't you worry about that. We'll sort it out.'

The commander knew that Higgins and Brian were mates; he had seen Higgins at Brian's place after Brian had shot an intruder who was trying to break into the house next door. Brian had seen the burglar trying to get through a side window, and when he ordered the man to stop, the guy came at him with a screwdriver. Brian responded with a gun; shot the guy in the foot. Higgins had arrived

The parlours

after the injured villain was taken to hospital, no doubt regretting the day he chose The Skull's next-door neighbour to rob. Bennett had turned up in an official capacity, and had seen Higgins there.

So Brian found the short exchange illuminating; he'd always suspected that Bennett was frightened of him. Brian wasn't averse to making threats against rogues and scoundrels; he reckoned Fat Harry might have begun to believe him capable of anything. Of course, Brian was happy for him to think that. Being unpredictable worked a treat. After the conversation, Brian realised that Bennett was driving the investigation into Higgins. That meant Higgins needed to be worried. Fat Harry had been educated in graft and corruption by Harry McMenamin, and he had also been a part of Slater's Breakers team in the 1950s and 60s. All these men, had risen through the ranks of the Victoria Police and were now in positions of power.

Brian walked away from that conversation knowing that he couldn't trust Fat Harry as far as he could throw him.

In the meantime, Bennett authorised two detectives to do an explosives course; Brian couldn't figure out why. They had the Mines Department and forensics teams who knew about explosives. Why did these detectives need to do a course in explosives? Brian had his suspicions about the several parlour explosions that followed.

Not long after, early one morning, Brian was reclining in the tub and Margaret was ironing a shirt for his day at work when she interrupted his ablutions, reporting what she had just heard on the radio.

'Joey Hamilton's place has just been blown up.'

Brian rolled his eyes. 'Maybe they'll blame me for that too,' he grumbled.

A short time later, there was another explosion that blew out a shop in Lygon Street. It had blown out windows in several other shops too. Brian found out that the man who owned the shop was a mate of Fat Harry's. While the words 'insurance job' never left his lips and he made no enquiries, his mental notes would have filled many notebooks.

There was no question in Brian's mind as to whether to tell Paul Higgins about what Fat Harry had said. He waited until they were alone and told him that he was the target of an inquiry that was ostensibly about Brian, Strang, Glare and him.

'What's he crook on you for?' Brian asked.

'Apparently everything,' muttered Higgins.

Every time Fat Harry saw Brian for weeks after that, he would pat him on the back and say, 'Mate, we are not after you.'

Soon after, the bosses at Russell Street received intel that a man by the name of Bob Slater had explosives in his house. The intel suggested that a massage parlour in Victoria Parade had explosives as well. One of the Superintendents asked Brian to search the two addresses after the warrants were made out. Higgins was called in as well from Consorting. A woman in the office typed out the warrants. When they were finished, she handed them to the superintendent for signing. Then he handed them to Brian. They were good to go.

Brian took his team to Slater's Housing Commission unit in Perry Street. The place was neat and clean, but not lavish. Considering Slater owned the parlour that would be searched later in the day, he could easily afford his own house, but people of his ilk didn't want to flash around wealth because the police became suspicious. It also made them targets for standover men. They searched the place and found explosives—detonators cords— among the kids' toys.

Two detectives from the Vice Squad turned up while Brian's crew were searching. Slater's wife was yelling and screaming and it became apparent that she had called in a favour. Hence the appearance of the two Vice Squad detectives.

'We were here this morning,' said one of the detectives. 'There's no explosives here!'

Brian took the high road. 'What are you saying?' he said right

The parlours

in his face. 'Are you saying we've loaded him up?'

The Vice officer stood his ground too. 'There's nothing here!'

'Did you search the place this morning?' Brian asked.

'No.'

'So how would you know? And even if you did search the place this morning—which you didn't—how do you know that someone didn't put something here after you left?' Brian hated this kind of interference. If the detective had taken him outside for a quiet word and explained that the couple were informants, they could have talked like gentlemen. Brian still would have searched the place for explosives, but might have given them the benefit of the doubt when preparing the brief and then let the court decide.

Once he'd declared his hand in front of the Slaters, it was impossible for the Vice Squad detective to back down. Or Brian.

'I'll catch you later,' the Vice Squad detective said to the Slaters, as he left in a huff.

Back at the office, a brief of evidence was prepared against the Slaters for possession of explosives and passed on to the bosses.

Along with Higgins, Strang, and Glare, Brian went to the Slaters' massage parlour that evening to execute the second warrant. They took a uniform policewoman in case there were any parlour workers who needed to be searched. The parlour—Twilight—stank of cheap perfume. They entered the place quietly so as not to spook people and send them running out the back. Intel was gathered much more successfully when there wasn't a panicked exit by half-naked patrons when police arrived.

During the raid, they herded all of the patrons and girls into a room and one detective started taking names. The others searched the rooms. The policewoman and Glare found a handful of sticks of gelignite and detonators on a hidden shelf under a billiard table. Despite the word of the Vice Squad detective, things were not looking good for the Slaters. It looked as if they were planning to blow up a rival parlour.

Once the search was done, Brian left Higgins, Strang and Glare to do the paperwork and compile the brief. He hated paperwork. His boss always said, 'Murphy, if there was a cover on a typewriter, you wouldn't know what was underneath it.'

Slater and his missus got charged, but were acquitted in court. Part of the problem was that Strang and Glare wouldn't meet with Higgins to answer the query sheet from the DPP in relation to the Slaters' trial. The DPP would later accuse Higgins of not answering the Prosecutor's queries. He only did this because he couldn't get a straight answer from Strang and Glare. They were always out when Higgins went to find them, and they wouldn't hand over their diaries to him. It didn't take long for Higgins to suspect their motives.

36

DENNIS ALLEN

Brian first met Dennis Allen in Chinatown in little Bourke Street. Someone had called the police because Dennis was having an argument with a restaurant owner. Dennis reckoned the food was bad and he wasn't going to pay for it. By the time Brian and his partner arrived, Dennis was pretty fired up. At first glance, he was not someone you'd want to tackle—foul-mouthed, covered in tatts, and wearing more gold jewellery than the Lord Mayor. After Brian calmed things down, he told Dennis that he got paid for what he did, and therefore, the restaurant owner should get paid for what *he* did.

'If your drugs are bad, you still get paid,' Brian reasoned.

That logic made sense to Dennis, and he handed over $200 to the restauranteur and told him to keep the change. The bill was only $120.

'And how much do I owe you?' asked Dennis, pulling out a huge roll of bills.

'You don't owe me a thing,' Brian said. 'You've behaved yourself, so you can go on your way.'

Dennis said, 'Well, who do I owe the money to?'

'Keep if for your bail,' Brian said, grinning. 'You're sure to get locked up sooner or later.'

Dennis laughed. 'There's plenty more where this comes from.'

Like every cop in Melbourne, Brian had heard stories about the Allen clan. Dennis was a violent drug dealer who was buying up half of Richmond. Dennis' mother, Kath Pettingill gained notoriety when she was shot through the eye by a prostitute when she attempted to re-pay a debt her daughter owed the woman. When Kath knocked on the door of the Collingwood Housing Commission flat, she had no idea the woman lay in wait with a gun. The bullet went through the door and hit Kath in the eye. Kath recovered quickly, got a glass eye, and resumed her position as a brothel madam at the front of her massage parlour.

In addition to the tattoos, Dennis dressed in bib-and-brace overalls and looked like a dero, or maybe Charlie Manson. He dressed to scare. Brian quickly took his measure; he was like a predatory animal—if he sensed fear in someone, he had them. If he met resistance, he either fought or backed down, depending on his likelihood of winning. On this night, he backed down.

Dennis stuffed the wad of notes back into his pocket.

'I'll be catching up with you,' said Brian.

'That won't be hard to do,' said Dennis as if his notoriety was a badge.

'You owe me one,' Brian said, letting the meaning sink in. He'd had a sudden realisation: if Dennis had done all the things he was rumoured to have done and was still free to terrorise Chinese restaurant owners, then he must be working as a police informant. Otherwise, there was no way he could have escaped jail.

'But you just knocked me back,' countered Dennis, as if money was the only currency.

Brian had a string of good informers, and decided on the spot to add Dennis Allen to his stable. But approaching Dennis would take some finesse.

A week later, Brian knocked on Dennis' door in Chestnut Street, Richmond. His house was a pigsty, full of overflowing ashtrays and spilt booze which made the place stink.

'This looks like the Hilton,' Brian said dryly.

Dennis looked around as if he had never noticed the filth he lived in. He turned to a woman sitting on a couch and screeched at her: 'Get off your fucken arse and clean this place up!'

The woman flew off the couch and scrambled to pick up an empty bottle nearby.

Dennis' violence towards women was legendary. He would belt them around and had been known to shoot them in the leg if they didn't do what they were told. The woman made a token effort to clear away the mess before he screamed at her to leave them alone.

Dennis looked at Brian. 'What are we going to talk about?' he asked.

'I'm only as good as what I can find out,' Brian said, 'and you know plenty.'

'What do you want to know?' Dennis was amiable. It was easy to see that he'd dealt with a lot of coppers before.

'I don't want any shit,' Brian warned. 'You know what I'm talking about.' They were two men sizing each other up. Both playing on opposite sides of the law.

'You got me playing a pretty dangerous game,' he said.

'You've played it before,' Brian said. 'It's going to cost you nothing. You can stick your money up your bum. I want good mail. Anything at all I can work with.'

'I'll give you a bell,' wheezed Dennis, following it with a lung-shuddering cough that only a big smoker and drinker can muster.

Brian handed Dennis his home phone number—the best way of contacting him—with the same disclaimer he gave all crims: 'If my wife is ever upset as a result of a phone call from you, I will act accordingly.'

'Nah, nah.' said Dennis, 'Sweet, mate. I understand.' He promised to ring soon.

Brian walked out into the bright light of day in Chestnut Street, knowing that Dennis' place was bugged and that their conversation would have been recorded. He wondered idly whether he would be approached by any bosses.

He wasn't.

The first job Dennis helped solve was an armed robbery.

Dennis had a stream of desperate people coming to his house to buy drugs and sell stolen property. Armed robbers would come promising money from their next job, and Dennis would ring Brian—after he'd been paid of course. For Dennis, informing on others served several purposes; it eliminated his rivals, and information was a currency he traded for his own freedom.

Sometimes, Brian would visit and ask about a particular crime and Dennis would greet him with his gravel voice: 'Hi mate, I was just fucken gonna ring ya.'

Dennis Allen knew everything that went on. He was such an avid dealer and he knew everyone and heard everything. His memory was incredible considering his drug usage.

In return for intel, Dennis was given a green light by Victoria Police to run his drug empire. Surveillance police were stationed in the nearby Rosella factory and sometimes Dennis would take a shotgun and fire it in their direction to show them he knew they were there. Police pretended they weren't there and didn't respond. He was being listened to 24 hours a day so Brian figured that he would milk Dennis for everything he could and let Victoria Police take care of the bigger picture.

It wasn't long before Brian met the matriarch, Kath when she wandered in one day, looking for Dennis.

'Hello love,' she said. 'Are you Brian Murphy? I've heard about you.'

Brian treated her respectfully which seemed to take her by surprise. In turn, she always referred to him as Mr Murphy. He called her Kath which was better than other coppers she dealt with who called her an old moll and treated her like a prostitute.

'I'll tell my Dennis that you called,' she'd say if her notorious son wasn't home when Brian came calling.

One of her kids got picked up in the small hours of the morning for doing a robbery. When Brian got to work, there was Kath in the corridor waiting.

'Hello, love,' she said.

'Who is it this time, Kath?' Brian asked.

'Jamie.' Kath was as worried as any mother about the fate of her son, which was surprising since they were all in trouble, all the time.

Jamie had been arrested for shooting someone during an armed robbery at the United Kingdom Hotel in Clifton Hill.

'But he didn't do it, love,' she said.

Brian promised to make some inquiries for her and let her know what was happening. He left her waiting in the foyer of the police station and went off to find his boss.

The boss didn't mince words. 'Piss off, Murph. None of your business.'

Brian took the matter up with another boss who gave Brian permission to go in and have a chat with Jamie. Before he went in, he said to Kath: 'If I go in there and talk to him and he admits it, will you believe he did it?'

'Yes love, I will,' she said.

In the interview room, Brian looked Jamie square in the eye. 'Kath's out there, protesting your innocence and they're going to lock her up,' Brian lied. 'Your mum's got a ton of guts and sincerity. If I wasn't married, I hope I'd marry a woman like her.'

Jamie looked at Brian and admitted the whole thing.

Brian went out to Kath, 'He's admitted it.'

'You're a fucken liar!' she snarled, suddenly showing her inner lioness.

'No, I'm not.' To prove it to her and put her out of her misery, Brian got permission to take her into the interview room.

'He's fucken belted you, didn't' he?' she screeched at her son.

'No, Mum, he didn't,' Jamie said, looking down.

'You didn't fucken admit to a robbery! Why?'

Jamie said, 'I didn't want you to get into trouble, Mum.'

Kath wasn't impressed with her son's attempt at chivalry. 'You're a fucken idiot!'

Once she and Brian left the interview room, Kath calmed

down a bit. 'You're a low bastard, getting him to admit that.'

Brian shrugged. 'That's what I get paid for, Kath.'

At that, she shook hands with him and said, sadly, 'See ya, love.' Then she walked out of the building.

The other detectives had Jamie for twelve hours and didn't get a thing out of him. Brian only needed a couple of minutes, the right words, and a devoted mother waiting in the wings.

37

TAKING DOWN THE PAINTERS AND DOCKERS

David Richards was a journalist and a little Pommy bastard whose legs Brian threatened to blow off the first time he met him. Richards had contacted Mick Miller to get permission to write an exposé on the Painters and Dockers for *The Bulletin*. Assistant Commissioner Bill Conn rang Brian and said that David Richards was coming to his office.

'Do everything possible to help him,' ordered the assistant commissioner.

'What's all this bullshit?' Brian spluttered. 'Since when has the press been kind to us?'

'Shut your mouth and do as you're told,' Conn said, then hung up.

At the end of the call, Brian stopped in his tracks. Was this a joke? Was it really Conn on the phone or was someone playing a trick. He rang Conn back and got his secretary. She said Conn didn't want to talk because he was still fuming at Brian's attitude.

Brian's mistrust of the press dated from the Collingburn trial when he saw how they twisted the truth to enhance the headlines, regardless of the real people they mowed down in the process.

When David Richards arrived at their door, one of the blokes announced him.

'There's a pommy bloke outside who wants to talk to you. Reckons he's a journalist.'

'Bring him in,' Brian said.

The journalist appeared in Brian's office. He had dark hair

with a sprinkling of distinguished grey at the side and he wore a fancy suit that looked Savile Row. That's why they all hated him before he had finished introducing himself.

'David Richards is my name, and I've been sent here to work on the Painters and Dockers with you chaps and do a story.' He was short and authoritative, with a posh pommy voice that went down like a lead balloon in the rough and tumble world of the Metropolitan Regional Crime Squad offices. There were a lot of stunned faces in the office that day.

'We have a few rules here, David,' said Brian.

'Yes. Yes. I understand,' said Richards.

'No you don't fucken understand,' said Brian. 'Will you just shut up for a minute.'

'Good. Good.' Toffy voice. Dismissive wave of the hand.

'You'll see things here that won't be print-worthy and if you print them, I'll blow your fucken legs off.'

'Good. Good.'

Brian couldn't believe this bloke. Normally, his threats to shoot people at least gave them pause. 'Go away and think about it so no one accuses me of not giving you a choice.'

The toffy pom was gone about thirty seconds before he was back, knocking on the door again. He'd thought about it and wanted in.

One of the reasons that Brian didn't shoot him in the legs was that if David could bring down the Painters and Dockers, that would be a win-win for everyone. Collingburn aside, the rorting and criminal activity around the union was the bane of every copper's existence. Another thing that angered Brian was that he suspected that a couple of cops who worked the docks undermined their colleagues by passing on information about raids and police activity in return for a buck or a favour.

David sat down and told Brian his plan. The more he talked about the Painters and Dockers, the more intelligent Brian could see he was. He had researched a fair bit of material that he had dug

Taking down the Painters and Dockers

up himself. And so, David began to spend a lot of time at the office and on patrol.

Whatever else David Richards was, he was keen. And he wasn't bound by police regulations or budgetary constraints. Mick Miller had authorised him to carry a gun when he accompanied the squad out on patrol—probably figuring that while the Painters and Dockers wouldn't have a go at police, a journalist was fair game. David organised a permit and bought a .38 snub nose revolver, Smith and Wesson, same as the police carried, for authenticity. Brian took David to the back of St Albans for target practice. The last thing he needed was the journalist firing off shots at random. The target practice went well and it turned out, David could handle a gun.

Word got round pretty quickly that there was a journo running around with a gun who was working on the Painters and Dockers. Brian wondered if the rumours came from David, himself—he was no shrinking violet.

Of the dozens of ideas David had to get information on the Painters and Dockers, one of his wildest was to climb the tower stack at Newport and set up surveillance cameras to trap the Dockers. He couldn't get permission to climb the tower, so his next crazy idea was to use a shipping container on the docks right opposite the office where the Painters and Dockers went to get paid. David brought down a photographer from Sydney and then disguised the shipping container with a huge tarp with holes cut into it.

One payday, David, a couple of Metropolitan Regional Crime Squad detectives and his photographer climbed into the container in the early hours before the Painters and Dockers arrived. The rest of the squad were hidden around the docks in case the ruse was discovered.

The operation was top secret. Brian told no one, especially not his bosses. When the bosses rang to see how David was going, Brian was always vague in his response. He knew that if word got out of the surveillance idea, he could end up with a couple of dead coppers and a dead Pom who he had grown rather fond of.

By the end of the day, David had photographs of blokes tearing the tops off half a dozen envelopes, tipping out the cash and pocketing it. This 'ghosting' had been going on for years. The union would quote that a job required 60 men, then send a fraction of that number to do the work. A dozen men would collect multiple pay packets. David, in his shipping container for a day with the support of Brian's crew brought the entire racket to a halt.

Brian took out warrants and prepared to raid all the Painters and Dockers joints on a particular morning. It was all going well until one of the bosses arrived to oversee the warrants. Brian handed them over to him and he put them in his folder.

'There are to be no raids this morning,' he said.

'*What?*' Brian could not believe his ears.

'Go about your business.'

'Where did these orders come from?' he roared, furious.

'Right from the top.'

Brian was furious. The boss and the warrants disappeared and no raids were carried out. In the end, it didn't matter, though. Once David's article hit the streets, all hell broke loose and it wasn't long before a Royal Commission was announced. In the fall-out Brian was worried that the Painters and Dockers would kill David. He may have been smart, but at the same time, he did dumb things like get himself cornered at a pub where Painters and Dockers drank. Which was what happened.

One night, David rang Brian from a pub where he was drinking with another copper, and explained in his toffy voice that they were cornered. His car had been blocked in in the car park by cars belonging to unionists.

'I'll be there in five minutes,' Brian told him. 'Sit tight.'

Brian wrapped a shotgun in newspaper and grabbed a couple of pistols. Outside the pub, he could see the Painters and Dockers by David's car. Brian walked in and surreptitiously handed over a weapon to the cop David was with. He then slowly unwrapped the sawn-off shot gun to the wide-eyed interest of the crowd. He said in a loud voice: 'if the gentlemen who have hemmed in these gentlemen's cars go out and move them now, there won't be any trouble.'

Half a dozen men scrambled out of the joint.

The cop checked outside minutes later, and all the cars were gone.

There were a lot of heart palpitations going on at the table in the wake of the mass exodus which gave Brian quite an appetite. Luckily everyone else at the table had lost theirs and he was able to enjoy a couple of lovely desserts for his trouble.

For all the threats he received, David Richards was left unscathed. If he was ever challenged or cornered, he liberally applied Skull Murphy's name to the conversation which kept things in check.

The Royal Commission investigating the corruption within the Federated Ship Painters and Dockers Union, marked the beginning of the end. The Commission attributed 15 murders and 23 attempted murders to the union power struggles. Billy Longley regarded that as conservative; he estimated there were between thirty or forty killed. Pat Shannon's assertion in 1972 that 'no stray bullet or bomb has harmed a non-Union member', did not remain true when in April the following year, a 10-year-old boy was caught in the cross-fire of a union hit at the Moonee Valley Hotel. Despite the death and mayhem they left behind, few Painters and Dockers were convicted.

No one mourned the union's demise.

38

A MAD BLOKE CALLED MAX

It was a cold June night in 1985 when the police radio burst with an urgent message: *Cheltenham 709! Urgent! Members shot! We need an ambulance! Quick! I've been shot in the arm. My sergeant has been shot at least three times with what feels like a bloody big gun. Please get that ambulance in a hurry!*

The fevered voice belonged to Peter Steele, and the sergeant he was talking about was Brian Stooke. Both men had been shot during a routine car check in Cheltenham. The driver they had pulled over minutes earlier was Max Clark. He was a cool customer until Steele and Stooke asked him to open his boot. Ropes and tools suggested that Max Clark might be the man responsible for a couple of factory burglaries in the area.

But Clark was not going to go quietly.

Before the sun came up, Max Clark—whose real name was Pavel Marinof—had shot and wounded five police officers. When Brian came on day shift, he could hardly believe the tale of horror that his police colleagues had suffered while he slept. He and his crew were put on the case to find Marinof, whom the press quickly dubbed Mad Max.

By shooting five members of the Victoria Police, Marinof had created a whole police force of enemies, all ready to shoot first and ask questions afterwards. And that was fine by Brian. By this stage of his career, he had shot 40 crims. None had died. He never worried about pulling his gun, never hesitated for a second. From the very beginning, he had never been willing to put a crim's life before his own, especially if the bad guy was pointing a gun at him.

Brian and his crew headed straight to Marinof's house in South Clayton. It was empty. His wife was visiting relatives overseas. The house was neat, but impersonal. There were few family photographs. After the shooting in Cheltenham, Marinof had headed home, and taken his pick from the arsenal of weapons in the garage. He switched cars, then rammed his way through a police road block. He had resurfaced to fire at two pursuing cops, then at a police handler from the Dog Squad whose dog had picked up Marinof's scent.

On the morning Mrs Marinof was due back from overseas, Brian and two colleagues met her at the airport. While his colleagues treated her almost as if she had done the shooting herself, Brian felt sorry for her. She looked just as shocked as anybody else about what had happened. He determined to take a gentle approach.

'If she knows anything, she'll tell us,' Brian told his colleagues in a low voice. He understood their anger, but they were aiming it at the wrong person.

They drove Mrs Marinof to Russell Street and questioned her. According to his wife, Pavel Marinof was a hard worker and the man of the house.

'I can't believe my husband would do that,' she said. She had never seen a gun in her husband's possession.

Brian's two colleagues snorted at the notion, but he believed her. He did the same thing with his own wife—protected her against a lot of what happened at work.

It quickly came out that Mrs Marinof's husband was not the man she thought he was. There was a girlfriend in Glenhuntly who first denied all knowledge of Marinof and then told Brian that she had gone out to dinner with him. It was clear she wasn't telling them the whole story. The girlfriend didn't believe Marinof could shoot at police—the detectives must be lying. Brian suspected she knew where Max was.

The next day, Brian asked Margaret to bake a nice orange cake for Mrs Marinof, which he took around to her house with a bunch of flowers. His interest was two-fold—he wanted to make sure she was okay, but he also needed to know whether she had heard from her husband. Mrs Marinof appreciated the kindness, but hadn't heard a word from Mad Max.

For months, Brian and his squad followed up report after report. Someone just moved into a boarding house; somebody who looked like Mad Max was seen out shopping. The problem was that while some of the sightings might have been genuine, they came too late for Brian and his crew to nab the fugitive. All up, they did 150 raids. The more they raided, the more writs appeared against police.

Raids began at 4 a.m. Police would kick in doors, wondering if an armed Marinof was standing behind pointing a gun in their direction. While the media was adverse in their reporting of the heavy-handed approach, the recipients of the raids also objected. One place they raided, a woman jumped out of an upstairs window, thinking they were the secret police. She broke both her legs.

The pressure was huge on everyone; the media, the bosses, and the fear of facing Marinof in the final gun battle, all mounted up. Brian and his squad were under the microscope. During this time, he lost about 20 kilos—his doctor blamed the pressure of the investigation. The police doctor said the same. A third doctor diagnosed an over-active thyroid and prescribed medication. He also gave Brian a month off work. As hard as it was to walk away from the Marinof manhunt, the rapid weight loss, his spiralling mood swings and lack of energy had worried him.

The day they caught Marinof, Brian was out fishing with a copper mate. When he got home with his bucket of fish, Margaret told him they had caught Mad Max; she had heard it on the news. He rang the office and while they confirmed Marinof had been caught, they were tight-lipped about the details. He was due back to work the following day, but figured he would head into the office to celebrate there and then.

A mad bloke called Max

When he arrived at Russell Street, one of his colleagues said to him, 'You shouldn't be here.'

'Is that right?' Brian was a little puzzled. Sure, he wasn't due back till the next day, but what was a day between squad mates.

Unbeknown to him, in his absence, a criminal called Thomas Joseph Fabian Erickson had fabricated a story about Brian and reported it to his bosses. This happened a lot so when Brian heard about it, he wasn't worried. Erickson was a pal of Christopher Dale Flannery and when the heat came down on his mate, dobbing in a copper eased the pain a little, especially when the copper was going to testify against Flannery, as Brian was.

This time, when Brian was hauled into the office, he entered at the same time as a young detective who was promptly told to leave the room. Something stirred in Brian's gut and he insisted the young man stay.

His boss, Fat Harry Bennett, pulled no punches. 'You're not going to Sydney to testify against Flannery. There've been allegations that you've killed somebody and buried the body.'

'That's bullshit!' yelled Brian. 'I bet that story came from Erickson! Every time I'm due to testify, he comes up with some ridiculous story about me.'

'Well you're not going to Sydney.'

Brian hit the roof. 'I'm telling you this: if this happens again, I'm going to put a bullet right through Erickson's head—whether it's in your office, or downstairs or in the court.' His threat to shoot Erickson went down like a lead balloon.

The fact that his bosses gave Erickson any credence, infuriated him. It was the beginning of his disillusionment with Victoria Police. And perhaps theirs with him. So after creating the successful Metropolitan Regional Crime Squad from a motley crew of 'rejects', one that had really made a difference, he was transferred. For 18 months, Brian had enjoyed a free rein with a good boss Max Williams who largely left him alone. Brian would report to him every Monday and the inspector was happy to let the results speak for themselves. Despite Brian's suspicion that he'd been given the Metropolitan Regional Crime Squad with the expectation he would stuff up, so that his bosses could get rid of him, he had made the squad successful. But it worked against him; the squad became something they could take away from him. And they did.

Brian was transferred back to Russell Street as the sergeant in charge of the muster room. That meant he was in charge of 30 detectives, and allocated jobs to them as they came up. It was a position of power on one hand, but it kept him confined to the office, on the other. Its saving grace was the opportunity it gave him to train the young coppers.

One day, one of the bosses said to him, 'How do you like it in here?'

'Love it,' Brian said. 'In fact I love it so much I'm writing a book.' He wasn't but he liked to put the wind up people.

'You're writing a friggin' book? What about?'

'Oh, you know,' Brian said vaguely. 'About all the experiences in here.' He waved his hands vaguely around the office and left the boss looking concerned.

Later, Brian could hear him on the phone talking loudly about writing a book. Suddenly, the boss was at Brian's elbow explaining in a nice voice that he wasn't stuck there and could apply anywhere he wanted to go.

Brian laughed to himself. The Major Crime Squad was where he wanted to go. The boss quickly agreed, even though they both knew Brian might not be welcome there. Brian asked the boss if he could address the Majors first. Soon, he was standing in front of a bunch of burly colleagues.

'I know why you don't want me here,' he told them. 'It's because I know that one of you is a raving homosexual who picks up male prostitutes in public toilets.' Brian caught the eye of the detective in question who kept his expression blank. 'Or it could be because I know that safe-cracker Vincent Keith Mendes has a detective in the squad who gives him advance notice when he's going to be raided.' Again, Brian looked around, catching the eye of the rat detective who passed on intel to crims and put his own colleagues in danger.

The inspector in charge stepped forward and cleared his throat. 'Um, I think you've vented your feelings.' He turned to the guys. 'Is there anyone who objects to Murph joining the squad?'

Of course no one said anything which was the purpose of Brian's rant. Anyone who stepped forward would have been immediately suspect.

39

HIGGINS

In 1987, a colleague, at the behest of Commander Bennett, approached Brian and talked about retirement. If you had been in the job for 30 years and were over 50, it was financially better to retire than to wait. Brian had been in for 33 years and was 55. He could get a golden handshake.

For someone who'd lived on adrenaline and coffee for three decades, Brian began to give serious consideration to life away from the Victoria Police. He didn't make the connection that Fat Harry might want him out of the way for what was about to go down.

At this time, Paul Higgins was in charge of Prahran as a senior sergeant. He had worked on the Great Bookie Robbery. He had chalked eleven commendations on his record sheet for such things as work performance, success, integrity, and knowledge. For eight years, Higgins had imagined that the whole Fat Harry episode was water under the bridge.

Higgins had not changed in the intervening years. He continued to tell it how it was, and like Brian, he refused to suck up to bosses if he didn't agree with them. In early 1987, Higgins was preparing to sit for his Inspector's exam, which might have the trigger for what unfolded. After all, if he reached inspector rank, his enemies would have found it harder to get rid of him. Also, if an inspector blew the whistle on corrupt colleagues, that couldn't be ignored.

Around March, Higgins got wind of a big enquiry against him. The name Lamb was mentioned in connection with it. Geoff Lamb was a massage parlour owner—his empire spanned over twenty parlours. Over the years, every parlour owner chose a cop who was their point of contact. Higgins was Lamb's. Higgins tolerated the insipid fellow who lived off the earnings of prostitution. If he was having problems with people standing over him, Lamb would call Higgins.

Brian was at Russell Street one night and heard that Lamb had made a statement to the inquiry. He told Higgins who replied that there was nothing Lamb or his family could say. But they said plenty.

About a month before Higgins was charged, a police colleague said to him: 'If I were you, I would take sick leave and go. Do yourself a favour, just go.'

Higgins had heard it all before. So had Brian. It was a tactic that had never worked for either of them. As such, they were both caught unawares.

When it happened, it happened quickly.

Inspector Ian Wynn and fellow officer Trevor Thompson who were running the enquiry picked Higgins up from the Prahran police station and drove him to his house. In 1980, Higgins had bought a two-storey house on Dandenong Road in East Malvern for $80,000. He had done it up nicely.

'What's going on?' Higgins asked, flabbergasted.

Wynn and Thompson gave nothing away. They had a warrant to search for a black mink fur coat. Photos were taken of the house and contents. The house would later be judged to be an Aladdin's Cave of antiques. Higgins father-in-law was an antiques dealer and much of the furniture had come from him. Higgins had been going to auctions with him for years. Higgins' wife was pregnant and had a toddler, but unlike many wives at the time, she had worked for years in an office. Nonetheless, the house was deemed too good for a copper's wage.

Higgins was taken back into the city to the police complex in Spencer Street. He was told he would be interviewed about disciplinary matters. He refused to talk because while he was obliged to talk about disciplinary matters, he was certainly not obliged to talk about criminal matters. Higgins was charged and locked up in the city watch house, but bailed on his own recognisance.

As a dedicated police officer, Higgins was devastated. His policing life was over.

Brian was also in shock. It all happened in the very same month he was in the process of retiring. Given that Higgins had just been charged, Brian was ready to leave. This was not what he had joined up for. He estimated that it must have cost the Victoria Police a fortune in the resources that were used to pursue Higgins, which only increased his own disenchantment with the senior echelons; the sense of disgust and betrayal, and he wanted no part in this.

When Brian finally spoke to Higgins, he was broken-hearted for his friend. Brian had no doubts at all that Higgins was a good man who had been set up by scumbags within the police department itself.

Higgins was charged with five counts of conspiring to obstruct the course of justice. He was accused of conspiring with a number of parlour owners to protect them in exchange for cash. A brothel owner made a statement claiming Higgins protected her from prosecution. A criminal called Alistair Farquhar 'Sandy' MacRae made a statement against Higgins too. There was a blip on the radar when MacRae was charged with a couple of brutal murders and found himself facing trial at the same time as Higgins.

With a parlour owner and a killer as star witnesses against a commended cop, Higgins didn't think the word of these kinds of people would stand up in court, but when he saw that the DPP were using top prosecutors, he was worried. The Police Association agreed to fund his defences.

Suspended without pay, Higgins spent his days looking for evidence to fight the allegations. He found out that Lamb had made a statement that he was paying the Consorting Squad $3,000 dollars a week. It was one of those things that was hard to prove one way or another. His word against Higgins. Even though the investigators went through Higgins' bank statements they couldn't find any money that couldn't be accounted for.

Higgins had to be very careful, however, when he was making his own enquiries because he was on bail. If he approached any of the witnesses, he could be charged with interfering with an investigation. On the other hand, while he was keeping out of the way, Geoff Lamb and Sandy MacRae courted the media, giving long interviews to reporters. TV journalist, Mike Willesee, ran a three-part series where Lamb and MacRae said that they paid up to $3,000 a week to Higgins and another cop at Vice. MacRae said that he would be falsely accused of murder and Higgins would walk into the interview room, demand $1,000 and then MacRae would be released. He told the reporters that these false accusations were just a greedy ploy to get more money.

The story sounded reasonable. Until police found the body of missing man Dominic Marafiote under Sandy MacRae's chicken coop.

A committal hearing began for Paul Higgins in October 1987, but after long delays, was withdrawn ten months later. The aborted committal hearing cost the Police Association nearly two million dollars in legal fees.

40

RETIREMENT AND CRIMS IN THE WOODWORK

With his retirement in 1987 happening virtually overnight, Brian spent the weekend thinking about his future. He was only 55 and had a lot of good working years left in him. He couldn't imagine an idle life. The first day he woke up a free, retired man, there were a couple of things on his mind. Over the years, he had cultivated a stable of informers who trusted him and knew they could talk to him about anything. He didn't imagine this would change simply because he took the uniform off.

Brian quite liked the idea of being a private eye. There were a lot of them on the periphery of the police force. Most of them had little training and he knew he would be in front of the pack if he joined their ranks. He could work from home, be his own boss, and if he stuffed up, he would only have himself to blame. All he needed was a phone and a car. And also a gun, even though he envisaged doing mostly insurance and industrial work rather than anything dangerous. But there were no guarantees.

Margaret liked the idea because she figured it would keep her husband out of her hair.

The first Monday of Brian's new-found freedom, he went into the city to get an application for a pistol permit. He parked his car in Flinders Lane near the permit office and noticed a car pulling up behind him. Greedy Smith and three of his drug-dealing heavies alighted from an Aston Martin just like the one in the James Bond movies. Dennis William 'Greedy' Smith had recently returned from the Philippines where for years, he had run the notorious

Retirement and crims in the woodwork

'Aussie Bar' in Manila—reported to have been funded by proceeds from the Great Bookie Robbery. The fall of the Marcos government in the Philippines had exposed two things of note: Imelda Marcos had an indecent number of shoes, and Greedy Smith was running a very indecent establishment. Both were ousted for their crimes. Greedy was a huge bear of a man draped with gold jewellery crammed on to his stubby fingers and chunky wrists.

'G'day, Mr Murphy,' he said in a friendly voice.

'G'day, Greedy,' Brian said.

'I know what you're here for! To get a pistol licence.'

Brian nodded. His retirement had been featured in the newspapers over the weekend and everybody knew.

'You don't need a fucken pistol permit,' he said, conspiratorially. 'You got any problems, you come and see me and we'll fix it up.' Greedy Smith was earnest. 'You just get in touch if you need my services.'

Brian burst out laughing. 'No worries, Greedy.'

He got back in his fancy car and so did his goons. And then they were gone.

Brian was suddenly glad that he had always been fair with Greedy and his ilk. Despite Greedy's generous offer, Brian went into the office to apply for his pistol licence the legal way, hoping it would be a cold day in hell before he ever needed anyone like Greedy to fight his battles. He filled in the application and soon, got a notification to appear before the Board.

Brian was savvy enough to employ a solicitor to come with him. His suspicion of trouble proved correct when he saw that the superintendent on the Board was the very same man whose partner had 'forgotten' to caution Neil Collingburn which led to his acquittal for the original breaking charge that had put him back on the streets for Stillman to pick him up on that fateful day in 1971.

Sure enough, as soon as the hearing began, the superintendent made his dislike quite clear. From where Brian was sitting, the other Board members, a solicitor and a public servant, looked as if they might be swayed by the pompous oaf.

'Why do you think you need a gun?' he asked.

Brian made sure he looked at the others on the panel rather than at the superintendent. 'I still get contacted by informers and I pass their information to the police.'

He looked at Brian suspiciously. 'When was the last time you were called out by an informer? You're retired.'

Brian had been waiting for this. 'Three o'clock this morning,' he said. 'In relation to a murder.' Before he could say anything, Brian added: 'I've passed the information on to the Homicide Squad. You can check if you like.'

'Mr Murphy,' he said, 'I think the best thing you can do is forget you were ever a policeman.'

'Is that right?' Brian asked him.

'Yes.' Sanctimonious smile.

Brian's blood boiled. After all his years of service, someone like the superintendent could cast him aside like rubbish. They couldn't take his voice though.

'In that case, you can stick my application up your arse.' Brian got to his feet, followed by his solicitor.

'It looks as if you've shut the door on your application,' said the solicitor.

'Good,' Brian said, relieved that this was the very last time that he would ever have to kowtow to the police hierarchy. He celebrated his freedom with a lemonade with his solicitor. Brian would never be granted a pistol licence, and if carrying a gun wasn't part of his life any more, he would have to live with that.

Not long after that, the Murphys' phone rang one night, around 10 p.m.. It was Alphonse Gangitano—known as the Black Prince of Lygon Street. Alphonse fancied himself a gangster and certainly played in the high-stakes world. Privately, though, the guy was crazy.

'Hello Mr Murphy,' he said. 'Can we meet? I have a proposition

Retirement and crims in the woodwork

for you.'

Thinking quickly, Brian didn't want him coming anywhere near his house so he gave directions to a tram stop nearby. He had heard stuff about Alphonse—he was a good fighter, but sneaky. He had a reputation for terrifying people. He had even picked up a solicitor friend of Brian's and had thrown him through a plate-glass window, accusing the solicitor of not trying hard enough in court for him.

Brian was curious. What did Alphonse want to see him for? Just to be on the safe side, he rang a couple of coppers he knew and told them where he was going and who he was meeting. Old habits die hard.

Under the cover of darkness, Brian walked around to the tram stop. Alphonse pulled up in a big black Ford with tinted windows 100 metres up the road and walked down to the tram stop. Alphonse was immaculately groomed in a dark tailored suit.

The two shook hands.

'What do you want, mate?' Brian asked him.

Gangitano looked earnest. 'I've discussed it with some of my friends and we would like you to come on board and be a consultant for us. You can tell us how to go about our business in a more ... productive manner.'

Brian wished he had a tape recorder. No one would believe this. He nodded as if considering the offer.

Gangitano continued: 'You know most of the police in the various squads and we believe that you could be our eyes and ears. You'll be handsomely rewarded and you'll want for nothing.'

Where were witnesses when you needed them? 'Mate, that's fantastic,' Brian said, shaking his hand. But then, a bit theatrically, he stopped, as if a thought had just occurred to him. 'But ...'

'What?' Gangitano said, bristling a little.

Brian scratched his forehead. 'On the other hand, anybody who took me on in that capacity would have a death wish.'

Gangitano looked puzzled. 'Why?'

'Because every copper in Melbourne with any brains would want to destroy you and me both. I could turn out to be the biggest thorn in your side that you could ever have. I don't think it would work.'

Alphonse laughed. 'Thank you very much for your honesty.'

'That's all right,' Brian said, trying not to laugh back in his face. The last thing he wanted was the gangster thinking that he had taken the mickey out of him.

'How much do I owe you for this meeting?' he asked.

'Nothing mate,' Brian told him.

The two shook hands and Gangitano thanked Brian profusely. 'I never thought of it that way,' he admitted.

They both went their separate ways.

It wasn't as if gangsters were beating a path to Brian's door, but not long after his late-night meeting with Alphonse, Brian got another phone call. This one was from a crim friend of Billy Longley's who told Brian that Bill was in a bad way, bitten by the black dog of depression.

'No one can talk any sense to him,' the crook said, concern in his voice. 'Maybe you could talk to him and help him.'

'I don't know about that,' Brian said, 'but if he rings me, I'll have a chat with him.' On the one hand, Brian had never turned down a fellow human being in trouble, but on the other hand, he didn't necessarily court crims either. Over the years, he had crossed paths with Billy who had of course protected the Murphys during the Collingburn affair. Brian had once got a call from a prison guard who told him that Billy wanted to see him. Brian had visited him in Pentridge where they chatted in a small interview room. He told Brian that one of the prisoners had been taken to the prisoners' ward at St Vincent's Hospital. Billy had intel that the sick prisoner was going to get a visit that afternoon from a man in a wheelchair and that the tubes of the wheelchair contained the components of a gun and the bullets. The plan was to pass on the gun to the prisoner who would then shoot his way out of hospital. Billy had thought

Retirement and crims in the woodwork

about it and wanted to tell Brian because he was worried that an innocent nurse or doctor could get killed in the crossfire.

'I don't think they deserve that,' Billy said quietly, 'not for just doing the job they're doing.'

In this, Billy rose in Brian's estimation. He was serving thirteen years for conspiracy to murder Pat Shannon, the secretary of the Painters and Dockers, but here he was, concerned about the safety of innocent bystanders. There was an honour about crooks like Billy who would break the sacred crim code to inform against a man who might kill an innocent nurse. Using the information, the ruse was exposed. Another time, Brian helped Billy out when he was in prison in Ararat. Billy received information that crims had stashed gelignite in a culvert close to the jail and were going to use it to blow a hole in the bluestone wall so they could break in and kill him. Brian drove up to Ararat with a colleague and interviewed Billy. After that, he contacted the Mines Department who recovered all the gelignite.

The phone call to say that Billy was suffering from depression didn't really move Brian. The two weren't friends, but it was in Brian's nature to reach out to people in need. If he could help, he would. A couple of days after, he answered the phone and recognised Billy's voice immediately.

'G'day, Chief,' he said. 'I'm ringing you.'

'I know that, Bill,' said Brian.

That broke the ice. He laughed.

'You're not travelling too well,' Brian said.

'A hundred precent correct, Chief.'

'I wouldn't mind having a chat with you,' Brian said.

'All right.'

He put his hand over the phone and asked Margaret if she minded him inviting Billy over for dinner. Even though Billy was a convicted murderer, Margaret knew her husband would never invite anyone into their home who would harm her. And she had never forgotten how Billy had protected her when Brian was on trial. Margaret nodded.

'What about coming over on Friday night and Margaret will cook you some fish for dinner?'

'Ferocious!' Billy said, sounding pleased as punch.

Brian got the impression that he didn't get too many invitations for dinner when Billy arrived with a bunch of flowers for Margaret, his trousers pressed, his shoes brightly polished, and wearing a crisp white shirt under a navy-coloured reefer jacket. He looked like a little boy who had been summoned by the Queen.

Billy came in and chatted to Margaret as she cooked the dinner and he told her about working in the prison kitchen and how he'd met a Vietnamese bloke in Pentridge who was waiting to be extradited back to Vietnam to be executed. This fellow used to cook special meals for Billy and a couple of other prisoners after the kitchen closed at night.

As Brian watched Billy talking to Margaret, he knew it was good for him to be out with regular folk. Margaret could see that Billy was a true gentleman, no matter what he had done in the past.

Over dinner, Billy described his one-room Housing Commission flat. 'It's like being in a cell, but worse. You never see anyone. You're on your own, but at least I've got a job.' He had been given a job cleaning offices at night so hardly had any contact with people.

Billy described how in prison, the wardens would slam doors on purpose, and the sound that echoed through the night and woke men who were nervous anyway. 'The worst thing that can happen to me,' he said sadly, 'is for someone to slam a door.'

Reflecting on his 13 years inside, Bill said philosophically, 'You can't beat the system.'

'I reckon the system saved your life,' Brian told him. 'If you'd been out, someone would have knocked you.'

'I think you might be right, Chief.'

When Margaret's niece arrived to join the dinner, Billy stood up and wouldn't resume his seat until she had sat down at the table.

Retirement and crims in the woodwork

She listened in fascination to Billy's tales of prison. Billy chatted away as if he hadn't talked to anyone much in ages. It turned out that he was an avid reader—ironically, he enjoyed murder mysteries. Sitting down in good safe company did him the world of good.

After Billy left, Margaret declared him to be the most courteous man she had ever met. Present company excepted, Brian hoped.

And so it began, that every couple of days the two men would ring each other. Billy explained how his applications to the Housing Commission to get transferred from Dandenong over to Ascot Vale where he grew up was an exhausting process. Brian offered to help in any way he could.

Before too long, Billy shifted into a block of units near the Showgrounds, and after that, rented a house not too far from there. He was soon back having coffee in Puckle Street, Moonee Ponds, a couple of days a week, just like the old days. Getting out and about did wonders for his state of mind. Once they realised who he was, the people in the coffee shop told him that they'd heard he had done a lot of bad things.

'It has been alleged,' Billy conceded with a nod.

And once word got around, Billy soon had a coterie of characters joining him for coffee which helped him became comfortable in his skin again.

One day he rang Brian and said that Graham 'The Munster' Kinniburgh was sitting outside the café. There was a long history of animosity between the two that went right back to the Painters and Dockers factions in the 1970s.

'You reckon I should give it to him?' Bill asked.

'Don't give it to him unless he comes in the door with a gun,' Brian advised.

'Fair enough, Chief,' said Billy.

Billy joined water aerobics at the Ascot Vale Aquatic Centre, and took ballroom dancing classes. He also started doing Weight Watchers, eventually becoming a lifetime member and lecturer.

He was selective about who he let know who he was, carefully choosing the ones he knew would tell everyone.

He loved being Billy 'The Texan' Longley.

As Brian caught up with Billy regularly, his admiration for the ex-crim grew. When someone invited Billy to a local school to talk to the sixth-grade kids, he asked Brian to go with him. While the kids seemed a bit bored when Brian spoke to them as a retired copper, when it was Bill's turn, a light seemed to go on.

'I got nothing,' Billy began. 'I've got the backside out of my trousers and haven't even got a decent chair to sit in. I'm 72.' Billy pointed to Brian. 'If you listen to him, he's got a house and a family. I have nothing and spent most of my life in prison. I was told when to get up and when to eat and when to go to the toilet.' Again, he pointed at Brian. 'He could go to the pictures whenever he wanted to, eat whenever he wanted to. In jail, you can't and that's no life.'

The little kids in front of him were wide-eyed.

'What do you reckon?' Bill asked as they left the school.

'I reckon you made a difference,' Brian told him.

And that was when they became friends.

When Billy turned 80, Margaret and Brian received an invitation to celebrate his milestone birthday. With the way he lived his life, Bill never thought he would make the distance. The guests made up a wild assortment of folk from all walks of life. An ex-governor of H-division mingled with murderers and regular people. A couple of ex-coppers, a couple of solicitors, journalists, and ladies and gentlemen from his dancing and water aerobics groups.

Margaret pointed out a killer. 'Who's that man over there?' she asked. 'He looks like a minister of religion.'

'He's one of Australia's most deadly assassins,' Brian told her.

Margaret couldn't believe it. The gentleman looked so respectable, just like the cleric she had taken him for.

It made Brian wonder. Perhaps ageing was the great leveller. The struggle was no longer against others, but with their own ageing bodies. Life became difficult enough with the aches and pains of ageing without clinging on to hatreds that age makes petty.

Looking around the room at Bill's eightieth, Brian realised he'd learnt a hell of a lot from villains. Through them, he saw how much they had missed the love of family which made him appreciate his more. There was a futility and stupidity about the way they carried on and like Bill, many ended up with nothing.

Perhaps a lot boiled down to the family you were lucky—or unlucky—to be born into. Brian's parents were unwavering in their quest to instil morals in their children. Billy once said that from the age of 14, all he ever wanted to be was a criminal. In later years, at their school visits, he spoke to the kids of his regret. He could see it too. He looked at Brian and his loving wife and family and could see the path his friend had chosen was a better one. He wasn't afraid to admit it.

There is not one thing that Brian would do differently. Everything that happened in his life, taught him something that he could use. Maybe if Billy hadn't carried the chip on his shoulder, but simply put things behind him, he might have lived a different life.

When Bill got sick, his biggest fear was that he would end up in a nursing home. In the end, he died in hospital in the presence of his family who loved him. He had a more peaceful death than some of the enemies he dispatched over the years which Brian said in his eulogy. A man is the sum of all his actions and he gave a warts-and-all eulogy with humour and affection that he imagined Bill would have appreciated. Through a strange twist of fate, he became friends with Bill when normally the two would have been mortal enemies.

Both lives were richer for that unlikely friendship.

41

HIGGINS IS CONVICTED

Brian could never understand the vehemence behind the force's pursuit of Paul Higgins. One day, during a barbeque in Brian's backyard, Higgins finally revealed the truth.

'What they're fucken doing to me is disgraceful,' said Higgins, nearly in tears. 'They've got a bloke accused of killing 20 people against me as a witness. They've got prostitutes that the police department had to pay thousands to persuade to become witnesses. Drug riddled massage parlour operators who've gone out of business and want to get even with the coppers.'

'And you're going to cop all this?' Brian asked him. 'About fucken time you levelled with me mate. Why is Fat Harry so crook on you?'

It was only then that the story of Commander Bennett asking Higgins to collect money from the massage parlours saw the light of day for the first time. Brian listened without speaking. And then he exploded: 'Well fuck me! That's why Fat Harry wants you and not me.' It finally all made sense. 'Why the hell didn't you tell me earlier?'

'I like to fight my own battles,' said Higgins.

'But this one's too big for you,' exclaimed Brian. 'Look where it's got you!'

Higgins admitted he had been worried what Brian might have done to Bennett if had he known.

Brian considered this. 'I might have made his life miserable, but to your advantage.'

Higgins is convicted

'You've got five kids and I didn't want you involved.'

Brian understood his concern, but he had something that Higgins didn't—a healthy mistrust. Higgins trusted everyone; he could never believe that coppers would go against coppers. Brian, on the other hand, had only ever trusted half a dozen cops in his whole career.

'I'll fix this for you,' Brian assured him. 'You'll never go to trial.'

'How?' said Higgins.

'We've got two detectives that we can charge with theft and conspiracy, and an officer we can charge with conspiring with the other two. We'll work out how to take out warrants and get them locked up and charged. Have their case heard before yours and have them convicted for conspiracy and theft. You'll never stand trial. There might be a Royal Commission but you'll never stand trial.'

Higgins shook his head. 'I couldn't do that to another policeman.'

'You said exactly the same last time and look how it turned out.'

Higgins had tears in his eyes. 'Sorry mate.'

Brian just couldn't understand Higgins misguided sense of loyalty and lack of self-preservation. His colleague loved his job and was so committed to it, that he could not contemplate the possibility that this blind faith in the system would eventually lead to his demise. In many ways, Higgins was a fighter, but never for himself.

It took five years for Paul Higgins' case to get to trial. Having failed at committal, the case was presented directly to the County Court. The size of the operation to charge Higgins was incredible. Officers from a special taskforce had travelled the country, interviewing 805 people, and calling 170 of them as witnesses. By the time of the trial, Sandy MacRae was doing a long stretch for murder, but had received concessions to be a witness against Paul Higgins, including an indefinite delay in a double murder charge in South Australia.

Brian made the tough decision not to go to court to watch the proceedings. He hadn't been charged or questioned, and he figured that it would be enough of a circus without him. Nonetheless, he promised to talk to Higgins daily on the phone in order to bolster his mate, and to discuss the case. Ever the strategist, Brian listened for hours as Higgins recounted each day's testimony, and gave advice where he could.

When Geoff Lamb testified, he told the court that he decided to make a statement against Paul Higgins after a sergeant at police internal investigations told him that Higgins had been responsible for Lamb's wife's fatal heroin overdose. The allegation was that Lamb's wife, Lorraine, had an affair with Higgins, then ended it and she overdosed. After hearing the link between his dead wife and Higgins, Lamb made a statement to the effect that between 1978 and 1983, he had been paying bribes and offering prostitutes to Higgins, Strang, Glare and an officer from the Vice Squad.

During the trial, Higgins met with his lawyer who told him that a deal had been offered. If he pleaded guilty to planting the explosives at Slater's house, they would drop all the other charges and he would get a non-custodial sentence. Higgins refused. His vehemence was later justified when Phil Glare confessed in 1990 to planting the explosives on Slater himself. His confession was not raised at Higgins' trial.

The trial lasted 420 days and the estimated cost all up was around $33 million. In the end, Paul Higgins was found guilty. In April 1993, he was sentenced to seven years in prison with a five-year minimum.

After Higgins' trial, Strang and Glare had an arrangement with the Crown solicitor which enabled them to plead guilty in the Magistrate's Court to one count of receiving a secret commission to the value of thirty dollars. Both received suspended sentences.

While the Police Association had funded Paul Higgins' defence, the cost proved almost too much and opinion was divided

Higgins is convicted

on whether to keep funding the case. Meetings were called to take a vote. By 1990, the Association was close to bankruptcy and the vote went against Higgins. That decision would cost Higgins his house, his superannuation, and ultimately, his family.

When Higgins was convicted, Brian was inconsolable. He couldn't believe the mate he'd worked with for years was corrupt. It was one thing to use a bit of dash to cut corners in an investigation for the greater good, but it was quite another to take money from crims. There were so many anomalies. Higgins bumped into a witness who suggested internal affairs had asked him to lie. Another investigator resigned over what he perceived as an unfair pursuit of Higgins. And most of all, Strang and Glare who always seemed close to Fat Harry got suspended sentences when Higgins got seven years.

Higgins did his time at Ararat and Brian visited him every month, religiously.

42

CLEARING THE LANEWAY

Brian had turned 60 and had long settled into a gentler pace of life, but once a copper, always a copper. That was how he knew the hotted-up black car parked in the laneway behind his house belonged to drug dealers, and the shifty types loitering at both ends of the laneway were druggies waiting to score.

The laneway adjoined a playground, and most days, Margaret would walk the cobblestones wearing rubber gloves and carrying a bucket. Armed with tongs, she would pick up all the syringes left by the druggies, and the condoms left by prostitutes who plied their trade in the laneways, drawn to the drug trade like flies to honey. Margaret didn't want the kids hurting themselves on used needles.

It was Good Friday and Brian had been out doing errands. When he drove into the lane, he saw the black car and made a quick decision. Instead of turning into his garage, he pulled up behind the drug dealers.

He sauntered up to the driver's side window, leant one arm on the roof, and tapped on the glass. An annoyed bloke the size of a jockey wound down the window and glared at him. A big guy in the passenger seat was a bloke Brian knew as Big Vince.

''Scuse me,' Brian said politely.

'What do you want?' the jockey snapped.

'Mate, you're dropping needles here every day. I've seen you around a couple of times. I don't want the coppers down here chasing you. Could you piss off and not come back.'

'Fuck off, baldy,' snarled the jockey.

Clearing the laneway

Baldy? He sure knew how to hurt a fella's feelings.

'All right, mate,' Brian said, raising his hands in supplication. 'I've asked you nicely. I'll do what you suggest.'

What the jockey saw was a 60-year-old bald man backing away, hands raised, placating. He no doubt felt a surge of power, this little ruler of lanes and alleyways, peddler of addictive poison. He perhaps thought he could infest any neighbourhood he liked and no one could stop him.

He was wrong.

Brian paced his garage, thinking. Blood slowly boiling. Probably lucky that the police force had denied him a gun permit; he might have taken it into the laneway and put a couple of bullets through the car—just to get their attention, of course. Then, an idea sparked. An idea that would tip the balance of power. The next best thing he had was a petrol can.

'It was filled with water, Your Honour,' Brian later said, one hand raised as if taking an oath. There was a twinkle in his eye.

He grabbed the can and walked back to the car. 'Mate! Mate! I wanna talk to you!' he said, knocking again on the car window.

The jockey wound down the window again; his mood unimproved. 'We told you to fuck off!'

Brian lifted the can, shaking it wildly, splashing the contents through the open window, soaking both the occupants.

Big Vince started squealing and flapping about like a demented cockatoo.

'Is this petrol?' High pitched jockey voice. Panicked beyond all measure.

Brian scrambled for his pockets. 'Where's my lighter?' he yelled. 'Give me your lighter, Vince!'

Big Vince tried to open his door but the car was parked too close to the fence and he was stuck. Brian leant against the driver's door, blocking the jockey's way out. There was a lot of screaming and he played it up. Teach them to call him *Baldy*.

The tactician in him wondered what the driver would do next.

Would he drive off and risk the car catching on fire? Or would he come out fighting?

He came out fighting.

Brian stepped back in order to get the first one in. Big Vince would be the problem; he was huge.

The squealing had brought a bunch of residents to their back gates. Including Margaret.

'For Christ's sake, ring the police,' Brian called to her.

'Why?' she asked.

'Just bloody do it!'

The jockey had stumbled from the car and was now advancing on Brian who made a tactical retreat into his garage. He dropped the petrol can and grabbed a shovel for a weapon. The little bloke ignored Brian and started going nuts on his car. He ripped off the side mirror and Brian realised he should've parked around the corner before approaching the drug dealers.

It was time to use the shovel to convince the jockey the error of his ways.

While this was going on, Big Vince, with the dexterity of a seal, wriggled his way over the centre console of the car and spilt out the door. As soon as he righted himself, he came at Brian like a bear. Brian held the shovel like a cricket bat. As Big Vince lumbered towards him, he swung the shovel and whomped him in the middle. There was a ripping sound as Big Vince's shirt tore opened and buttons pinged onto the bluestone laneway. He staggered backwards. Brian just had time to land another blow on Big Vince when the cavalry arrived. And they were just in time.

A cop car screeched to a halt beside him and he slipped the shovel back in the garage.

'Look what he's done to me!' yelled Big Vince pulling open his shirt to reveal a stomach covered with more hair than Brian had ever had on his head. Branded onto his middle was the exact shape of the shovel.

Brian had certainly left an impression.

Clearing the laneway

The drug dealers accused Brian of pouring petrol over them.

'This is disgraceful!' the young copper exclaimed, staring at Brian. 'I could get you fifteen years for that!'

'They're drug dealers and you're taking their word over mine!' Brian was seething. 'They come in here and deal drugs in my lane and you do nothing about them!' He was on a roll and quite possibly a soapbox.

'You poured petrol over them,' said the cop, towering over Brian's soapbox from his high horse.

'*Allegedly* poured petrol over them,' Brian said.

Like a cross parent, the cop pointed to Brian's back gate and ordered him to go inside. 'I'll deal with you later.'

Brian was happy to oblige. He was filled with adrenaline. He closed the garage door and left them to it. Once inside, he grabbed the petrol tin and took a sniff. Whoops. It did smell more like petrol than water. He headed straight for the gulley trap at the back of the house and turned on the tap above it. He filled the tin with water and emptied the contents onto the garden. Then he did it again. And again. He kept sniffing the tin. There was definitely the smell of petrol but it was getting fainter. He half-filled the tin with water and put it back in the garage.

After a couple of minutes, there was a knock on the back gate.

'Who is it?' Brian snapped.

'It's the police,' said the voice of the young copper. 'We want to talk to you.'

'Well I don't want to talk to you!'

'If you don't open the gate and talk to us, we'll come around and lock you up.'

Brian didn't want to take the chance of getting locked up. It was Good Friday and he had to drive Margaret to Mass later that afternoon.

He begrudgingly opened the gate and went out into the lane, half suspecting they would throw him in the divvy van.

'Look, I've been speaking to these gentlemen—'

'They're fucken drug dealers!' Brian corrected him.

'Just shut your mouth and listen.'

Brian shut his mouth.

'I've been speaking to these *gentlemen* and if you pay them $250 to clean their clothes and get their car detailed, they won't press any charges. Can you help us with that?'

Brian was outraged but his natural ability to strategise clicked into gear. He figured the drug dealers didn't want to take things further because they wouldn't be good witnesses. The cop had taken the path of least resistance. It was a good solution. For everyone except Brian.

'Sweet. No worries,' Brian said amicably.

He saw the drug dealers grin at each other. Not only had they won, but they would get a quid out of the old bald bastard.

Brian hurried inside and searched for a little brass coin—a one-cent piece he knew he kept in a box when the coins were discontinued. He found the next best thing—a two-cent coin—and tucked it in his pocket and returned to the laneway.

'Have you got that money with you?' asked the cop.

'Yep.' Brian grabbed his hankie in a way to look like a pile of notes, and pinched the coin in between his thumb and pointer finger.

'Give it to him,' encouraged the cop.

Big Vince held his hand out expectantly. Brian opened his fingers and dropped the coin into his palm. It was very satisfying to see Big Vince's expression change. Brian grabbed his hand and pulled him close.

'That is twice the value of what you're worth,' he told him before spitting in his face.

'Oh, that's disgraceful!' said the cop, as if he'd never seen anything worse than a law-abiding citizen spitting at a drug dealer.

Big Vince was dumbstruck. And Brian was ordered inside again. As he slipped smugly through his gate, he heard the policeman say, 'Come on gentlemen, we're going to the police station.'

Clearing the laneway

Facing the wrath of his wife was a little harder than the collective wrath of Big Vince, the jockey and the cop.

'What on earth is going on out there?' she said.

'I don't want to discuss it,' he told her petulantly.

Margaret could read him like a book. She knew he was in no mood to talk. He announced that he was going for a lie down. Minutes later, she checked on him and found him sleeping like a baby. Less than an hour later, Brian woke up fresh as a daisy. But he realised he had a bigger problem. The drug dealers knew where he lived.

'If those drug dealers come back, and go to do anything to this house,' he told Margaret, 'I'm going to give it to them, more than they'll ever expect. I want you to go to church and I'll stay here.'

Margaret tried to protest. 'What are you going to do?'

'What you don't know, won't hurt you,' Brian assured her.

Margaret got ready for Mass and Brian was just about to drive her when there was a knock on the door. It was the young copper. He was with a partner—a bloke Brian recognised.

'We'd like you to come to the police station with us,' he said in a stern voice. 'It looks as if you're going to be charged.'

'If you don't mind,' Brian said in his politest voice, 'I have to take my wife to Mass.'

They agreed to follow the Murphys to church, then meet back at the house. Brian led them into the backyard for a chat. At the same moment, two detectives he knew arrived through the back gate for a visit. Their timing was fortuitous as it turned out. There was Brian with a backyard full of coppers.

'Come back in a couple of hours,' he told his detective mates. 'We'll have a cuppa then.'

'What's going on?' one of them asked.

'Mate. Later,' Brian said, pointedly, nodding slightly towards his uniformed visitors. They guessed he was in a spot of bother and made a hasty retreat, winking at him on the way out.

Once Brian was alone with the two coppers, they asked where

the petrol can was. He pointed to the tin in question and the young cop picked it up and sniffed it.

'There's an odour of petrol here,' said the cop.

'Give it to me,' Brian said. 'It's water! I'll drink the bloody thing.'

'No, that won't be necessary,' he said.

His partner stood nearby shaking his head. They were more polite on this visit, and he guessed that when they took the drug dealers to the police station, the young cop had been told that the old bald guy was the legendary Skull Murphy. But despite any feelings of camaraderie, Brian wasn't about to make their job any easier.

'We'll go to the police station,' said the cop in a placating voice, 'and we can sit down and talk about this.'

'Yes, that's a good idea,' Brian said, feigning a meekness that he had never felt.

Heading off in the police car was a familiar feeling. So was walking into the South Melbourne police station. All activity seemed to stop when Brian entered; there was an awkward silence. Some of the cops knew him, and all of them would know *of* him. He had no doubt they were all wondering if he was going to behave himself.

Doing the opposite to what people expect really throws them. So that's what Brian did; he behaved himself.

'What am I going to be questioned about?' Brian asked the young cop once they had settled in the interview room.

'You threw petrol over somebody,' he said.

'No I didn't,' Brian said.

'We are going to question you about it.'

'Am I going to be cautioned?' Brian asked, voice like a simpleton.

'Yes,' said the young cop and then he politely read the caution. Whatever Brian said would be taken down and used in evidence against him in a court of law.

Clearing the laneway

'Do you understand this?'

'Yes, I do,' Brian said.

'What is your full name and address?'

'You've just cautioned me and told me I don't have to answer any questions. Thank you for being so polite about it. I'm not going to answer any questions.'

The young cop looked at his partner, then said, 'We are duty bound to ask you some questions.'

'Good,' Brian said, nodding, smiling at him.

He asked what had occurred in the lane.

'Thank you for being so polite about it. I'm not going to answer any questions,' he said.

Brian did this for the next hour until the young cop terminated the interview. They stood to leave the room and asked him to wait. Brian told them he was happy to wait. Not a care in the world.

Ten minutes later, the cops returned with the shift sergeant—a copper Brian knew to say hello to.

'Mate, howya going?' The sergeant wrapped a friendly arm around Brian's shoulder. Buddies.

'Good!' Brian beamed at him.

'Mate, just between you and me, what happened today?' said the sergeant.

Brian looked him in the eye and smiled. 'Mate,' he said, 'I've got blokes ten years in jail with that opening.'

The sergeant burst out laughing. 'They'll take you home now.'

'Thank you very much,' Brian said politely.

He walked out to the police car, and bumped into the two detectives who had visited him earlier. They offered to drive him home. Brian bade farewell to the young copper. Back at his place, they had a cup of tea and a good laugh.

Margaret arrived home from church and Brian assured her that everything was okay. She was cross because she'd had to field questions when the good parishioners asked: 'Where's Brian?' She told them that he had come across a couple of drug dealers in their laneway and he had gone to the police station to help the police. Which, technically, was true.

'You were in the right place to pray for me,' Brian said.

After dinner that night, Brian told Margaret that he had to go and see a fella. That was code for things she didn't need to know. He didn't tell her that the drug dealers would be feeling mighty annoyed with him at that moment, and obviously, they knew where he lived. He couldn't leave things up in the air like that. He had never lived his life looking over his shoulder and he wasn't about to start now.

Brian went into the garage and retrieved a special knife that he had collected years earlier. It was designed for people with rheumatoid arthritis; the handle was thick and looked like the grip of a pistol. He ground down the blade on his emery wheel and took all the edges off it till it was little more than the handle. He wrapped the stump of the blade in duct tape, then tucked it into his belt with just the handle showing. And then he took an evening stroll down to St Kilda and up Fitzroy Street. The smell of the sea breeze, the wind in his hair … well it would have been if he had any. He stopped to pass the time of day with the friendly citizens of St Kilda; working girls and drug dealers alike. He asked the same question of all of them.

'Have you seen Big Vince? I want to talk to him.' Each time he asked the question, he let his sports coat fall open just enough for them to all see the handle of the knife tucked into his belt, and gave them a moment to imagine it was a gun they were seeing. Then he went home.

'What on earth have you been doing?' cried Margaret as soon as he stepped in the front door.

'Nothing!' Brian said in the innocent voice that Margaret had never fallen for.

'Everyone's been ringing for you!'

'Have they?' he asked, letting his eyes go wide in surprise.

Margaret handed him a sheaf of messages. He started at the top and rang D24 and asked for the detective who had rung while

Clearing the laneway

he was out.

'Murph! What the bloody hell have you been doing? Going up and down Fitzroy Street with a gun?'

'I was making sure that something doesn't happen which might,' Brian told him. 'And I was not carrying a gun … even though it might have looked like one.' He let that hang in the air.

The bloke realised what Brian was doing and the bluster left his voice. 'You sure it's not a gun?'

'It's a knife for arthritis sufferers,' he said, 'filed down so it's just a handle.'

At the end of the line, a pause, then, 'I heard about what happened today. All the best.'

Brian rang Paul Higgins who had also left a message.

'What the fucken hell's going on? Every bastard's ringing the station saying you've gone off your nut going up and down Fitzroy Street.'

'Yep.'

'My bloke's got Big Vince under control. He heard you were looking for him and he just wants to forget this ever happened.'

'Good,' said Brian.

And he answered the same way to the next four coppers who rang with the same message: Big Vince will keep away if Brian let things drop.

'Good,' Brian said, smiling serenely.

There was a rumour at the station. It was said that the police station washing machine was quite busy that Good Friday night. There was another rumour that an old mate of Brian's who still worked at the police station paid his mother a visit and her washing machine was quite busy too.

When the clothes were forensically tested for petrol, the results identified only the enzymes found in washing detergent. Tests found the clothes to be exceptionally clean.

Brian never saw the drug dealers ever again. And they all lived happily ever after. At least he did.

43

LOSING HIGGINS

Ever since he was released from prison, Paul Higgins had been fighting to clear his name. He had also been fighting cancer. He and Brian spoke almost daily on the phone. Brian would ring to check up on him and see how he was. Towards the end of his fight there was a moment of false hope. Higgins was declared in remission. But Brian didn't quite believe it—perhaps it was because Higgins didn't look any better, or perhaps there was an air of death around him.

And it turned out his intuition was correct.

Jack the Dancer returned for a final waltz.

Brian went to visit Higgins in a palliative care hospital and was shocked at his friend's gaunt face, but tried not to show it. He got out his phone and took a photo of Higgins who now looked like a white-bearded prophet. The two spoke for a long while; Higgins was still angry about what had been done to him and the way he had been treated. Looking at him, Brian was reminded of his mum, Maggie; they always said she suffered from Irish Alzheimer's—she forgot everything except the hate.

Brian realised this. 'Mate,' he said, 'you have to die your own death. Let all that stuff go.'

Higgins met his eyes. 'Every time you've given me advice and I've ignored it, you've turned out to be right.'

'Let me carry it for you,' Brian offered. It was the last thing he could do. 'I'll carry the hate for you, mate.'

Higgins nodded and looked relieved.

Losing Higgins

They had weathered so many storms in their career with Victoria Police—on the streets with dangerous criminals, and inside the organisation with some equally dangerous colleagues; staying loyal to their friendship and their principles despite monumental betrayals by others. Higgins was a good man and a good friend, and in the end, that's what mattered. He could've pointed the finger right back at his colleagues, but it wasn't in his nature. If anyone did to him what they did to Higgins, Brian would've come out swinging, naming names. Perhaps that's why no one ever did point the finger in his direction. People in glasshouses always avoided a loose cannon.

Higgins spoke about his two older sons. He was rapt with the way they had turned out. One of them was a police officer; both were hard-working good men. His youngest son excelled at martial arts. Higgins was a very proud father.

Higgins appreciated the visits from a small handful of close mates. One colleague, Dougie Lewis, was an ex-Consorter who had worked with Higgins. He told Brian that he didn't want Higgins dying alone; so he visited nearly every day and would ring Brian with daily updates.

The day before Higgins died, Brian saw him, and he was as bright as a button. He wanted to sit up in bed, then get out of bed. Up until then, Higgins had long periods of unconsciousness. The nurses said that this activity was an indication that the end was near—his last hurrah.

'I wonder what it's like,' Higgins said, talking about where he was headed.

'Dunno, mate,' Brian deadpanned. 'Nobody's come back to tell us, yet.'

Higgins laughed.

As the two old men sat together, Brian reflected on how similar they were— men who'd gone where angels feared to tread. Back in the day when everyone sat around the office planning this raid or that, Higgins and Brian would give each other the eye and they'd be out the door making the arrests while the others were still scratching their backsides.

Brian looked at his friend and once again shook his head at the way he had been treated.

When he got the call that Higgins had breathed his last, he felt relieved. All the shit in the world had been lifted from his mate's shoulders. He imagined him in a place better than earth.

A year later, Brian still had to stop himself reaching for his phone to call Higgins.

44

BUY GREEN BANANAS

Brian always had energy to burn. He retired over a quarter of a century ago, but never stopped. People still ring and call around all the time, wanting his advice. He reckons it's in his soul to help people. He was also born with the kind of uninhibited personality with the ability to find a positive in every negative and learn from his mistakes and the mistakes of others. He has reached a reflective stage of his life and is at an age where many hesitate to buy green bananas. He's buried a lot of friends and family and every time he does, he better understands that it's the inevitable end for all of us.

When a man can sit down and look at his children and know that he has done a good job. When his grandkids seek him out for advice, he can consider himself a lucky man. His children and grandchildren are his legacy, much more than his legacy in the police force.

In the telling of his story, Brian wanted the world to know that he thought his friend Paul Higgins was a good man, and an innocent man.

He also wanted the world to know about the sexual abuse he'd suffered at the hands of Bob Taylor when he was a boy. Brian has seen so many men carry the pain into middle age. Sexual abuse has a devastating effect on victims. His advice: seek help, seek counselling. Living in silence is like living in a prison.

Brian feels lucky to have been a policeman.

In recent years, he did something he'd been thinking about for a while. He waited until all his family were sitting at the Christmas table and stood to make a speech. With great emotion, he told them that he wanted to give his Valour Award to his oldest son Reg. Brian explained that it wasn't because he was the oldest, but it was because when Reg was 12, he offered to step up and be the man of the family the day of the verdict that might have sent Brian to jail.

As Brian handed his son the small box that held the medal, Reg looked a little shocked.

'We are only the way we are because of our parents,' he said.

Brian is of an age where tears flow as easily as laughter. Many flowed that day.

'That was long overdue,' said one of his daughters, dabbing at her eyes.

www.ingramcontent.com/pod-product-compliance
Lightning Source LLC
Chambersburg PA
CBHW062242300426
44110CB00034B/1179